Visitor's Guide
INDIA:
DELHI, AGRA & RAJASTHAN

*The author 'Christopher Turner' wishes to express his gratitude for their
hospitality to Thai Airways, the Taj Group of Hotels, the
ITC WelcomGroup and Oberoi Hotels Group*

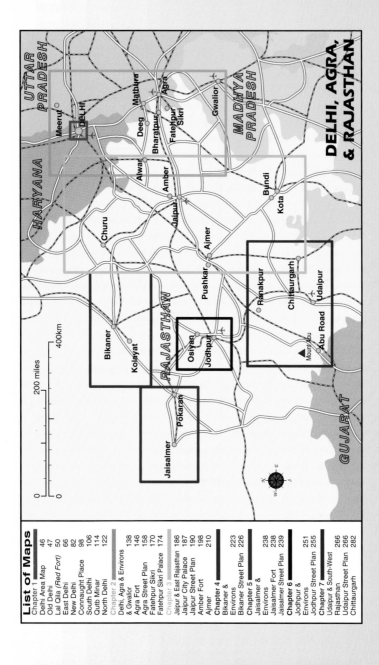

DELHI, AGRA,
& RAJASTHAN

VISITOR'S GUIDE

INDIA:

DELHI, AGRA & RAJASTHAN

Christopher Turner

MPC

HUNTER

Published by:
Moorland Publishing Co Ltd,
Moor Farm Road West, Ashbourne,
Derbyshire DE6 1HD England

ISBN 0 86190 516 4

British Library Cataloguing in Publication Data:
A catalogue record for this book is available from the British Library.

Colour origination by: Reed Reprographics, Ipswich

Printed in Hong Kong by: Wing King Tong Co Ltd

Cover photograph: Taj Mahal, Agra *(C. Turner)*
Rear Cover: A 'charming' scene in Jaisalmer *(C. Turner)*
Page 3: A working camel *(C. Turner)*

The illustrations have been supplied by:
Daphne Cartledge pp30 top, 126 bottom, 198, 199; Bob Kemp pp39 bottom,
55, 99, 127, 139, 287; Oberoi Hotels Group pp126 top;
Inspirations pp23 top (for a free colour brochure on India ☎ 01293 820207);
by Phil Addyman, courtesy of © Somak Holidays pp 62 ,63, 90, 94;
remainder by Christopher Turner

MPC Production Team:
Editorial: Tonya Monk
Editorial Assistant: Christine Haines
Design: Ashley Emery
Cartography: Alastair Morrison

CONTENTS

Key to Symbols Used in Text Margin and on Maps

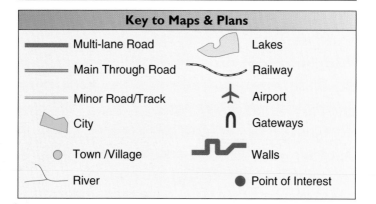

⛪	Tomb	🏛	Museum
🏰	Fort	🏢	Building of Interest
🕌	Temple/Mosque/Shrine	🐦	Birdlife
✳	Place of Interest	🦌	Nature reserve / Animal Interest
⚱	Ecclesiastical Site	�𝕿	Archaeological Site
✿	Garden		

Key to Maps & Plans

▬▬▬	Multi-lane Road	〰	Lakes
═══	Main Through Road	⌇	Railway
───	Minor Road/Track	✈	Airport
◇	City	∩	Gateways
○	Town /Village	⨆	Walls
⌣	River	●	Point of Interest

How To Use This Guide

This MPC Visitor's Guide has been designed to be as easy to use as possible. Each chapter covers a region or itinerary in a natural progression which gives all the background information to help you enjoy your visit. The important places printed in bold, and a comprehensive index enable the reader to find the most interesting places to visit with ease.

At the end of each chapter an Additional Information section gives specific details such as addresses and opening times, making this guide a complete sightseeing companion.

At the back of the guide the Fact File, arranged in alphabetical order, gives practical information and useful tips to help you plan your holiday before you go and while you are there.

The maps and plans for each region show the main towns, villages, roads, and places of interest. However always use a good, recommended map when touring and exploring.

Introduction

Undeniably, a first visit to India provides a series of cultural shocks — but most of them will be shocks of delighted astonishment. Astonishment at the vivid colours of the sky, the clothes, the bazaars, the parakeets and peacocks; astonishment at the tolerant proximity of man and animals, even in the streets of large cities, where monkeys play, elephants parade, camels strut, and cows meander absent-mindedly. Nothing is bland, nothing is predictable, no-one is bored or lonely.

Most visitors are primarily attracted to Delhi, Agra and Rajasthan by the justifiable fame of their exotic buildings — Mogul palaces and mausoleums, Rajput forts, Jain temples and, in Delhi, the architectural splendours of the British Raj. Few will depart without having paid homage, at least once, to Agra's Taj Mahal, the magic of which unfailingly moves all who see it. Scenically, the sand dunes of west Rajasthan's desert, and the serene lakes of Udaipur are the high spots.

preceding page; School children pose for a group photograph in front of the marble shrine of Sheikh Salim Chishti at Fatehpur Sikri

To visit everything described in this book at a reasonable pace would take around 3 months. Few, unfortunately, will have this amount of time available; be very selective, therefore, as not only will an over-ambitious schedule be physically exhausting, but India's wonders are likely to merge into a confused, unsatisfying blur, dominated by memories of long waits in spartan airport lounges.

On returning home, many Westerners experience a depressing reverse cultural shock. Where have all the animals gone? Why is everyone clad so dowdily? What has happened to the smiling faces? How can everything be so expensive? Above all, where are the perpetual blue skies and sunshine? Withdrawal symptoms can take some time to disappear — arrange a few treats to help speed up the process, and start planning a return visit to this uniquely invigorating part of the world.

For those making their first trip to India, the 'Golden Triangle', formed by Delhi, Agra and Jaipur, is by far the most popular destination. The three cities are located relatively close to each other, they are connected by good transport systems, and they boast excellent hotels. Jaipur is the capital of India's most picturesque state — Rajasthan — home of the turbaned, warrior Rajputs, and most will wish to explore some of its fascinating outlying regions. Great Mogul buildings and Rajput forts are found within the area covered by this book, together with the lesser-known, but exquisite, temples of the Jain religion.

Throughout the pages which follow this introduction, the region is broken down into manageable itineraries, and suggestions are given for reducing their extent for those with limited time at their disposal. Even holidaymakers on escorted tours will find that many of the directions given are indispensable for simplifying their 'free days'.

Although transport will be needed for exploring most of Delhi and Agra, which spread over vast areas, the centres of Jaipur, Bikaner, Jaisalmer, Jodhpur and Udaipur, the main cities of Rajasthan, are clearly defined, and may be explored easily on foot.

History

The history of Delhi, Agra and Rajasthan is extremely complex, some of it having repercussions on the entire region, some on parts of it only. To aid comprehension by non-historians, much has had to be simplified, or omitted; as this book is a guidebook, priority is given to incidents which have some connection with what the visitor is able to see. The following outline of historical landmarks is backed up by additional information as relevant locations are reached.

To avoid tedium, only the most important of the literally thousands of battles fought in India are referred to. It should be borne in mind that all Indian people and places shown in Roman lettering are transliterated, which means that various sources spell them slightly differently. Try not to be put off by Lodi, for example, being spelt elsewhere as Lodhi, or Sultan Iltutmish being spelt Altamish. Some of the early Muslim, and most of the Rajput dynasties tend to repeat or only slightly vary the names of each sucessive ruler; this means that it is often necessary to give the full, sometimes lengthy name in order to avoid confusion.

A BRIEF RESUMÉ

Rajputs, part of the Hindu warrior caste, ruled most of north India from 647 to 1193, when Muslims arrived to form the Delhi sultanate, which would vary in extent depending on the military capabilities of its leaders. It was the Muslim Moguls (or Mughals) who were to provide a more stable period of administration from 1526 until decline set in following the death of Aurangzeb in 1707. With no undisputed power in control, a return to internecine warfare was inevitable, the Mahrattas emerging as the most successful protagonists. The country was now an easy target for a powerful invader, and the British, who had already gained a trading foothold, had taken control of most of India by the end of the first decade of the nineteenth century, imposing a Pax Britannica on the warring factions. India was to remain under British rule until 1947, when the long sought-for independence was at last granted. At the same time, the sub-continent was divided into the Hindu majority Republic of India, and the Muslim majority Islamic Republic of Pakistan. In 1971, after a short war, East Pakistan, with the support of India, obtained independence, forming the People's Republic of Bangladesh.

EARLY HINDU RULE

Aryans, probably from the Iranian regions, began to invade the Indian sub-continent around 2000BC, gradually pushing back the indigenous Dravidians to the far south (where they still form the majority). It was from Aryan legends and beliefs that Hinduism evolved, to become the pre-eminent religion of India.

According to the epic book, the Mahabharata, a city known as Indraprastha (Indra's Abode), stood on the west bank of the Yamuna River around 1450BC. Many believe that it occupied the site of Delhi's Purana Qila fort, remnants of which survive; pottery frag-

Local costumes are worn throughout Rajasthan

ments recently excavated have given some credence to this view. However, the first Delhi which is known with certainty to have existed, was located 12 miles (19km) further south, where the Qutb Minar tower now stands. It was a settlement called Dilli, ruled by Tamar Rajputs, and probably built in the eighth century. In 1052, the Tamars constructed a fortress known as Lal Kot; this subsequently fell to another Rajput clan, the Chauhans, whose leader, Prithviraj III, a great hero to all Hindus, extended it in 1180; this larger citadel became known as Qila Rai Pithora. Only fragments of the walls of Lal Kot and Qila Rai Pithora have survived.

Northern India had already known foreign invaders, the Sind and Punjab becoming part of the Persian empire of Darius, and subsequently, in 326BC, of Alexander the Great. From that empire, Sind was taken by Arab invaders in 712, who introduced Islam to India but did not extend their territory.

It was another Muslim, the Turkish Shahab-ud-din Ghori (or Muhammad-bin- Sam-Ghori) who was to prove a more significant conqueror, taking Ajmer in 1191. He failed, however, to defeat Prithviraj at the first attempt, but was successful the following year, the Hindu warrior being killed by his army, which was commanded by Qutb-ud-din Aibak. In 1193, Qila Rai Pithora fell and for 3 months it was commanded by a Hindu vassal. Aibak then took control, establishing the citadel as his base in India, and demolishing its complex of Jain and Hindu temples, which he replaced with Delhi's first mosque. It was to be 754 years before Delhi would again be under the permanent control of Hindus.

THE DELHI SULTANATE (1206-1526)
The Slave Dynasty (1206-1290)
Aibak proved to be an unusually faithful subordinate but, in 1206, Ghori was assassinated and he proclaimed himself Sultan of Delhi. Although his family name was Muizzi, Aibak's dynasty became known as the Slave Dynasty, because he had originally been a slave of Ghori (one of his own slaves would, coincidentally, succeed him also). Aibak's capital, however, would be Lahore, not Delhi.

Dying in a polo accident in 1210, Aibak was succeeded by Iltutmish (or Altamish)-ud-Daulah, who had married one of his daughters. Iltutmish is regarded as the most important of all the early sultans, ruling not just Delhi but a large part of India: from Bengal in the east to Gujarat in the west and the Deccan in the south. It was Iltutmish who transferred the capital from Lahore to Delhi, where he enlarged his father-in-law's mosque and began to construct the adjacent Qutb Minar. At his death, in 1236, the Delhi sultanate was the most powerful state in north India.

Iltutmish's eldest son was already dead and, as his others were judged unfit to govern, the sultanate passed to Raziyyat, his daughter. This was in defiance of Islamic law, which forbade women to rule, and Raziyyat was forced to abdicate after 4 years by the doctrinaire nobles. She fought to regain her throne but was killed in battle: the next woman to rule Delhi would be Queen Victoria.

A period of turmoil followed, with various descendants of Iltutmish occupying the throne for short periods. In 1246, Ghiyas-ud-din Balban became de facto ruler, but 20 years were to pass before he would be proclaimed sultan. At his death, in 1287, Balban was succeeded by Kay Qubadh.

The tombs of Aibak (ruined) and Iltutmish are within the Qutb Minar complex, that of Balban lies just to its east. Far away to the north, within the confines of Old Delhi, is the tomb of Raziyyat.

Khalji (or Khilji) Dynasty (1290-1320)

Qubadh, who proved to be an indecisive leader, was overthrown after just 3 years by an elderly Afghanistani of Turkish origin, Jalal-ud-din-Firoz Khalji, who formed the second, but short-lived dynasty of the sultanate.

In 1296, Jalal was assassinated by his son-in-law Juna Khan who, as Sultan Ala-ud-din Khalji, would reign competently, but ferociously, for 22 years. Intent on forcing the submission of the Rajput princes, Ala-ud-din gained impressive victories at Ranthambore in 1301 and Chittaurgarh 2 years later. It was during this period of expansion that the Delhi sultanate virtually became an empire. In 1309, Ala-ud-din founded a third Delhi, slightly north-east of the original settlement, which was named Siri; only important for 11 years, it was probably never completed. As at Lal Kot/Qila Rai Pithora, fragments of walls are all that exist.

Qutb-ud-din Mubarak Shah became sultan in 1316, following the death of Ala-ud-din, but he proved to be the last of the Khaljis, being murdered by his general, Khusraw Khan, a Hindu convert, in 1320. Khan only ruled for 4 months, his own assassin, Ghazi Malik, founding the next dynasty.

Tughlaq (or Tughluq) Dynasty (1320-1413)

The Tughlaqs ruled for less than a century, but founded three new Delhis, and their Delhi sultanate was again expanded to cover most of India. Ghazi Malik, as Sultan Ghiyas-ud-din Tughlaq, was a firm but popular leader, who immediately founded the fourth Delhi, which bears his family name. Situated a few miles east of Siri, the extensive walls of Tughlaqabad are still one of the capital's most impressive sights. On returning from a victorious campaign in Bengal, Ghiyas was killed at Afghanpur when a wooden pavilion collapsed; it was alleged that his son and successor Juna Khan Tughlaq had engineered the 'accident', but this was never proved.

Juna Khan, on becoming sultan Muhammad Guri in 1325, began work on yet another Delhi, the fifth, which he called Jahanpanah. It was sited to the west of Tughlaqabad but, within 2 years, well before it was ready for occupation, Muhammad Guri ordered the emigration of his subjects to Daulatabad in Maharashtra in order to create a second, more central capital. Rebellions in the north soon led to the Sultan's return, but it is not clear if Jahanapanah was ready for his occupancy. Due to the alleged murder of his father, and the migration that he had enforced, Muhammad Guri was one of the least popular of the Delhi sultans; however, as so often seems to be the case with historical 'baddies' he died a natural death and, even more surprisingly, shares the same tomb as his father, facing the entrance to Tughlaqabad. During his reign, virtually all India acknowledged the suzerainty of the Delhi sultanate.

Firoz (or Feroz) Shah succeeded Muhammad Guri, his uncle, in 1351, and soon lost the Deccan. As territories in south India had also broken free, the sultanate's area of control diminished considerably in a short period. The most important achievement of Firoz Shah's 37 year reign was the founding of Firozabad, by far the largest Delhi had yet built. This was a major step as, for the first time (discounting the Indraprastha of prehistory), Delhi's location moved to the west bank of the River Yamuna. No doubt it was the advantage of the waterway as a means of transport that provided the impetus for this move. Due to subsequent demolition and rebuilding, the precise boundaries of Firozabad are unclear, but it is known to have encompassed part of what is now called Old Delhi.

Firoz Shah had not prepared a successor, and on his death in 1388 a dispute arose. Nazir-ud-din Muhammad Tughlaq became sultan but, in 1394, a rival had appeared who also claimed the sultancy. It matters little, however, because the Mongolian Timur (or Tamburlaine, a corruption of Timur-i-Leng, meaning the lame), was on the rampage. In 1221, an earlier Mongolian warrior, Genghis Khan, had reached the Indus River, but declined to cross it. Not so Timur, who had already taken Baghdad and advanced to within 200 miles (322km) of Moscow. He invaded India in 1398, bent on pillage, and executed 50,000 prisoners immediately before the battle for

Firozabad, which quickly fell, Timur's mighty army meeting little resistance. Most of the city was sacked, and its rubble would be used as building material more than 200 years later for the construction of Humayun's Dinapanah. Only the walls of Kotla Firoz Shah, the city's fort, bear witness to the existence of the great city. The tomb of its builder, Firoz Shah, lies not within the limits of Firozabad, but adjoins the madrassa (college) which he established to the north of the Qutb Minar complex, at Hauz Khas. Timur spent only one year in India, and appointed a vassal, Khizr Khan Sayyid, to control Delhi on his behalf.

Sayyid Dynasty (1414-51)
The Sayyid dynasty was not to play an important role in the history of the Delhi sultanate. The tomb of Muhammad Shah, the third of the Sayyids, who died in 1450, lies in New Delhi in what are now known as the Lodi Gardens. Alam Shah, the last of the dynasty, lived until 1478, but resigned the sultanate in 1451 to an Afghan subordinate, Bahlul Lodi, who already ruled much of the Punjab.

Lodi (or Lodhi) Dynasty (1451-1526)
Bahlol Lodi, who reigned 1451-89, annexed most of Jaunpur in 1479, thus re-establishing the sultanate's control over north India. His successor, Sikandar Lodi (1489-1517), was a devout Muslim who, like the future Mogul emperor Aurangzeb, persecuted followers of other religions. In 1504, he refounded Agra, a city of ancient Hindu origin, which had been taken by Muslims in 1115. It was named Sikandarabad, and a fort constructed. The reason for this move appears to have been Agra's proximity to Rajasthan, which Sikandar Lodi intended to subdue. Delhi was no longer the capital, which would remain at Agra until the reign of Aurangzeb.

Sikandar's successor, Ibrahim Lodi (1517-1526), proved to be a harsh ruler, and revolts spread among the Afghan nobles who had migrated to his court. Ibrahim's uncle, Alam Khan Lodi, together with Daulat Khan Lodi, governor of the Punjab, asked Babur, Mogul leader of Afghanistan, to help them overthrow Ibrahim. Babur enthusiastically complied and, with their assistance and the great advantage of gunpowder, defeated Ibrahim's army at Lahore in 1524. Two years later, the Sultan was killed by Babur at Panipat, north-east of Delhi; the Delhi sultanate was at an end, and Mogul rule in India commenced.

The tombs of Sikandar's Lodi, and probably Ibrahim Lodi, survive in Delhi's Lodi Gardens, that of Bahlol Lodi, now rather dilapidated, is in South Delhi

THE GREAT MOGULS (1526-1707)
Babur (1526-1530)

Mogul is a corruption of Mughal, the Persian word for Mongol. Babur's ancestors had long ago moved west to Afghanistan from Mongolia and his warrior lineage was impressive: a father who had been a fifth generation descendant of Timur, and a mother who was a fourteenth generation descendant of Genghis Khan. The language spoken by Babur was Turki, and this remained the private written and spoken language of Mogul royalty until 1760. The court language which developed, however, was Urdu, a combination of many tongues, which would eventually spread to much of Muslim India and was the most commonly used language in Delhi and Agra until partition: it is now the official language of Pakistan.

Babur made Agra the capital, but spent most of his 4 year reign battling elsewhere, notably against the Rajputs, gaining important victories at Khanua and Bayana, where he defeated Rana Sanga of Chittaurgarh. Partly due to these excursions, but also to his passion for gardening, no buildings of importance remain from his period.

The first Mogul emperor, a Sybaritic man, was little impressed by his new kingdom, finding it lacking in culture, food and amenities; he did, however, revel in its quantities of gold and silver.

Allegedly, Babur constructed a palace on the east bank of the River Yamuna at Agra, facing the site of the future Taj Mahal; there is, however, no evidence to corroborate this. All that exists in Agra of Babur's work are two gardens which he laid out.

Babur, although devout, was certainly no Muslim bigot, wisely advising his son and successor, Humayun, to show religious tolerance. He died near Lahore in 1530 and was sufficiently orthodox to insist

A welcoming musician within Jaisalmer Fort

that he should lie in a simple grave, according to the teachings of the Koran: the next four Moguls were to disregard that edict in spectacular fashion. Babur's body was eventually brought back to Agra, where it lay 4 years before being transferred to Kabul in 1540, just after his son Humayun had been deposed by Sher Shah Sur.

Humayun (1530-1540 and 1555-56)

Like his father, Humayun was cultured and clever. However, he also exhibited sentimentality, a rare quality at the time, and found it difficult to exert authority over his three rebellious half-brothers. Humayun was also extremely superstitious, and would make no move unless the stars confirmed that it would be propitious. He became addicted to opium, taking it in pellet form.

Humayun's first capital was Agra, where he completely rebuilt Sikandar Lodi's fort. In 1533, however, he laid the foundation stone of Dinapanah (Asylum of Faith) on what may have been the site of Indraprastha: yet another Delhi was established.

The north-eastern provinces of Bengal and Bihar were ruled by an Afghan, Sher Khan who, sensing Humayun's lack of resolution and his fraternal difficulties, decided to contest the Mogul empire. His army defeated Humayun at Bilgram in 1540, and Mogul rule was to be interrupted for 15 years.

The Sur Interregnum (1540-1555)

Sher Khan, as Sher Shah Sur, controlled the former Mogul empire until his death at the siege of Kalinja in 1545, and proved to be a wise and powerful leader. Much of his administrative system was to be adopted later by the greatest of all the Mogul leaders, Akbar. Sher Shah Sur appears to have demolished Humayun's citadel at Dinapanah apart from its walls and gateways. He extended the city, renaming it Shergarh, and rebuilt the citadel, where two of his structures have survived. Islam Shah Sur succeeded, on his father's death in 1545, and reigned for 8 years but was a far less effective leader. His own son, Firoz Shah, was murdered by his uncle after ruling less than a year, and the throne was then disputed.

Humayun's Return (1555-56)

After his defeat by Sher Khan, poor Humayun wandered from Lahore to Sind to Rajputana (now Rajasthan), back to Sind, and then, in 1543, to Persia, where he became dependent on the hospitality of Shah Tahmasp. The Shah was a devout Shi'ite Muslim and insisted that Humayun, a Sunni Muslim, should convert to his sect in return for assistance said elsewhere.

News of the turmoil within the Sur dynasty had reached Humayun and, in 1554, he returned to India with a re-organized force. On this occasion, there was no brotherly strife to weaken his endeavour — he had forgiven his siblings as usual — and the Moguls were victorious at Lahore in the February of that year; Delhi and Agra were regained in 1555 by Humayun's outstanding general, Bhairam Khan. It appears that, as a tit-for-tat, Humayun demolished most of the fort within the walls at Shergarh, keeping only its mosque, for reasons of religion, and the small Sher Mandal tower, in which he is said to have housed his library. In many ways, Humayun was the most appealing of the Great Moguls, and it seems sad that within a few months of regaining his lost empire he accidentally fell down the internal stairway of the Sher Mandal, dying of his injuries 3 days later. There had been no time for Humayun to begin rebuilding work at Shergarh, which he presumably renamed Dinapanah once more, and his successor, the 14-year-old Akbar, would rule, at least initially, from Agra.

Little of architectural note has survived from Humayun's period, due to his long absence. The walls and gates of the Purana Qila are probably his work, at least in part, and a small mosque, which he built at Agra, now facing the Taj Mahal, has survived. His great tomb, at Delhi, was not planned during Humayun's lifetime, due to his recent return and sudden death. Humayun's great gift to his dynasty was miniature painting, which he introduced to India on his return from Persia.

Akbar (1556-1605)

The name of Akbar, meaning great, was prescient, the third Mogul emperor proving to be the greatest ruler of India since the Buddhist emperor Ashoka (274-222BC). Bayram Khan suppressed the news of Humayun's death for 2 weeks, in order that Akbar could return from the Punjab to claim the throne without dispute. He was appointed Regent, and defended the young Emperor in battle against the last of the Sur dynasty, Sikandar Sur, whom he defeated. From an early age, Prince Akbar had exhibited great personal bravery, which would soon be augmented by exceptional physical strength. As a scholar, however, he disappointed, and never learnt to read or write with facility.

Initially, Akbar was involved full-time in fighting to expand and stabilize the Mogul empire, achieving his prime aim of subjugating the Rajputs by 1570, only Udaipur and Bundi of the princely states being permitted to remain independent. A Muslim enclave was established in the heart of Rajasthan, at Ajmer, which was ruled directly by Akbar as a provincial capital.

Akbar had gained Rajputana in battle, but held it by diplomacy. He permitted complete freedom of religion, and the Rajput princes were allowed to remain in direct control of their territories (although they had to pay taxes to swell the Mogul coffers). Rajputs were appointed to important positions in both the army and the state, and intermarriage between Muslims and Hindus was encouraged — Akbar himself marrying a Jaipur princess. The *jizya*, by which non-Muslims had been treated as second-class citizens and required to pay a poll tax, was abolished in 1564.

For all his lack of education, Akbar had an enquiring mind, and spent much of his time studying comparative religions. His free-thinking attitude may owe its origin to the fact that his own mother was a Hindu, but it was Akbar's teacher, Mir Abdul Latif, who convinced him that this was the correct and most pragmatic philosophy to adopt. In India, with its many beliefs, religious tolerance was essential from a leader who wished to unite the people and gain their co-operation.

Initially, Akbar ruled from Agra, rebuilding its fort and probably replacing all his father's work there. However, the Emperor, still in his twenties, decided to create a new capital a few miles to the west, which was to be called Fatehpur Sikri. Its palace and great mosque were completed but, in 1569, Akbar left the new city to do battle in the Punjab; his base was Lahore, and this was where Akbar would remain until returning to Agra in 1599, just 6 years before his death.

Akbar created a new religion, known as Din Ilahi, and decreed that he, not the Islamic elders, would pronounce on dogma. He overruled many of the strictures of the Koran, a notable example being his insistence on washing the body before, rather than after making love. Akbar encouraged painting, and ignored the Islamic tradition that neither human nor animal life should be depicted. Most of the subject matter of paintings during Akbar's period consisted of historical events, including the Akbarnama, the official history of his own reign. The Emperor also commissioned a translation into Urdu of the great Hindu epic, the Mahabharata. All this, of course, led to much disapproval from Muslim religious leaders, who regarded Akbar as a heretic.

Apart from a palace and a gateway in its fort, there are no buildings from Akbar's period to have survived in Agra, although the gateway of his tomb nearby, in Sikandra, may have been designed in the Emperor's lifetime. In Delhi, the young Akbar appears to have played no part in the erection of his father's great mausoleum,

This superb torano arch forms the entrance to the Jain Temple at Lodurva, near Jaisalmer

Humayun's widow having taken all responsibility for the project. All that survives of Akbar's work in the present capital is a handful of insignificant tombs and mosques. Fortunately, the extensive palace and mosque of Fatehpur Sikri exist in pristine condition, Akbar's city having been virtually unoccupied since he left it. A unique feature of most architecture from Akbar's reign is its emphasis on Hindu rather than Islamic themes, an expression, perhaps, of the Emperor's own lack of religious bigotry.

Jahangir (1605-1627)

Prince Salim, as Jahangir was called before inheriting the throne, was addicted to alcohol and drugs, as were his two brothers, and it was with some reluctance that Akbar appointed him successor, initially preferring Khusrau, Jahangir's oldest son. As had become almost a tradition, Salim rebelled against Akbar in the Emperor's last years, but was forgiven.

The empire was stabilized during Jahangir's reign, the last Afghan-controlled state in Bengal capitulating and the Rajput Sisodias of Udaipur being finally subjugated in 1614. Conflicts with the Muslim sultanates in the Deccan continued in a rather desultory way, neither side gaining much ground. Jahangir's personality was mercurial, possibly due to his addictions — unnecessary cruelty alternating with magnanimity. Overall, however, Jahangir's reign appears to have been surprisingly successful, although he depended more and more on the assistance of his favourite wife, Nur Jahan, who, together with her father and brother, virtually ran the empire in his final years.

Like his great-grandfather, Jahangir was an enthusiastic gardener, and the aridity of Agra and Fatehpur Sikri held little appeal. Most of the Emperor's time was therefore spent further north, in the moister, cooler climates of Lahore in winter and Kashmir in summer. Reputedly, Prince Khurram, Jahangir's third son, was not favoured to succeed by the influential Nur Jahan and, like his father before him, he rebelled against the Emperor. Reconciled after 3 years, Khurram was forgiven and, following his victory in the Deccan, in which a horde of gold and jewellery was acquired and presented to Jahangir, Khurram was appointed by his father to succeed him.

Jahangir had been an even more enthusiastic patron of the arts than his forbears, insisting on higher quality painting at the expense of output from the royal studios. Mansur, generally regarded as the greatest Mogul artist, produced his exquisite natural history paintings during the Emperor's reign. Jahangir appears to have had little interest in architecture, although he is believed to have been responsible for much of Akbar's tomb at Sikander — generally regarded as a hybrid monstrosity. Nevertheless, his reign did see the introduction in India of buildings faced entirely with marble, and with petra dura inlay work, both hallmarks of the great buildings of his successor's reign.

Shah Jahan (1627-58, died 1666)

As Prince Khurram (Joyous), Shah Jahan (Ruler of the World) had proved himself an able military leader, and it was partly due to his successes on behalf of Jahangir that his own reign proved to be the most peaceful of the entire Mogul period. Shah Jahan certainly had greater mental stability than his father and, in spite of his outstanding military ability, proved to be far more interested in cultural pursuits than in expanding the empire. Nevertheless, it should be noted, in view of what was to transpire, that he had gained the throne with unsentimental viciousness, as was considered normal at the time: he already appears to have killed his partially-blind brother, Khusrau and, on becoming Emperor, blinded and imprisoned his surviving brother Shahriyar. Not content with this, Asaf Khan, Shah Jahan's father-in-law, was instructed to put to death all other males of royal blood who might contest the throne; for these horrific acts he was appointed chief minister. It will already have been observed that the law of primogeniture was not invariably followed in Muslim India.

Shah Jahan immediately settled at Agra, where he began the great architectural set-pieces for which the Mogul dynasty is renowned. All the palaces within the fort except one were replaced, the Jama Masjid (Friday Mosque) was constructed and, following the death of his adored wife Mumtaz, the Taj Mahal built in parkland to the south of the city. In spite of these expensive projects, Shah Jahan, on coming to power in 1638, had immediately begun to plan a completely new city at Delhi, which would bear his name. The foundation stone of Shahjahanabad was laid the following year, during the Muslim holiday of Muharram, as suggested by his astrologer and, on completion of its Red Fort and the adjacent Jama Masjid, in 1648, Shah Jahan transferred to his new city.

It would seem that the Emperor had scant interest in painting, but was riveted not only by architecture, but also by jewellery design, which reached its peak with the extraordinary Peacock Throne, commissioned to display his gem collection. When Mogul architecture is considered, it is generally the buildings of Shah Jahan's period which come to mind. During his reign, both Mogul and Hindu features were modified and synthesized to create a unique style. Makrana marble, basically white, but with veins of grey and cream, became the standard building material for royal projects, most of

Tomb of Akbar, Sikandra

Tomb of Itimad-ud-Daulah, Agra

Tomb of Humayun,
East Delhi

Examples of stages which led to the design of the Taj Mahal

Taj Mahal, Agra

which were decorated with the inlay of semi-precious stones in floral or geometric patterns, known as petra dura. The majority of the outstanding buildings of the period are to be seen in Agra and Delhi, but there is also a set of delightful pavilions which was constructed by the Emperor at Ajmer, in Rajasthan. Others survive at Srinagar in Kashmir, and Lahore, both favoured summer destinations of the Emperor as an escape from the intense heat of Agra and Delhi.

In 1657, Shah Jahan fell desperately ill, and it was believed that he would die. He bequeathed the empire to his oldest son Dara Shukoh, whose three brothers, as was usual, contested the decision. Of all his sons, Shah Jahan favoured Aurangzeb the least, but it was he who triumphed. Almost miraculously, the Emperor recovered, but Aurangzeb's position had become too strong, and he deposed his father, putting him under house arrest at Agra.

Aurangzeb's treatment of his elder brother Dara Shukoh was typically appalling: he was paraded through the streets of Delhi in rags on the back of a dirty elephant, and then beheaded. Other princes were treated with varying degrees of harshness, Aurangzeb apparently exonerating himself by quoting the barbarism exhibited by his father in acquiring the throne. Rather surprisingly, Aurangzeb did not put Shah Jahan to death, permitting him to spend the last 8 years of his life as a prisoner in Agra Fort — with a harem but few clothes or writing materials.

Aurangzeb (1658-1707)

Unusually, none of Shah Jahan's sons had drink or drug problems, but Aurangzeb (pronounced Aw-rang-zheb) was considered to be the most competent. His great drawback was a religious bigotry (in spite of having a Hindu mother) which appeared to increase as his reign progressed. Nowadays, Aurangzeb would be considered a fundamentalist, his strict Muslim orthodoxy being reminiscent of that of Iran's Ayotollah Khomeini. Initially, he forbade Hindus to repair their temples or build new ones, but eventually, a programme of active destruction of temples was launched, and the *jizya* tax on non-Muslim 'heathens', which had been abolished by Akbar, re-introduced. The alienation of Hindus was inevitable, and Aurangzeb's son Akbar remonstrated with the Emperor over his divisive acts, eventually aligning himself with Rajputs against his father. In the case of the Amber Rajputs, Aurangzeb was sensible (or hypocritical) enough to retain close relationships. In return, its ruler, Jai Singh I, showed great 'diplomacy' in capturing for the Emperor Dara Shukoh (who was executed) followed, in 1665, by the heroic Mahratta leader Shivaji (who escaped).

It must be admitted that the Mogul empire reached its greatest extent during Aurangzeb's reign, the Deccan at last having capitulated. It was the great size of the empire, however, which was partly to contribute to its imminent downfall, lack of communications making effective defence impossible.

The ascetic Aurangzeb, in spite of his long and reasonably peaceful reign, showed little interest in cultural pursuits, even going so far as to ban music on religious grounds. Royal patronage of painting virtually ended, and the studios broke up, their artists founding schools in Rajput areas. It is said that a reason given by Aurangzeb for deposing his father was Shah Jahan's excessive expenditure on architecture. Little of importance, therefore, as might be expected, was built during his reign, nevertheless, one example, the Moti Masjid mosque within Delhi's Red Fort, already indicates the decline of Mogul architecture into fussiness of detail at the expense of well-regulated form.

Even for the times, Aurangzeb was undoubtedly a monster — although some Indian Muslims who are unaware of the facts still regard him as an evangelical hero but, like so many evil leaders, he died of natural causes, at an extremely advanced age of 89. It is recorded that, as death approached, racked with guilt, Aurangzeb at last showed remorse for his wicked deeds — rather too late, unfortunately, to significantly affect an unbiased appraisal of his life.

FROM THE GREAT MOGULS TO BRITISH RULE (1707-1803)

Great empires frequently collapse due to over-expansion, the passing of a tyrannical ruler, or widespread disaffection: in the case of the Moguls all three occurred following the death of Aurangzeb. Bahadur Shah I (Muazzam) succeeded his father, but without Rajput support, and provinces quickly began to break away to form separate Hindu kingdoms. No Muslim-controlled states remained outside the Mogul empire, Aurangzeb having already disposed of the last of them, Bijapur and Golconda.

The Mahrattas, low-caste Hindus, were founded by Siraji (1630-80), who was distinguished by great military ability and a religious tolerance unique for the time. His heroic exploits convinced Hindus that by uniting they could expel their Mogul overlords from India. Siraji inflicted many defeats on the Moguls in south India, and dramatically escaped from imprisonment at Agra. The first major defeat of the Moguls, however, occurred at the hands of the Persian, Nadir Shah, who sacked Delhi in 1739, slaughtering most of its inhabitants and returning to Persia with loot which included the Peacock Throne. Another Muslim invader, Ahmad Shah Abdali, sacked Delhi three times (1756-57), and the Moguls were now terminally weakened. A newly-formed Hindu group, the Jats, peasants from north India, contested Delhi with the Mahratta leader Rao Scindia, and ruled the capital in turn between 1771 and 1803.

A French general commanded Scindia's Mahratta garrison at Delhi, but surrendered the city to General Lake of the British East India Company in 1803. In the following year, Jaswant Rao Holkar led a Mahratta army that besieged Delhi, Colonel William Burn forcing its retreat. The British were now to rule Delhi, Agra, and soon the rest of India, apart from a handful of French and Portuguese enclaves, until 1947. When the British took Delhi, Shah Alam II, inheritor of the Mogul dynasty, was permitted the title King of Delhi, although his 'kingdom' consisted of little more than the Red Fort. This act was typical of the sentimental respect shown by the British for Indian royalty: most rajas were permitted to retain their titles and an element of direct rule over their territories. In the case of Shah Alam, the man was not only of an advanced age, but had been blinded by a rival 15 years previously; it is not inconceivable that these factors elicited sympathy from the new conquerors. Unfortunately for the Moguls, their next leader, Bahadur Shah II, permitted himself to be proclaimed emperor by the mutinous sepoys in 1857, and the dynasty was finally brought to an end by his banishment to Rangoon.

FROM THE 'JEWEL IN THE CROWN' TO INDEPENDENCE (1857-1947)

The British Crown took over from the East India Company in 1858, following the suppression of the Mutiny and, by Proclamation, Queen Victoria gave Indians equality with British subjects: the Governor General was appointed Viceroy. English manners and behaviour were introduced to the sub-continent, and they quickly became fashionable; it was not long before an Indian Prince, Ranjitsinji, would be distinguishing himself at cricket, wearing an England cap. Close friendships between the British and Indian aristocracy were forged, many blossoming from youthful associations at English public schools. The higher echelon of princes became intimates of the British royal family, a vast number of wild animals and birds being slaughtered at 'sporting' events held in each other's honour.

At the 1911 Coronation Durbar of George V, the transference of India's capital from Calcutta to Delhi was announced — to everybody's surprise.

Indian troops were to fight bravely for the British Empire in both world wars, but a strong nationalist movement, inspired first by

Mahatma Gandhi and later by Pandit Nehru, began to pressurize for independence. This was strongly resisted by the British, both Gandhi and Nehru being imprisoned repeatedly for their 'sedition'. When Clement Attlee's Labour government won control of the United Kingdom in 1945, plans were immediately drawn up to grant India independence, and this was finally put into effect in 1947, simultaneously with partition. Surviving physically from the Raj are the British 'cantonments' of Agra and North Delhi and, of course, New Delhi, where the triumphal avenue, Raj Path, and the official buildings round it, particularly the former Viceroy's Lodge, have a certain imperial grandeur.

By stages, the princely states of Rajputana (Country of the Rajputs) were integrated to become, in 1956, Rajasthan (Abode of the Rajas), with Jaipur the new state's capital. In 1970, all royal titles were officially abolished, but former maharajas and maharanis are often still respectfully addressed as such.

Geography, Flora and Fauna

Both Delhi and Agra lie in a flat plain, on the banks of the River Yamuna. North-west of Delhi, The Ridge marks the beginning of the long Aravalli range of hills, which runs south-westward for more than 400 miles (644km) , terminating at Udaipur. It is at Jaipur that most visitors will first see the higher ground. Outside the monsoon season and the short period that follows it, the landscape is predominantly arid. To the west of Rajasthan, straddling the Pakistan border, the Thar (or Great Indian) Desert contains great stretches of sand dunes. Virtually all Rajasthan's lakes, including those at Udaipur, are man-made.

The entire region lies north of the Tropic of Cancer, and cannot be considered tropical in spite of the intense summer heat; many of the plants grown will therefore be familiar to western visitors — the roses at Delhi, in particular, are splendid in March. Bougainvillea, however, which cannot grow in northerly climates, is the most spectacular of the flowering shrubs. Many trees will be unfamiliar, particularly the banyan (Indian fig), with long roots suspended from its branches creating an umbrella effect. Another type of fig tree, the pipal, its leaves tinged pink, was the tree under which the Buddha gained enlightenment. Cactii thrive in the dryer parts of Rajasthan.

The animal and bird life of India is a great attraction for many visitors; even in urban streets it is common to see monkeys, peacocks, striped-back squirrels, vultures and kites, in addition, of course, to animals that in other countries are restricted to the farmyard. Snakes are now a rare sight in major towns, apart from the snake-charmers' cobras (with fangs removed). In Jaipur, elephants will be seen in the streets at certain times, but are rare in Delhi or Agra, apart from state processions. Camels are used as work animals in Rajasthan and are commonly seen in the town centres. For the more exotic creatures, such as crocodiles, bison, hyena, deer (of many types), bears, and, of course, the big cats — tigers, leopards and panthers — it is necessary to visit the wildlife sanctuaries at Sariska or Ranthambore. Outside Bharatpur, the Keoladeo Bird Sanctuary is a mecca for ornithologists.

The People

India's population has almost doubled in the last 30 years, and now approaches a billion, with little sign of the birth rate falling. In spite of increasing industrialization, the vast majority still live in the country. In Delhi, which being the capital is naturally cosmopolitan, Indians of all types, from the light-skinned Kashmiris of the north, to the dark-skinned Tamils of the south, will be seen, as will many oriental-featured Nepalese. In Rajasthan, the taller Rajputs, with their turbans and bristling moustaches, remain in the ascendancy.

Much of the delight of a visit to India stems from the people, who seem much friendlier and happier than ex-patriate Indians. 'Yob' behaviour is virtually non-existent, and the country is undoubtedly one of the safest in the world for an unaccompanied tourist to visit. A great advantage for all readers of this book, is that the majority of Indians speak English, and 'meeting the locals' will not be a problem. However, do not make the mistake of thinking that all Indians are proficient in English, or that they will answer your questions strictly truthfully. Sometimes a 'No' response may just mean that the person is telling you he does not speak English. In general, never ask a question that can be given a simple yes or no answer, and do not give any hint of the answer that you would like to receive. Indians always wish to please, and many prefer to give an answer that will make you happy, than another, albeit the truthful one, which will not.

Indians love fanciful stories, and will exhibit much ingenuity in embellishing prosaic facts. It would appear that this has always been so, and the reader will find in this book a great number of equivocations, viz: it is said, allegedly, by tradition, possibly, a popular story is...., reputedly, etc. This indicates that a great deal of Indian history, at least prior to British rule, is dependent on myths, many of which are contradictory, and the exact truth will never be known. Some of the fanciful stories told by 'guides' indicate that the tradition still flourishes.

One tradition which will not please visitors is haggling: most find it aggravating and embarrassing. Unfortunately, it is absolutely necessary (except in shops where prices are fixed by the government). Usually expect to pay one-third of the first price quoted.

Indians claim that their infamous bureaucracy is the fault of the British administrators who introduced it many years ago. It never seems to occur to them that if this were so, the United Kingdom, and its other former colonies would be riddled with red tape in a similar way. A more likely reason for this infuriating addiction is that Indians have an unusually convoluted and pedantic way of thinking, which is perfectly expressed by reams of unnecessary forms for members of the public to fill in. What other country insists that a lengthy questionnaire is answered before a seat reservation can be made on a train? It is essential that short-fused visitors should be psychologically prepared for all this form-filling; to explode in a fit of temper, although understandable, will gain nothing, and possibly result in even more forms for 'difficult customers' being produced. India is paranoid about building up its reserve of hard currencies, and many of the forms that foreigners are required to fill in are aimed at achieving this. A further point to take into consideration is that the processing of these forms does at least provide much-needed employment. Visitors should avoid, as often as possible, banks, post-offices and railway booking offices — agents charge a small fee for making reservations, but it is a worthwhile price to pay.

A combination of the caste system and memories of the Raj has resulted in a servile over-politeness in some Indians, which can be almost as trying as the bureaucracy. Elderly retainers in luxury hotels are the worst offenders, apparently believing that their constant bowing and leering will elicit a stream of tips; it seems strange that they appear to have no clue that all this effusion has a negative effect. Try to remember that in spite of their smart hotel dress, the few rupees that can be spared for them are much needed to alleviate their relative poverty.

Languages

As there is no single language in India, English has been maintained as the lingua franca, and will be spoken by all well-educated people — sometimes to the exclusion of a native tongue. Hindi is the predominant Indian language in Delhi and Agra, while in Rajasthan, a local variant, Rajasthani, is still heard. For daily use, Muslims frequently speak Urdu, which before partition was the most commonly spoken language in Delhi and Agra. In spite of the many

In the streets of India's large cities monkeys play

On important occasions, elephants and their mahouts are richly garbed

different languages of India, those in the north have a Sanskrit root and a speaker of Hindi, for example, can usually understand Punjabi. It is in the south of India, where the tongues such as as Tamil have a Dravidian root, that speakers of north Indian languages are unable to communicate without English. Unless extremely proficient, it is not recommended that foreigners should attempt to speak an Indian language to a stranger, nor to ask if he or she speaks English. To do either might be regarded as implying that the Indian is not well-educated, and it would therefore be offensive.

Religions

Nowhere else in the world does the population of a single country follow so many disparate religions. An outline of the most popular follows.

HINDUISM

Many Westerners come into contact with Hinduism for the first time during their holiday in India, where two-thirds of the population is Hindu. It is one of the most complicated of the world's great religions, and much study and tuition is necessary before it can be properly understood.

Hinduism evolved from Vedism, a form of nature worship introduced by the Indo/Europeans to the Indus valley (now in Pakistan) when they settled there about 1,200BC. Although it is supported by many holy books, which are primarily narratives of epic events, Hinduism is not a doctrinaire religion, and no all-powerful body exists to pronounce dogma. Because of this, Hindus are eclectic, tolerant, and wide-ranging in their beliefs. To precisely define a Hindu is, therefore, impossible; many followers claim that Hinduism is more a philosophy than a religion in the accepted sense. Hindi, incidentally, is the name of India's official language and not directly connected with any religion.

Most non-Hindus are surprised to discover that, in spite of numerous 'gods', Hinduism is, like Judaism, Christianity and Muhammedism, a monotheistic religion. Brahmin, The Almighty, is revered as 'one that is the all', and the gods that Hindus worship represent different aspects of him. Similarities with the adoration of their patron saints exhibited by Roman Catholics have been noted.

The trinity of primary gods comprises Brahma (not to be confused with Brahmin) the creator, Vishnu the preserver and Shiva the destroyer and reproducer. When represented in human form, each has four arms.

Although Brahma is always depicted somewhere in Vishnu and Shiva temples, few Indian temples are primarily dedicated to him, probably because his work as creator of the world is finished. Only one Brahma temple, at Pushkar, is to be found in the area covered by this book. Brahma's consort, Saraswati, goddess of learning, is also depicted with four arms; she rides a peacock, and holds a *vina* (musical instrument).

Vishnu as himself rather than one of his earthly incarnations is usually shown bearing a quoit and a conch shell; occasionally he holds a club and a lotus flower in his other hands. A more complex but popular depiction of Vishnu illustrates him floating on the ocean, his vessel formed of coiled serpents; Brahma emerges from a lotus blossom growing from the god's navel. Laxmi (or Lakshmi), Vishnu's consort, sits at his feet; she is the goddess of wealth, and was created from the ocean. Closely associated with Vishnu is his vehicle, the half man/half bird Garuda. Vishnu is accredited with nine incarnations on earth (*avatars*); in chronological order these are: Matsya the fish, Kurma the tortoise, Varaha the boar, Narasimha the man/lion, Yamana the dwarf, Parashurama, Rama, Krishna and Buddha; his tenth incarnation, that of Kalki, is yet to come. The belief that Vishnu's last earthly appearance was as the Buddha (Siddhartha Gautama) about 500BC, neatly links Hinduism and Buddhism. Followers of Vishnu are known as Vaishnavites.

Throughout India, Vishnu is primarily worshipped in two of his earthly incarnations: Krishna and Rama. Krishna's life is documented towards the end of The Mahabharata epic. When depicted, he is blue in colour, which is why birds with blue plumage, such as pigeons and peacocks, are regarded as sacred. Krishna is often shown trampling serpents and playing a flute or holding a lotus blossom.

Vishnu, as Rama, is the subject of the epic poem *The Ramayana*; he is usually shown carrying a bow and a sheaf of arrows. The monkey Hanuman, who assisted Rama, generally appears in Vishnu temples as a secondary god.

As the member of the trinity of gods who has the powers of destruction and reproduction, Shiva (meaning auspicious) inspires great awe and trepidation amongst Hindus, who therefore wish to placate and please him. By tradition, he dwells in the Himalayas. When depicted in human form, Shiva has a third eye and wears a tiger skin; he may be holding an antelope, a trident, a noose or a drum. More commonly, Shiva is symbolized by a *linga*, usually a carved block of stone. This takes the form of a phallus, a reference to the god's reproductive powers. Shiva's vehicle, the bull Nandi (joyous), normally guards the shrine in Shiva temples. Followers of Shiva are known as Shaivites.

Parvati, goddess of beauty, and Shiva's consort, is the most revered of all Hindu goddesses. In her form as Durga, ten-armed and riding a tiger, or as the even more terrible Kali, with a protruding tongue and demonic appearance, she is also the most feared, and inspired the murderous thugee cult of the nineteenth century. It appears that Parvati now accepts more responsibility for cosmic violence than Shiva himself.

Shiva and Parvati have two children: Kartikkhaya, god of war, whose vehicle is a peacock, and Ganesh (or Ganpati), the elephant-headed god of learning, whose vehicle is a large rat. Ganesh, with his endearing, slightly comical appearance, is the best-loved of all the gods. He possesses none of the violent traits of his parents or brother, preferring to pacifically eat the sweets and fruits of which he is so fond, and with which his followers so liberally provide him. It is said that Shiva, returning to Parvati after a long absence, surprised her in the company of a young man, whom he failed to recognise as their son, and in a jealous rage decapitated him. On discovering his tragic error, Shiva was only able to replace the head of Ganesh with that of the next creature that he saw — it was an elephant.

A precept of most Hindus is that all creatures are reborn continuously until a perfect life has been led. The form of each reincarnation may be higher or lower, depending on the deeds performed in the previous existence. *Moksha*, the reward for a perfect life, is relief from this onerous cycle, ie non-existence. A similar reward nirvana is sought by Buddhists, but it seems a strange aim to the followers of the world's other major religions, all of whom believe that there is only one life on this earth, which will be followed, at least for the virtuous, by an eternity in paradise. A goal of non-existence seems equally surprising to those atheists and agnostics who expect it, no matter how well they have lived, but would prefer, in their heart of hearts, not to be totally extinguished.

Events and moral codes are believed to be established by a universal law (*dhurma*), which all Hindus must accept. Every Hindu is born into one of four main castes: Brahmins, the priests; Kshatriyas, the military and rulers; Vaisyas, the tradesmen and farmers; Sudras, the artisans. Those without caste, the Harijans (the untouchables), are still generally regarded as unsuited for any but the meanest of tasks, even though the law of India now expressly forbids discrimination. It is believed that membership of a caste is divinely ordered and cannot be changed; intermarriage between castes, although legally permitted, is rare. Muslims, Sikhs and of course foreigners, have never been part of the caste system.

Hindus hold all life sacred, and many are therefore vegetarians; the cow, as provider of milk to human children, being particularly sacrosanct. A devout Hindu would not kill a poisonous snake, even if it had bitten his child! Cremation, rather than burial, is virtually universal for Hindus, and their ashes, whenever possible, are scattered on sacred waters, such as those of the River Ganges. Pilgrimages are also made to these holy watering places, as it is believed that by bathing in them the soul as well as the body is cleansed. The accredited curative powers of the waters when drunk are a further reason for pilgrimages — pollution dangers notwithstanding.

Fretwork jali screens frame the views of Lake Pichola from the rooms at Udaipur's Lake Palace Hotel

Males who wear the *tilak*, a red spot marked on the centre of the forehead, are usually members of the Brahmin caste, but those from other castes may also wear it, and often do so, just for good luck. When a female wears the *tilak* it indicates that she is married and her husband is alive.

The swastika emblem is associated with Hinduism as a sign of good fortune, but it is also important to Buddhists and Jains. When the top bar faces right, the swastika symbolizes the day, when it faces left, the night; only rarely will the swastika be seen in the latter style. On its formation in 1919, the German Nazi Party adopted the swastika as its emblem (the top bar facing right), and between 1935 and 1945 it was Germany's national flag.

A good introduction for those who wish to learn more about this ancient religion is the book *Hinduism* by K. M. Sen (Penguin, 1961). Although it is not possible to become a Hindu by conversion, only by birth, Westerners are able to seek spiritual guidance from a guru.

Camels at the approach to Jaisalmer Fort

ISLAM

Around 10 per cent of Indians now follow Islam; the percentage was, of course, much higher before partition, when the majority of Indian Muslims migrated to Pakistan. Islam was founded by the prophet Muhammad (570-632) at Mecca in a pagan region, now part of Saudi Arabia. Muhammad had a series of visions, beginning in 610, in which the angel Gabriel revealed the wishes of Allah (God). The Koran is a compilation of what transpired in these visions as dictated by Muhammad, who could not write. Islam is a strictly monotheist religion, and the Koran specifically orders tolerance of both Judaism and Christianity, which are similarly monotheist. Much of the Old Testament of the Jews is, in fact, incorporated in the Koran, and Moses and Jesus are regarded as prophets, although subsidiary to Muhammad. Muslims, like Jews, do not believe that Christ was the son of God.

Unlike Hinduism and Judaism, the followers of which do not attempt to gain converts, Muslims from the start actively strove to proselytize their religion — by force if necessary. All Arabia had been converted within 20 years of the Prophet's death, and was eventually followed by Byzantium and much of Spain. The battle of Poitiers, France, in 732, stopped its advance westward, and the Roman Catholic Inquisition eventually banished the religion from most of western Europe. Expansion of the Ottoman Empire had introduced Islam to eastern Europe and, even after its collapse, some pockets, such as parts of Bosnia, have retained the faith. Islam's eastern spread had greater staying power and still holds sway in Malaysia and much of Indonesia. From the eleventh to the nineteenth centuries, most of north India was under Muslim rule, and it is surprising that greater inroads were not made into other faiths. Undoubtedly, India's greatest Muslim leader, Akbar, who showed great tolerance towards native religions, even those that were idolatrous, was partly responsible for this.

As yet, there is little sign of a strong Islamic fundamentalist movement developing in India, and disturbances of a religious nature are, fortunately, rare. When they do occur, a great deal of media coverage is given to them, but tourists are unlikely to be affected. Apart from Ajmer, for long a Muslim stronghold, visitors will see few signs of Islam in Rajasthan. In Delhi and Agra, however, the greatest architecture is almost entirely Muslim-inspired. Friday is the Muslim holy day, and the premier mosque in every city is known as the Jama (Friday) Masjid (Mosque).

The majority of Indian Muslims are Sunni, followers of the descendants of the Governor of Syria who claimed the caliphate succession to Muhammad in 661 after assassinating the prophet's son-in-law, Ali. Muslims who follow the descendants of Ali, Shi'ites, are now concentrated in Iran, Iraq and the Lebanon; they are generally more orthodox and have led the return to fundamentalism. Ritual bathing before prayer is important for all Muslims, as it is for Hindus, and washing facilities will be found in the courtyards of mosques.

JAINISM

Few who have not visited India will know much about Jainism as it has only around three and a half million adherents. Nevertheless, for those who travel to south and west Rajasthan, the religion is extremely important, due to its exquisite marble temples, the carving of which is unsurpassed in its delicay on the sub-continent — even at Khajuraho. Jainism is not as old as Hinduism, but roughly contemporary with Buddhism, with which it has many similarities. There have been twenty-four tirthankaras (pathfinders or prophets), the last of whom, Mahavira, lived around 500BC.

Like Buddhists, Jains believe that the universe is infinite, and was not created by a god or gods. However, their belief in reincarnation and the quest for salvation of the soul by eventually leading a perfect life is not dissimilar from that of Hindus. More than all other religions, Jainism stresses reverence for every form of life; followers are strict vegetarians and opposed to artefacts made of leather. There are two sects of the religion, the Shevetambara being the most common. The other sect, Digambara, is more ascetic, its members observing complete nudity (Digambara means sky clad).

Jain temples are distinguished by minute, almost filigree carving, particularly of their columns. Decorative themes include sensual pleasures, some of which rival Khajuraho in eroticism. Jain temples are usually built in clusters, each one honouring a tirthankar, and located in remote districts to avoid destruction by iconoclasts of other religions.

BUDDHISM

Buddhism has more followers in India (around five million) than Jainism, but many of them are emigrés from neighbouring Buddhist countries, such as Tibet and Sri Lanka. Most Indian Buddhists live in the north-east, centred on Darjeeling; few are to be found in the area covered by this book, the only Buddhist structure of interest being the Tibetan temple in Delhi. Siddharta Gautama (624-544BC), a prince, founded Buddhism in north India by forsaking earthly pleasures and achieving enlightenment by eliminating desires. Known as The Buddha, he apparently had three predecessors and another is expected to follow. Buddhists believe that only by extinguishing all desires throughout a series of rebirths (karma) will a state of nirvana be reached and release from further rebirths achieved. The spread of Buddhism owed much to the Mauryan Emperor Ashoka (274-232BC), but its sphere of influence contracted after his death, most of the country quickly returning to Hinduism. To help reclaim converts, Hindus announced that Buddha was one of the incarnations of their god Vishnu, and a merging of some aspects of both religions followed.

SIKHS
Guru (Teacher) Nanak (1469-1538) founded the Sikh (Disciple) religion, and nine gurus followed. The majority of Sikhs live in the Punjab, where their holy centre is Amritsar; extremists wish to break away from India to form their own country of Khalistan, and from time to time there are disturbances connected with the Sikh desire for greater autonomy. Sikh temples are called gurdwaras, and there are examples in most large Indian cities. The Sikh religions, although basically Hindu, incorporates elements from Islam and Buddhism. Its holy book is the Granth Sahib. Idols are not worshipped, the caste system was abandoned by Guru Govind in 1675, and pilgrimages to holy waters are frowned on.

Sikh males are distinguished by large turbans, which protect their uncut hair (kesh), which is tied in a bun. The four other *kakkars* are: *kangha*, a wooden comb; *kaccha*, short trousers; *karra*, a steel bangle; and *kirpan*, a dagger around which the hair is wound. For much of the Mogul period, Sikhs rebelled against the emperors, and many of their temples were demolished.

Since the sixteenth century, in honour of Guru Gobind Singh, all Sikhs have adopted the surname Singh (Lion). They are particularly adept at technology and provide a high percentage of India's airline pilots.

Industry and Agriculture

As in Mao's China, India's bureaucratic centralization and reluctance to invest in modern technology from abroad led to industrial stagnation. Policy has changed only recently, but a greater sense of dynamism is already apparent, and unbiased prognostications for the economy are encouraging. Major development of iron ore excavation has unfortunately coincided with the worldwide recession, but the clothing industry has continued to expand and is now the main earner of hard currency. Virtually all motor cars in India are locally manufactured, but based on ancient British models: the ubiquitous Ambassador is a virtual continuation of the Morris Oxford, last produced at Cowley in 1959. In late 1994, plans were

Oxen draw water the old-fashioned way in south Rajasthan

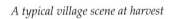

A typical village scene at harvest

announced to build the Rover Montego in India, after a period of component assembly, but this 10 year-old model is hardly likely to earn appreciable amounts of foreign currency. To rival the export achievements of Asia's Western Pacific Seabord countries, India's manufacturers must become more innovative, and familiarize themselves with the latest computer technology — a willing, low-cost workforce is waiting.

As has been said, the majority of Indians still live in the country and consequently work on the land. Here, some modernization has taken place, particularly in the use of fertilizers, but India's monsoons are notoriously unreliable, and failures in the late 1980s led to a great deal of hardship, particularly in Rajasthan, where drought conditions prevailed. Protection of cows, for religious reasons, means that more than 100 million beasts produce vast quantities of milk, but nothing else, apart from the not unimportant service of clearing the streets of rubbish (by eating it). Strict Hindus are vegetarians, and the quality of meat in India is not generally high. India, at last, has no need to import food, but its production of rice and fruit is insufficient to form the basis of a major export industry.

Indian Architecture

Try not to be overwhelmed by Indian architecture; it is not as complicated as it at first seems. Most will find it fascinating to observe how the building styles evolved and their elements merged, resulting in some of the world's greatest architectural gems. Chronologically, what will be seen are 'pure' Muslim buildings, with simple, pointed arches and domes in Persian or Afghan styles, Muslim buildings which incorporate Hindu features, and Mogul buildings, which fuse Muslim and Hindu features into a unique style. Mosques generally comprise a courtyard (*sahn*), with an ablutions tank (*hauz*), minarets, arched screens incorporating a much higher central archway (iwan) and leading to the domed prayer hall (liwan), the east-facing wall (*qibla*) of which is indented with niches (*mihrabs*).

Hindu buildings, the finest of which will be seen in the form of palaces and forts in Rajasthan, do not exhibit their evolution of style in such a clear way as Muslim buildings, and an expert eye is generally needed to distinguish periods and regional variations. The following elements occur in Hindu buildings, but all have been adopted by Muslims with enthusiasm: cusped arches; chajja eaves, deep and sloping; *chattri* kiosks, in the form of cupolas supported by slender columns; *jali* perforated screens; *jarokha* balconies, canopied and extending from windows in a wall.

Much more detail is given throughout the text as particular features are seen.

Food and Drink

HOTELS AND RESTAURANTS

Splendid Indian food is now available in the west, particularly in Great Britain where it has become almost the national cuisine from the point of view of eating out. Because of this, standards in the best Indian restaurants overseas, such as London's Bombay Brasserie, will not be bettered and only rarely approached in India; outside large cities, such as Delhi, the visitor will be hard put to find anything approaching gourmet standards. In the area covered by this book, the most sumptuous treats will be found in the luxury hotels of the capital, where the tandooris (particularly in the Maurya Sheraton Hotel) are guaranteed to be outstanding. Many visitors on accompanied tours that include meals will find that they are usually restricted to buffets, most of which are specially prepared for tourists and rarely soar above average in quality — an occasional splash out on à la carte will cost very little and certainly relieve the monotony. Delhi, due to its position as India's capital, has a range of restaurants outside the hotels, but most are geared to Indian standards and pockets.

Throughout India, smaller restaurants often indicate Non-veg or Veg, indicating that they do or do not serve meat. As might be expected, the greater the tourist appeal of the town the better the restaurants; Jaisalmer and Pushkar, for example, although small, have some first-rate rooftop establishments. Do not expect Western standards of service outside top-grade venues, and try to be patient. No matter how high the hotel is graded, prices will be astonishingly low compared with what would be paid at home. Those on budgets, however, should remember the iniquitous 20 per cent tax levied on all services offered by luxury hotels before committing themselves.

FOOD

Many Indian dishes found in Western restaurants (which are nearly all run by Bangladeshis) will not appear on menus in India: no-one has ever heard of Chicken Bombay or Madras, for example. These terms were invented to give foreigners an idea of how much chilli is used in the dish similarly, the word curry itself will not be seen in north India; its origin appears to be the Tamil word *kari*, which describes a sauce of mixed spices combined with various foods, primarily intended for flavouring rice. The sauce does not necessarily include chillis, which were not introduced into India until the sixteenth century by the Portuguese from South America. Those who are addicted to extremely 'hot' dishes will be disappointed to find that these are unpopular in north India, where the emphasis is on tandooris, biryanis and 'Mogul' cuisine, with their subtle blends of spices, chillis being either non-existent or kept to a minimum. Incidentally, vindaloo is a Goan dish of pork marinated in vinegar, its only connection with the overseas version being a copious amount of chillis — it is very rarely found in India outside Goa. Phal, the name given in England to the hottest of all curries, is unknown in India. The thin, crispy bread known in Bengal and Bangladesh as a poppadum is simply called papad, and sweet mango chutney will only be found in the restaurants of international hotels, as it is not favoured locally.

DRINK

Filtered water served in the better hotels is usually harmless; it is, however, always safest to purchase mineral water; bear in mind that this can be hard to find off the beaten track. Only in luxury hotels should ice be risked. All Indian soft drinks are too sweet for foreign tastes, but the sweetness may be reduced by mixing with soda water and a squeeze of lime juice. Bottled mango juice served ice-cold is the most palatable of India's soft drinks.

As an accompaniment to meals, either mineral water or *lassi*, a yoghourt-based drink, slightly salted, are the best options. *Lassi* with sugar added is also a pleasant sweet drink. Special versions of *lassi* made in Jodhpur and Bikaner are referred to in the text.

Alcoholic beverages in India (apart from Goa) are less than riveting. Due to taxation they are also extremely expensive, and well-known foreign brands are hardly ever imported. Most beers are rather weak and gassy, such as Kingfisher, but Delhi does possess a 'head-banger' beer appropriately known as Bullet — take care, two bottles are the recommended maximum. Indian whiskies and gin only approximate to Scotch and Gordons, the best being Peter Scott and Royal Challenge whiskies, and Aristocrat, Forbes and Blue Ribbon gins. Rum is a better bet, particularly when mixed with a combination of Thumbs Up (Indian cola) and soda water. Off-licences in India are known as English Wine Shops.

Indians boil up tea, water, milk and sugar together into a strong, extremely sweet brew, which few foreigners enjoy. Insist that tea, milk and sugar are served separately. Also emphasize that cold, not boiled milk is required. This will puzzle most waiters, but persevere.

A glossary of selected food and drink items is included in the Fact File on pages 291 to 293.

Delhi

1

✳ Few of the world's major cities possess as many historic
monuments as Delhi nor, at least for 6 months of the year,
such a pleasant climate in which to view them. Although a
few museums do exist, Delhi is not a 'museum city', neither does
Delhi possess a nightlife.

Apart from a ridge north-west of the city, the landscape is dead
flat. Formerly, there were no doubt picturesque viewpoints around
the ghats bordering the River Yamuna, but the course of this has
gradually moved eastward, and few will even glimpse it. Primarily,
therefore, what the visitor to Delhi is offered, is architecture, some of
the most splendid in the world, and most of which is a combination,
and later a fusion, of Islamic and Hindu styles.

Those who are on escorted tours are generally restricted to a few
days in which to explore this enormous, rambling city, whereas at
least 2 weeks are needed to do it justice. Fortunately, Delhi may be
are designed to lead the visitor through each of them from one
location of interest to another, following either an approximately
circular route or a straight line. The order in which the itineraries are

preceding page; Delhi's Crafts Museum displays regional buildings and costumes; folk music and dancing from all parts of India are performed daily

described has been planned so that the most important sights are seen in the first 3 days; but those particularly interested in the historical development of the ten separate Delhis may prefer to vary this order for the sake of chronology to South Delhi, East Delhi, Old Delhi, North Delhi, New Delhi.

The epic Hindu book, the Mahabharata, refers to Indraprastha, a city founded on the banks of the River Yamuna around 1450BC, and some have identified part of its location as the site of the Purana Qila in East Delhi. However, although fragments of pottery from the first millenium BC have been discovered, no archaeological traces of an important settlement from that period appear to exist.

The first five Delhis known for certain to have been built lie west to east, almost following a straight line, in what is now South Delhi: Lal Kot, Qila Rai Prithora, Siri, Tughlaqabad and Jahanpanah. Sections of the walls of each of them have survived in various states of preservation, by far the most impressive being at Tughlaqabad. The great Qutb Minar complex, incorporating Delhi's oldest Muslim buildings, occupies part of the Lal Kot and Qila Rai Prithora sites.

Little more than the citadels of the sixth and seventh Delhis, Firozabad and Dinapanah/Shergarh, have survived, and these, known as Kotla Firoz Shah and the Purana Qila, stand adjacent to each other in East Delhi. East Delhi's most famous sight, however, is the Tomb of Humayun, the first important Mogul structure to be built in Delhi, and the prime inspiration for Agra's Taj Mahal. The picturesque Nizamuddin, an 'oasis' village, with its revered shrine to a Muslim saint, is nearby.

Old Delhi (Shahjahanabad) not only includes the Lal Qila (Red Fort) and the immense Jama Masjid (Friday Mosque), but also the city's most fascinating bazars, running south from Chandni Chowk, Shahjahanabad's 'High Street'. Stretches of the city wall and many of its original gateways have survived.

North Delhi begins immediately north of the Lal Qila. With its historic Indian Mutiny associations, this sector is of greatest interest to British visitors; others, pressed for time, may prefer to omit the itinerary, although everything may be seen in half a day.

New Delhi, planned by Lutyens from 1911, is the largest of Delhi's sectors. It was laid out spaciously, from scratch, with tree-lined avenues, parks, and housing for the wealthy (primarily British administrators). Its commercial centre, Connaught Place, is Delhi's great meeting point, sited, as it is, where the old and new cities meet.

Most leading shops, tourist offices and restaurants (apart from luxury hotel restaurants) are to be found in this area, but even so, Delhi's 'Picadilly Circus' is practically deserted by 10pm.

Further south, Lutyens constructed his great imperial way, Raj Path, with, at the west and east ends respectively, Viceroy's House (now Rashtrapati Bhavan) and the India Gate memorial. Architecturally, this is by far the most important heritage left to a former colony by the British. Almost all of Delhi's museums are located in New Delhi, including the National Museum, which should not be missed, and the houses in the gardens of which Mahatma Gandhi and Mrs Indira Gandhi were assassinated.

Most of Delhi's de luxe and luxury grade hotels are situated in New Delhi, but the majority of them, although splendid, are located on its southern periphery, thereby entailing tedious journeys to and from the city centre. Conveniently-sited exceptions include the Imperial, Le Meridien, Janpath, Holiday Inn and Park hotels. In Connaught Place itself, there are several lower grade but comfortable hotels, such as Nirula's and Marina. Budget establishments of varying standard are located around New Delhi station in the area known as Pahargani.

Auto-rickshaws are significantly cheaper than taxis, especially if advance bargaining is firm, but they have drawbacks in Delhi, the chief of which is their open sides, which offer no protection either from the cold or from the black exhaust fumes emitted, so it seems, by almost every vehicle. An additional advantage of taxis is that their drivers usually, but not always, know the city better, and they are also, of course, faster, quieter and more comfortable. It will certainly be more economical and convenient to arrange a daily rate for visiting South Delhi, and a half day rate for North Delhi. Much of Old Delhi, and parts of New Delhi such as the west end of Raj Path and the Connaught Place area are best toured on foot. In East Delhi, where several lengthy halts are made over a not very long distance, hire of a vehicle for a day or half a day is uneconomical. Cycle rickshaws are only permitted to operate in Old Delhi; they are suitable for short journeys and are great fun except, perhaps, for the cyclist — help him by dismounting on a steep incline.

Although Delhi is now primarily occupied by Hindus, Muslims had provided the majority of the population for hundreds of years before the partition of India, in 1947 and virtually all buildings of historic and architectural interest that survive in the city, apart from those of Lutyens, were built by its Muslim rulers. Undoubtedly, ancient Hindu (and Jain) temples once stood in Delhi, but repeated sacking and rebuilding of the city, combined with the intolerance of other religions by Aurangzeb in the seventeenth century, meant that

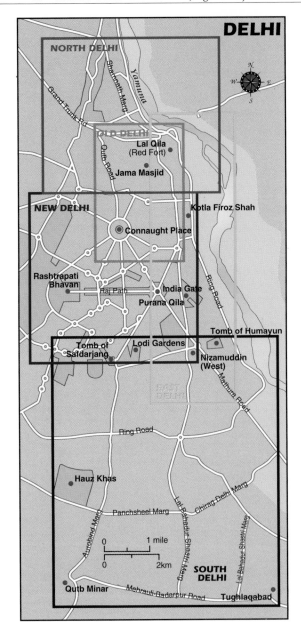

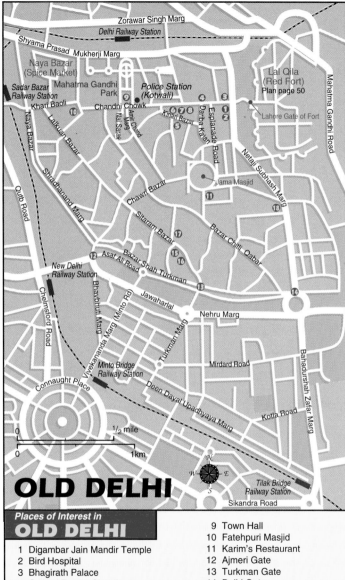

OLD DELHI

all were destroyed. Of primary importance in Delhi are the three forts, the palaces within the Red Fort, and the innumerable mosques and tombs. It is particularly fascinating to observe the evolution of the Mogul style of architecture, which reached its highest point in Shah Jahan's period, and the stages of development in tomb design, leading eventually to the sublime Taj Mahal, which many visitors will see immediately after leaving Delhi.

Unlike most Indian cities, Delhi is not particularly noted for its animal life, apart from the venerated cow, which appears to be as contented meandering amongst heavy traffic on the highways as it would be in a field. For the more exotic specimens of India's fauna, it is necessary to visit the parks and grounds of the historic buildings, where striped-back squirrels, peacocks and, on occasions, monkeys, can be spotted. Elephants are supposed to be barred from the Delhi area, but occasionally one can be seen, laden with timber, his mahout sublimely ignoring the regulations.

All cities seem to have their own particular aroma; Delhi's is immediately apparent outside Indira Gandhi International Airport, and it will remain with the visitor until the city has been left. The aroma is not, thankfully, of motor vehicle exhaust or cow dung, nor is it of heady spices; it is, surprisingly, of new mown hay.

✳ OLD DELHI

Old Delhi is the name by which the mid-seventeenth-century walled city of Shahjahanabad is now generally known. It incorporates the Lal Qila (Red Fort) at its eastern extremity, Chandni Chowk, the main shopping street, with its warren of fascinating alleyways, in the centre, and the Jama Masjid (Friday Mosque) to the south. This is the most confusing as well as the most colourful sector of the huge, sprawling city, and a personal guide is recommended (for a maximum of 2 hours) in the Chandni Chowk area. Shahjahanabad, the penultimate Delhi to be built and the most northerly located, was originally bordered to the east by the River Yamuna, but the course of this has gradually moved away, leaving mud flats, most of which have been transformed into commemorative gardens, in sections of which the great and the good are cremated.

A start is recommended at the entrance to the Red Fort, declining the offers of 'guides', many of whom know very little about the buildings or their history. After the fort has been seen, a circular route is followed, ending at the Jama Masjid, just south of where the itinerary began.

Lal Qila (Red Fort)

Shah Jahan selected the site of the Red Fort in his new city of Shahjahanabad in 1638; the foundation stone was laid the following year, and the fortress/palace ready by 1648 for the court to begin its transfer from Agra. The fort then nestled against the west bank of the River Yamuna, and the royal pavilions were set in a straight line, north to south, to take advantage of the river breezes. Two gateways faced the main arteries of the new city, Chandni Chowk and Faiz Bazar (now Netaji Subhash Marg).

When Aurangzeb deposed his ailing father, in 1658, Shah Jahan had not completed transferring his seat of power from Agra, and Aurangzeb became the first and last Great Mogul to rule entirely from Delhi's Red Fort. Precious material was looted from the fort's pavilions by its various eighteenth century invaders, including the Jats and the Mahrattas. It was the British, however, who must accept most blame for the altered layout of the fort, in particular the demolition of the arcades surrounding the two main courtyards, the western section of the women's quarters, and the formal gardens to the north. This iconoclasm took place following the Indian Mutiny and was explained away as being essential for defence purposes. However, retribution seems to have been an equally important factor.

The red sandstone castellated wall, which inspired the name of the fort, extends for 1½ miles (2½km) and reaches a height of 60ft (18m). It is said that half the construction cost of the entire project was incurred by this wall.

Tickets are purchased at the kiosk facing the Lahore Gate, from where the fort is entered. The **Barbican**, wrongly inscribed Lahore Gate, through which visitors pass, was erected by Aurangzeb in 1666 to strengthen the defences. Its heavy appearance certainly spoils the architecture, concealing, as it does, the **Lahore Gate** itself; Shah Jahan (who never said it) is reported to have complained from his prison at Agra that it was like throwing a veil over the face of a beautiful bride. From the Barbican, the road bends sharply towards the gate, thus depriving any aggressor of a direct approach. It was on the Lahore Gate that the flag of independent India was first hoisted, in 1947. A tradition has been established that the Prime Minister speaks to the nation from here on Independence Day (15 August).

Ahead lies a vaulted arcade of shops, **Chatta Chowk**, originally known as the Meena Bazaar, and where courtiers made their purchases. Most shops now sell souvenirs or refreshments to tourists; those of better quality are sited at the far end. **Goel**, number 35, **Tula Ram**, number 36, and **Gulzari Lal**, number 38, are of particular

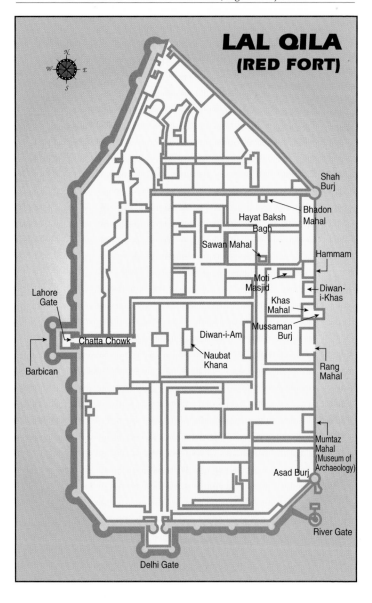

LAL QILA (RED FORT)

Shah Burj
Bhadon Mahal
Hayat Baksh Bagh
Sawan Mahal
Hammam
Moti Masjid
Diwan-i-Khas
Khas Mahal
Lahore Gate
Mussaman Burj
Chatta Chowk
Diwan-i-Am
Barbican
Naubat Khana
Rang Mahal
Mumtaz Mahal (Museum of Archaeology)
Asad Burj
River Gate
Delhi Gate

Only in Old Delhi are cycle rickshaws permitted to operate within the capital

Delhi's Red Fort gained its name from the red sandstone used for its massive ramparts

interest. The shops end at the west side of the outer courtyard, which is now much altered from its original appearance when arcades completely enclosed the area. A path from the courtyard led southward to the fort's Delhi Gate (not to be confused with the Delhi Gate in the city wall, which lies further south).

Once standing in the centre of the courtyard's east wall, but now isolated, the **Naubat Khana**, ahead, was the official entrance to the palace; at this point, all except the royal princes were required to dismount and proceed on foot, a tradition observed until 1857. Musicians played on the first floor gallery whenever an important guest arrived. A panel, delightfully carved with a floral design, should be noted immediately left.

This gateway now accommodates the **Indian War Memorial Museum**, where weapons, uniforms and badges from ancient times are displayed. To the east of the Naubat Khana, trees have replaced the arcades of the inner courtyard, where guards were formerly mounted; the area is now grassed.

Immediately ahead, on the same axis as the Lahore Gate, stands the **Diwan-i-Am** (Hall of Public Audience), where important state functions were held. From his throne in the central recess, the emperor sat in judgement over those accused of crimes, and considered grievances aired by his subjects; the marble bench beneath the throne was occupied by the emperor's wazir (chief minister). Sessions were held every day from 12noon until approximately 2pm in the afternoon, and punishments meted out on the spot, including whippings and executions. As may be imagined, great crowds gathered to witness the gruesome spectacles. The emperor was always accompanied by his sons and members of the nobility. On major occasions, the marble throne was replaced by the even more splendid Peacock Throne, which normally stood in the Diwan-i-Khas.

The panels of petra dura work lining the recess were commissioned from Austin of Bordeaux; it is said that the artist depicted himself as Orpheus in the small panel above the throne. All were removed by British soldiers following the Mutiny of 1857, eventually becoming exhibits in London's South Kensington (now the Victoria and Albert Museum). Lord Curzon, when viceroy, returned them, and ordered the restoration of the Diwan-i-Am; this was executed by the Florentine Menegatti in 1909. Unfortunately, the precious stones that had originally studded the panels, have been lost, presumably looted.

Columns supporting the hall are twelve-sided and set in pairs on the outer perimeters. The Hindu-style cusped arches, which link them, are a feature of the Shah Jahan period. Originally, the columns and arches were decorated to resemble white marble, and sumptuous material was draped between them.

The Diwan-i-Am projects into what was primarily the military zone of the fort; behind it, skirting the straight section of the east wall, are the five surviving royal pavilions of the palace. The **Asad Burj** is the most southerly of the three watchtowers that punctuate the east side of the wall.

It was in this corner that the zenana (women's quarters) was sited. Two of its three pavilions remain; the first, the **Mumtaz Mahal**, has been converted to a **Museum of Archaeology**. Manuscripts and Moghul miniatures are on view, but the rooms are very dark. A pavilion, which once stood immediately to the north, has completely disappeared.

The name of the next pavilion, **Rang Mahal** (Palace of Colour), derived from its brightly painted interior, which has been lost. This appears to have been the most important of the women's pavilion, and was possibly occupied by the chief sultana. The ceiling was originally of gilded silver studded with gold flowers, but most was stripped by the Jats, only traces remaining in the end pavilion. Paving, and the walls carved with reliefs, are of marble. Arches divide the area into rooms, through each of which passes a marble water channel, known as the Nahr-i-Bihist (Stream of Paradise), leading into a lotus-shaped pool in the central hall. Apparently, the floral shaping of the pool agitated the water in a picturesque manner. This water channel passed through all the private pavilions, its cooling effect being of great importance during Delhi's blisteringly hot summer months. The Rang Mahal lies immediately behind the Diwan-i-Am, stressing its importance; much more accommodation was originally provided for the royal ladies but to the south, all was demolished by the British in 1857.

Facing the north side of the Rang Mahal is the verandah of the **Khas Mahal** where, it is believed, the emperor spent much of his recreational time including, possibly, his four-hour lunch period, during which he would be offered at least fifty separate dishes. The verandah (baithak) appears to have been used as a lounge. Its outstanding decorated ceiling, in floral geometric patterns, is well preserved. The three central rooms of the building are believed to have formed the emperor's bedroom suite.

Protruding eastward from this is the **Mussaman Burj**, an octagonal tower surmounted by an open gazebo, from where the emperor watched elephant fights and other entertainments held below on a narrow strip of land between the fort's walls and the river; the Yamuna's course has since moved further east. A riverside location was essential for these, so that the animals could be cooled down after their exertions. On this gazebo each day, at sunrise, the emperor made a public appearance, in order to prove to his subjects that he was alive, a ritual known as Jharoka-i-Darsham, intended to prevent subversion. It must be presumed that the emperor retired early, as it is recorded that the royal musicians played in the gazebo when the morning star appeared, heralding the first calls of the muezzins from the city's mosques (hence the name Mussaman Burj). On the north side of the Khas Mahal, three rooms were set aside for private prayer. Above an intricate screen, a carved alabaster panel depicts the scales of justice, proclaiming that Mogul rule was fair.

The **Diwan-i-Khas** (Hall of Private Audience), which follows, is generally regarded as the most splendid of the Red Fort's pavilions. It was here that the emperor conferred with his ministers and nobles. Comprising a single hall with flanking aisles, the Diwan-i-Khas is entirely faced with marble, and has a five-arched façade. Petra dura work, incorporating semi-precious stones (some missing), forms a dado to the columns, the tops of which, together with the arches, are painted and gilded. Calligraphic panels above the inner side arches at the north and south ends, facing inward, repeat the phrase, in Persian, 'If there be a Paradise on the face of the earth, it is here, it is here, it is here'. The marble pavement reflects the cusped design of the arches. Originally, the ceiling was of silver with gold inlay, but this was removed by the Mahrattas in 1760. Lord Curzon commissioned the present timber ceiling, supported by iron girders, in 1911.

The fabulous Peacock Throne was brought here from Agra Fort when Shah Jahan transferred the court to Delhi; on state occasions, however, it was moved to the Diwan-i-Am. Nadir Shah looted the throne in 1739, taking it with him on his return to Persia, where it was broken up following his murder 8 years later. Contemporary descriptions and miniature paintings are all that exist to convey an impression of its glories. Made of solid gold inlaid with precious stones, the throne was approximately 6ft (2m) long by 4ft (1m) wide, and stood beneath a gold canopy fringed with pearls. Behind the throne, more precious stones represented the tails of two peacocks, closely matching the birds' natural colouring. Between the tails stood a parrot, carved from a single huge emerald. The Peacock Throne eventually became synonymous with the ruling Persian dynasty.

An early description refers to the splendid Diwan-i-Khas, surprisingly, as the *ghasl khana* (washing room); it is assumed that this was because the next pavilion to it was the *hammam* (bath house). This consists of three rooms, one of which is a Turkish style sauna. Fine

Delhi street scenes

marble and petra dura work survive, but the baths have been under restoration for some years and remained closed to visitors at the time of writing.

Immediately west of the baths is the **Moti Masjid** (Pearl Mosque), the only mosque ever built within the fort. The devout Aurangzeb commissioned this tiny mosque in 1659 in the manner of a royal chapel, thus saving himself regular journeys to the Jama Masjid, outside the fort. The building is regarded as defining the stage when Mogul architecture began to decline from its zenith, which had been reached in the reign of Shah Jahan. The courtyard is not large enough, the three domes are cramped, and the decoration is too heavy and excessive. The present name of the building comes from its smoky, white marble, resembling a pearl, but the mosque's domes were originally of gilded copper, and not replaced by marble until 1857. The finials to the domes are unusually dominant, calling to mind a Buddhist stupa. In spite of these criticisms, however, the craftsmanship exhibited throughout, particularly the petra dura work of the cornice, and the prayer hall's pavement remains superb. The fine bronze door to the courtyard should be noted. Token donations on entry (except Fridays) are expected.

A Persian-style formal garden (*charbagh*) divided into four parts by water channels, occupies the north-east sector of the fort. It is known as the **Hayat Baksh Bagh** (Life-Giving Garden). On its west side this was formerly linked with another garden, now lost, the Mahtab Bagh (Moon Garden). Two small garden pavilions survive: the **Bhadon Mahal** (August Pavilion) to the north, and the **Sawan Mahal** (July Pavilion) to the south. Their names refer to the months of Delhi's monsoon, when it was considered pleasant to sit within enjoying the cooling rain and breezes, which brought relief from the heat. In the central tank, the small island pavilion was added by the last Mogul emperor, Bahadur Shah Zafar II, in 1842.

The **Shah Burj** watch tower, at the north-east corner of the fort, served as a further viewing point for the entertainments below. Water was drawn up to this tower from the River Yamuna via an aqueduct, and chanelled directly southward through the royal pavilions.

A return to the Lahore Gate leads to the forts' exit. Ahead is Chandni Chowk, Old Delhi's famous shopping street. At the entrance to the thoroughfare, on the south side, the corner site is occupied by the **Digambar Jain Mandir**, a temple built in 1656 for worship by members of the Digambar branch of the Jain religion in the new city of Shahjahanabad. It is closed 2.30-5pm. Steps ascend to the hall, which is supported by marble columns. This, in turn, leads to the *vedi*, the gilded throne room, where the image of Tirthankara (prophet) Adinath is venerated. Jains have a deep respect for all forms of life and will not kill any living creature: priests will be seen wearing masks so that they cannot harm flying insects by swallowing or inhaling them accidentally.

Directly south of the temple is the famous **Bird Hospital**, run by Jains who care for the wounded birds. Many of the 'patients' are injured by domestic fans in the summer months, when around sixty a day are admitted. Every Saturday, the birds are examined, and released if fully recovered. As may be expected, donations from visitors are welcome.

It is now time to charge into the claustrophobic hustle and bustle that is **Chandni Chowk** (Moonlight Crossroads), the onomatopoeic quality of the thoroughfare's name being undoubtedly apt. Shah Jahan's daughter Jahanara laid out the street to form the processional thoroughfare for her father's new city in 1648, and it stretches westward from the Red Fort to the Fatehpuri Mosque. Chandni Chowk was originally tree-lined, and a water channel ran through its centre. Shops are closed on Sundays and the many public holidays, but the smaller entrepreneurs then take over, selling from the sidewalk, and the street's vivacity is maintained. Alleyways run southward, accommodating speclialized bazars which should not be missed. Cycle rickshaws ply along Chandni Chowk itself, but most of the side streets are best explored on foot; visitors are recommended to employ a guide who knows Old Delhi well to conduct them for an hour or two through the maze, otherwise much will be missed. While hotels and tour agencies can provide professional guides, at a price, many young men will be willing to assist for a small fee — ensure that whoever is chosen speaks good English and knows the locations sought. Make it absolutely clear that a shopping expedition is not required.

On the north side, the **Bhagirath Palace**, with its colonnade, now accommodates traders in electrical goods on its ground floor, and a budget-grade hotel above. It was built as the Delhi residence of the Begum Samra early in the late-eighteenth century. Her husband, Walter Reinhhard, was a Christian mercenary, locally known as Sambre, hence Samra, which is a corruption of it. Also on the north side is the **Central Baptist Church**. Formerly, at this point in Chandni Chowk, there stood a gate which gained the name Khuni Darwaza (Gateway of Blood) when, in 1739, the bodies of victims of Nadir Shah's massacre were piled against it.

Opposite the church, **Dariba Kalan** runs southward. On its corner with Chandni Chowk is a famous kiosk, Nain Chand Jain, where jalebis, hot and crisp, but not excessively sweet, are fried. Dariba Kalan (meaning large, incomparable pearl), is renowned for its jewellers and perfumeries. At number 1659 (opposite number 257), **Shri Ram Hari Ram**, on the west side, is an extensive basement-level bazar, where watches and precious jewels are sold. Further down, on the opposite side, Gular Singh stocks a wide range of perfumes.

Returning in the direction of Chandni Chowk, but well before this is reached, **Kinari Bazar**, left, leads diagonally north-westward. Kinari, meaning braid, refers to the accessories sold in the street for celebrations and festivals.

A short street, left, leads to another **Jain temple**, this one catering for the Svetambar sect. Its domed stone façade imitates wood; particularly noteworthy is the delicately carved porch. Marble columns and gilding provide a sumptuous interior — note the prophet's ivory canopy.

Return to Kinari Bazar, turn left and right, following **Paratha** (or Paranthe) **Walan**, so-named because paratha cooks formerly occupied most of the establishments. A few are left, and a cheap, but satisfying vegetarian snack in this lively street can suffice for lunch.

A return to Chandni Chowk, ahead, is now made. Almost immediately on the right is the renowned sweet shop **Ghantewalla**. The name means bell and, by tradition, a processional elephant of the emperor jangled his bell outside the shop for a sweetmeat whenever he passed.

Standing in line on the same side of the road, are the Sunehri Masjid and are the Sisganj Gurdwara. The **Sunehri Masjid** (Golden Mosque) was built between 1714 and 1722, and its dome, cupola and finials remain gilded. It is said that Nadir Shah observed the slaughter of Delhi's citizens by his troops from the mosque's roof in 1739. Initially, the Mogul emperor, Muhammad Shah, ingratiatingly welcomed his Persian conqueror, his troops, but the crowd attacked when they demanded free food. Nadir Shah summoned his main force, camped outside the city, and in 6 hours, much of Shahjahanabad was devastated and most of its inhabitants slaughtered. Nadir Shah soon returned to Persia, bearing the Peacock Throne and the royal treasury. Some assert that this included the Koh-i-Noor diamond, but others believe that Humayun had presented this two centuries earlier to the Shah of Persia, in gratitude for his hospitality. It is primarily due to the desolation created by the Persian army that so few of Old Delhi's buildings remain from the Great Mogul period.

Immediately east of the mosque, the **Sisganj Gurdwara**, a Sikh temple, marks the traditional site where, in 1675, Aurangzeb beheaded the ninth guru Teg Bahadur, who had rebelled against the Emperor. Here also, it is believed that Aurangzeb exhibited the corpse of his elder brother Dara Shukoh, whom he had executed as part of his struggle to gain the throne. Immediately prior to his execution, Dara Shukoh had been paraded ignominiously along Chandni Chowk, clad as a beggar, on the back of an elephant plastered in mud. Flower stalls congregate outside this temple, adding a colourful note.

Returning westward, on the north side, the **Kotwali** (police station) faces a small plaza. Outside this building, following their suppression of the Indian Mutiny in 1857, the British displayed the severed heads of three Mogul princes, and the corpses of those that they had hanged within the building. Both the Kotwali and the **Town Hall** (1860-65), on its west side, are classical in style, with stucco frontages. Formerly, a bronze statue of Queen Victoria stood outside the Town Hall; it can now be seen in the College of Arts.

The section of Chandni Chowk between here and the Red Fort was once called Urdu (meaning camp). The Urdu language evolved from the mixture of tongues in the royal residences (camps) and is an abbreviation of *zaban-i-urdu* (camp language). To the rear of the Town Hall stretches **Mahatma Gandhi Park**, formerly Queen's Gardens. The Public Library within its grounds was built to commemorate a former viceroy, Lord Hardinge. Behind the park is Delhi Railway Station.

Chandni Chowk, the heart of Old Delhi

Nai Sarak runs southward at an angle from the Town Hall's plaza and contains many bookshops, some of which sell handmade paper of fine quality.

Chandni Chowk at its west end, is closed by the **Fatehpuri Masjid**; the mosque was commissioned in 1650 by a wife of Shah Jahan, Begum Fatehpuri. Of red sandstone, it has a single dome and there is little embellishment apart from the screen of seven arches. Dried fruit kiosks are set in the outer walls.

The **Naya Bazar** (Spice Market) lies just north of the mosque; great bales of exotic herbs, spices, dried fruits and nuts fill the shops. Here is a good place to buy cashews and saffron at give-away prices. Adjacent to the market is **Giani Ice Cream**, renowned for its home-made produce. Pistachio is an all-year round favourite; equally delicious is mango, but this variety is only available in late spring and early summer. Hot lentil halva, a crisp, nutty-tasting sweet, is also made on the premises.

Shah Jahan, as was normal, enclosed his city with a wall. Its eastern stretch followed the River Yamuna, and part of it on that side also served as the Red Fort's east wall. There were fourteen gates to Shahjahanabad, few of which have survived. The watchtowers that punctuated the wall were converted into bastions by the British following a raid on the city in 1804. This was just as well, as they had to repulse a much more formidable attack, by 70,000 Mahrattas, 3 years later.

A suggested route from the west end of Chandni Chowk passes the Ajmeri, Turkman and Delhi gates, following what remains of the southern section of Shahjahanabad's wall. It might have been expected that Shah Jahan would have commissioned splendid entrances to his new city, but none is particularly outstanding. This has suggested to some that the Emperor may have sensed impending trouble, and therefore wanted his defencive wall completed as quickly as possible.

A brief pause at **Ajmeri Gate**, the western entrance to Shahjahanabad, will suffice, before continuing eastward along Asaf Ali Road to **Turkman Gate**. From here, follow Sitaram Bazar northward; a left turn leads to the **Kalan** (or Kali) **Masjid**. This is one of the most ancient buildings in Old Delhi, having been constructed by Firoz Shah Tughlaq within his extensive city of Firozabad in 1386. The mosque is designed in the Arabian style, it is two-storeyed, battlemented and surmounted by small domes. The square courtyard is cloistered, and a stern, fortress-like appearance prevails.

To the east of the mosque is the **Tomb of Turkman Shah** 'Sun of Devotees', who died in 1240. Another tomb, contemporary with Turkman Shah's, is located immediately to the north and reached from the opposite side of Sitaram Bazar. Here lies the only female Sultan of Delhi, Sultan Raziya, daughter of Iltutmish. She ruled from 1236 to 1240, lost her throne, and was killed fighting to recover it.

Return to Asaf Ali Road and continue eastward to **Delhi Gate**, the south-east entrance to Shahjahanabad. For some reason, like Trafalgar Square in London, this has become a popular venue for feeding pigeons. Immediately northward from the gate stretches **Netaji Subhash Marg**, the main artery of the Daryaganj quarter. It follows the route of Faiz Bazar, Shahjahanabad's north/south artery. **Moti Mahal**, passed on the left, is a famous Old Delhi restaurant, very economically priced. The building was restored in 1993 and offers a rare Delhi opportunity for winter al fresco dining in its walled patio. *Tandooris* and *chicken murgmasalam* are specialities. Very soon the great bulk of the Jama Masjid is seen, lying west of the main road; its elevated site, known as the Bhojla Pahar, is an outcrop of the Delhi Ridge.

Jama Masjid

The Jama Masjid (Friday Mosque), is one of the largest and finest mosques in India. It was the last major work commissioned by Shah Jahan, who laid the foundation stone in 1650; 5,000 workers took 6 years to complete the project. Although it is contemporary with Agra's Jama Masjid, the building bears a greater resemblance in its plan to the Moti Masjid within Agra Fort, although it is embellished with two minarets and is much more ambitious in scale. There are three entrances, but it is preferable to approach the mosque from the east side, with parkland to the right and the great complex symetrically positioned ahead, impressively fronted by a broad flight of steps. Formerly, the east gate was closed to all except the emperor, who would often ride to it on the back of an extravagantly decorated elephant from the Red Fort's Delhi Gate. The return route was always varied, as a precautionary measure. Even when Aurangzeb built his Moti Masjid within the fort's complex, he continued to worship at the Jama Masjid on Friday evenings for the week's most important prayers, the streets being watered in the dry season to lay the dust as he approached.

The building is set on a red sandstone plinth on which rest arcades. The three octagonal entrances are sited in the centres of the north, east and south sides, and pavilions mark the four corners. It is obvious that pains were taken to provide the Jama Masjid with an harmonious and appealing exterior, in contrast to the majority of Indian mosques, where only the interior is regarded as architecturally important. At certain periods, non-Moslems are re-

The last great architectural masterpiece of Shah Jahan's reign, the Jama Masjid in Old Delhi

fused entry to the mosque, and a check should be made in advance to ensure that no holy festival is being celebrated.

The doors of the main gate are decorated with bold arabesques of brass; at this point, shoes must be left or carried in a bag. Within the walls, the great courtyard (*sahn*) is almost 300ft (91m) wide and can accommodate 25,000 worshippers. In its centre stands a marble ablutions basin (*hauz*) incorporating a fountain.

Unusually in a royal Mogul building, we know the name of the architect: it was Ustad Khlil, who combined sandstone and marble for the exterior of the prayer hall (*liwan*). As is normal, the high central entrance (*iwan*) dominates, providing a focal point for worshippers in the courtyard whenever there are too many for all to be accommodated in the hall itself. Of all the great Mogul buildings, only the Taj Mahal was designed with a dome large enough to 'float' above its *iwan*. The Jama Masjid's three domes of white marble are decorated with strips of black marble, thus accentuating their onion shape.

Surmounted by marble kiosks, the slim towers of the *iwan* are echoed by the two loftier minarets flanking the hall. Serving as Delhi landmarks, they are each 130ft (40m) high and constructed from alternate strips of white marble and red sandstone. It is usually possible to ascend the minarets, for a small fee, with a supplement required for photography. Ladies should heed the notice insisting that 'women must be with reliable men relative.' From the courtyard's east arcade, the splendid views of the Red Fort's walls are a reminder that the original name of the mosque was Masjid-i-Jahan Numa (Mosque with a View of the World).

Within the north-east pavilion are housed much-venerated relics of Muhammad brought from Mecca: a footprint of the prophet, one of his sandals and a tract from the Koran — these will be shown on request. Originally, Shah Jahan inserted the prophet's footprint within the prayer hall.

The prayer hall is entered by passing through the marble screen of cusped arches. Steps, right of the central niche (mihrab), lead to the pulpit (*minbar*), which has been carved from one slab of marble. Exit from the mosque via the south gate.

Old Delhi's most famous restaurant lies immediately south of the mosque, in a courtyard approached from the street, appropriately named Gulli Kabab-i-yan (Kebab Street). Just ask for **Karim's**, everyone knows it. Established here in 1913, this restaurant bears the name of its Muslim founder, Hafiz Karim Uddin, and is still run by his descendants. A Muslim-style tandoori oven, of iron rather than clay, reputedly gives an additional crispness to breads, such as *nan* and *kulcha*. Other speciality breads, uncommon elsewhere, are *khameeri* *roti*, *sheermal* and *roomali* (handkerchief). However, it is the succulent *lamb kebabs* for which Karim's is famous. Adventurous diners might also like to try *lamb's trotters* (popular for breakfast) or *sheep's brain curry*. Another, much more up-market, but rather less authentic, branch of Karim's was opened in 1971 at Nizamuddin village, to the south of New Delhi.

It may now be appropriate, if dusk has fallen, to return to the Red Fort for the *son et lumière* performance. The English version always follows the Hindi, but programme times vary according to season.

EAST DELHI   ❈

Beginning just north of the Red Fort, this route proceeds southward, virtually following a straight line formed by Ring Road (Mahatma Gandhi Marg) and Mathura Road. Remains are seen of the citadels of Firozabad and Dinapanah, the sixth and seventh Delhis to be built in the fourteenth and sixteenth centuries respectively. The great mausoleum of Humayun, which was the precursor of the Taj Mahal, and the picturesque village of Nizamuddin basti end the route. All the locations are easily found, and it should not be necessary to hire a driver for the whole day. At the village of Nizamuddin, however, it might prove useful to acquire the services of an English-speaking resident who knows the intricate maze of streets and the precise location of the monuments sought. A bag is particularly recommended for carrying footwear within Nizam-ud-din's *dargah* (shrine), which is quite extensive, thus avoiding a return to the original entrance to collect it.

A short distance north of the Red Fort, on the east side of Ring Road (Mahatma Gandhi Marg), **Nigambodh Ghat** is now parkland. Ghats are steps leading to bathing areas from a river or lake, but although the name is frequently retained in Delhi, the course of the River Yamuna has moved back from them; many have areas set aside for important cremations.

Immediately north of the Red Fort stands the **Salimgarh Fort**, built a century earlier, its site now bisected by the railway, which crosses the Ring Road by a bridge. Islam, the son of Sher Shah Sur, built this island fortress between 1545 and 1554 to defend his father's city of Shergah, located further south, against the projected return of Humayun; it therefore predates the Red Fort and Shahjahanabad. Only part of its defensive wall has survived.

Vijay Ghat, also parkland, faces the east wall of the Red Fort and incorporates a memorial to India's second prime minister, Lal Bahadur Shastri, who died in 1966, and was cremated here. Immediately south of Vijay Ghat, in **Shanti Van**, India's first prime minister,

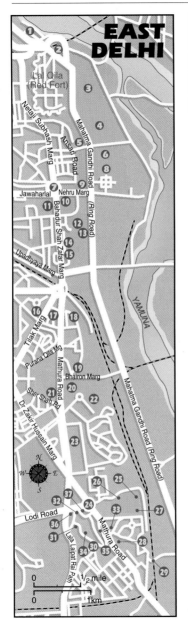

Places of Interest in
EAST DELHI

1 Nigambodh Ghat
2 Salimgarh Fort
3 Vijay Ghat
4 Shanti Van
5 Zinat-ul-Masjid
6 Shakti Sthal
7 Delhi Gate
8 Raj Ghat
9 Gandhi Memorial Museum
10 Ambedkar Stadium
11 Khooni Darwaza
12 Firoz Shah Kotla
13 National Rose Garden
14 The Times of India
15 International Doll's Museum
16 College of Art
17 Supreme Court
18 Pragati Maidan
19 Crafts Museum
20 Purana Qila
21 Khair-ul-Manzil Masjid /
   Sher Shah Sur Gate
22 Zoological Gardens
23 Sundar Nagar
24 Sabz Burj
25 Tomb of Humayun
26 Tomb of Isa Khan Niyazi
27 Nila Gumbad
28 Tomb of Khan-i-Khanan
29 Barapula Bridge
30 Nizamuddin Basti
31 Dargah of Nizam-ud-din Aulia
32 Tomb of Mirza Ghalib
33 Tomb of Arab Sarai
34 Chaunsath Khamba
35 Kalan Masjid
36 Tomb of Khan-i-Jahan
37 Karim's Restaurant

Jawaharlal Nehru, who died in 1964, and his grandson Sanjay Gandhi, killed in an air crash in 1980, were both cremated and are commemorated.

Against the Shajahanabad wall, on the west side of Ring Road, stands the **Zinat-ul-Masjid**, now in a dilapidated state. The mosque was built for a daughter of Aurangzeb in 1710, and its design was obviously influenced by that of the Jama Masjid. The striping of the domes, however, is far less delicate.

Shakti Sthal, together with Raj Ghat to its south, is the most visited of India's memorial grounds. Here are commemorated three Indian leaders, all bearing the name Gandhi and all assassinated by extremists. Most visitors are moved, some to tears, by this poignant reminder of such wanton destruction of peaceful, democratic lives. Shakti Sthal is also of interest to geologists, as specimens of rock from all India are exhibited in the grounds, many of them formed when the then island of India collided, on its northward drift, with the continent of Asia.

Prime Minister Mrs Indira Gandhi, assassinated in 1984 by two of her Sikh guards, was cremated here, and a great rock marks the spot. Foreign visitors should bear in mind that the ashes of cremated Hindus are scattered over holy water, such as the River Ganges or Pushkar Lake, and therefore, unlike Muslim, their monuments are examples not tombs but cenotaphs. Some confusion also exists over the name Gandhi. Mrs Indira Gandhi was the daughter of Jawaharlal Nehru, and gained her surname through marriage to Feroze Gandhi,

Mahatma Gandhi is commemorated in Delhi's Raj Ghat, on the spot where he was cremated following his assassination in 1948

who was not related in any way to Mahatma Gandhi: a strange historical coincidence! Her son Rajiv, Prime Minister of India (1984-89), was killed in south India by a bomb during his election campaign of 1991. It is believed that the assassin was an elderly Tamil woman, who also died in the explosion after presenting him with a bouquet of flowers in which the bomb was concealed. A brick plinth to the north-east commemorates Rajiv Gandhi: note that it is forbidden to mount the steps.

Raj Ghat, where Mahatma Gandhi is commemorated, lies a short distance to the south. International leaders, including Eisenhower and Ho Chi Minh, have made pilgrimages to Raj Ghat and planted trees, which are labelled with their names. Beneath a footbridge, a path leads to the enclosed garden, created to mark where Mahatma Gandhi was cremated and where his monument now stands. A simple, black marble platform indicates the precise site of the cremation; it bears the single Hindi word *Rama* (God), and a flame burns continuously in a lamp at its head. Every Friday, the day on which Gandhi was killed, a ceremony takes place here during which offerings (puja) are made to his memory,

Facing Raj Ghat, on Ring Road, at its junction with Jawaharlal Nehru Marg, is the **Gandhi Memorial Museum**. Of greatest interest to most visitors are the meagre personal belongings of the Mahatma, which include his stick, sandals, spectacles and watch. Also displayed, a grisly exhibit, is the bullet that killed him.

Follow Jawaharlal Nehru Marg westward to its junction (second left) with Bahadur Shah Zafar Marg. Immediately left is the Ambedkar Stadium, followed by the Firozshah Kotla cricket ground, where Delhi's occasional Test Matches are played. A short distance ahead stands the Kabul Gate, now more generally refered to as the **Khooni Darwaza** (Bloody Gate), where the British executed the sons of the last Mogul emperor, Bahadur Shah Zafar II, in 1838, following the uprising. The gate lies outside the Old Delhi wall and is believed to have formed a north entrance to Shergarh, the city built over Humayun's Dinapanah by his Afghan conqueror.

🏰 Firoz Shah Kotla

Firoz Shah Kotla, the citadel of Delhi's sixth city, Firozabad, is entered from the gate beside the Khooni Darwaza. Firoz Shah, the third Tughlaq sultan to rule Delhi (1351-88), was, like Shah Jahan, who would follow him three centuries later, an enthusiastic builder, but he appears to have had limited funds available, as much of his city consisted of restored structures, and plastered rubble predominated over sandstone. Nevertheless, Firozabad covered a large area, which comprised most of Old Delhi. It is said that some secret passages led from the citadel to: the river, the North Ridge hunting lodge and a location near the Qutb Minar in south Delhi, where Firoz Shah is buried. Timur (Tamburlaine) defeated the last Tughlaq ruler of Delhi, Nasir-ud-din Tughlaq, in 1398, and some of his troops were killed attempting to collect ransom from the citizens. In revenge, Timur slaughtered the 3,000 inhabitants of Firozabad and razed the city to the ground. The ruins would later serve as building material for the cities of Shergarh and Shahjahanabad.

Nothing of Firozabad survives apart from this citadel palace, which was built, possibly for the first time in Delhi, on the west bank of the river. Much later construction makes it difficult to appreciate the original layout of the complex, which consisted of three separate enclosures. Nevertheless, its Ashoka pillar and mosque are important Delhi monuments.

The **Ashoka pillar**, a 46ft (14m) high monolithic column of sandstone, was carved in the reign of the Buddhist king Ashoka (273-236BC) and originally stood at Topra (Haryana), over 62 miles (100km) to the north. Firoz Shah arranged for it to be transported down the River Yamuna to its present site in 1356. The pillar, wrapped in silk, reeds and animal skins, was laid on a long carriage and pulled by 200 men to the river bank. Perhaps Firoz Shah was inspired by the pharaohs, who had floated their granite obelisks down the Nile from Aswan to Lower Egypt in a similar way. The column was raised as each stage of the stepped-pyramid platform was completed.

Firoz Shah believed that the pillar had mystic powers, but in fact, Ashoka's words, sandwiched between later inscriptions, simply commanded his subjects to follow the teachings of Buddah. The edict, in Brahmi, was not understood until 1837, when James Princep deciphered the characters. Immediately above and below it, further inscriptions, dated 1163, refer to the victories of Visaladeva, a Chauhan prince. Although Firoz Shah did not record his own deeds on the column, unimportant Nagri, Sanskrit and Hindi inscriptions were added later; the date 1524 refers to the year in which the pillar was rediscovered. A second Ashoka pillar, which is contemporary with it, stands on Delhi's North Ridge, within the former site of Firoz Shah's hunting lodge.

The ruins of the site are only meaningful to archaeologists, although the existence of a well, south of the pillar, is apparent. Also ruined is the **Jama Masjid** (Friday mosque of the citadel), the largest of the seven mosques built by Firoz Shah. The proximity of the River Yamuna prohibited the usual main entrance from the east side, and it was transferred to the north. Timur is believed to have prayed in this mosque following his victory in 1398, and was so impressed by the building that he modelled his great mosque at Samarkand on it. In spite of the ruined state of the structure, prayers are still offered here on Fridays.

In the south-east corner of the complex, the **National Rose Garden** is at its best in late February and March, Delhi's early summer, when most varieties are in bloom.

Bahadur Shah Zafar Marg (the 'Fleet Street of Delhi') continues southward, parallel with Ring Road, passing, on the left, the offices of *The Times of India*, the country's most influential daily newspaper. On the same side of the road, Nehru House accommodates the **International Doll's Museum**. This is an amusing, as well as an instructive display of dolls, dressed in around 500 local costumes from the Indian sub-continent. However, the collection is, as implied, international, and the museum claims to possess over 6,000 dolls from eighty-five countries. Although the sources are named, the periods of the dolls and their costumes are not. Particularly appealing are the examples from Japan.

Continuing southward, the thoroughfare splits after the railway bridge has been passed: to the right. Tilak Marg, to the left, Mathura Road. A short distance south, on Tilak Marg, the **College of Art** appears to be the last resting place of the bronze statue of Queen Victoria, which originally stood outside the Town Hall in Chandni Chowk. It was moved to Coronation Park after independence, but vandalized and transferred here. In extensive grounds between Tilak Marg and Mathura Road, stands the Supreme Court, opened in 1958. Prior to its construction, the courts sat in Parliament House.

Return northward and follow Mathura Road, first right. Entered from Gate 4, on the east side of Mathura Road, **Pragati Maidan** is an exhibition and entertainment complex, founded in 1972. Exhibits, in a series of pavilions, represent the Indian states in the manner of an EXPO. Included within the complex is a children's park, known as Appu Ghat, reached directly from gates 3 or 2. Appu was the elephant mascot of the 1982 Asian Games, held in Delhi. There are more than twenty rides, many of them quite spectacular (some terrifying); popular with all are the Toofan Mail dragon roller-coaster, aeroplanes that can shoot each other down (Uran Kharola), Mini Flight, and Appu Columbus — for those who do not get seasick.

Within the park there are several restaurants of varying grades, cinemas, showing Indian and foreign films, and shops. Temporary fairs, both national and international, are accommodated in some of the larger buildings. Particularly important is the International

The Crafts Museum in East Delhi

Trade Show in November. A noteworthy example from an architectural viewpoint is the **Hall of Nations**, a pyramidal structure designed by Raj Rewal. As may be expected, most of the trade shows close at weekends.

The superb **Crafts Museum** occupies part of the 7-acre (3-hectare) Pragati Maidan Village Complex. Its main entrance is from Bhairon Marg, the next left turning off Mathura Road. Vernacular buildings, typical of various Indian regions, are ranged around a central group of exhibition halls and demonstration areas. Many of them have been transferred here from their original locations, and there is a strong sense of authenticity, enhanced by praiseworthy reticence in the use of caption boards. Charles Correa, the internationally renowned Goan architect, designed the museum, which was founded in 1951 with the aim of encouraging and maintaining the traditional skills of Indian craftsmen. Over 20,000 individual items are exhibited, many of them antique; they include textiles, ceramics, enamels, jewellery, masks, toys and carvings. Musicians and dancers in traditional dress perform throughout the day free of charge, and craftsmen may be observed at work. There is a restaurant and shops, but no hassling of visitors is permitted.

₩ Purana Qila

Facing the Bhairon Marg entrance to the Crafts Museum is the Purana Qila complex, entered from Mathura Road. The Purana Qila (Old Fort) was the citadel of Delhi's seventh city, Dinapanah (Shelter of the Faith), founded by Humayun in 1534. Humayun's rule as emperor (1530-56) was interrupted between 1540 and 1555 by his defeat at the hands of Sher Shah Sur. Most of the surviving 1 mile (2km) stretch of the fort's wall was probably built by Humayun but this is not certain. The mosque and Sher Mandal tower, all that remains within, are undoubtedly the work of his deposer.

Best observed from Mathura Road is the north-west gateway, **Talaqi Darwaza** (Forbidden Gate). A moat, fed by the River Yamuna surrounded the entire wall of the fort. Public access is by **Bara Darwaza** (Great Gate), the monumental south-west entrance. Apart from the truncation of a flanking tower, this is in remarkably good condition, the delicacy of its Hindu *chattris* and *jarokhas*, contrasting strongly with the structure's predominating Muslim vigour. Lutyens intended that the Purana Qila should serve as the impressive termination point of Raj Path's east vista when he laid out New Delhi, but the National Stadium was eventually built in front of it — a town planning disaster permitted by Lord Willingdon, who was encouraged, it is said, by his philistine wife. Within the enclosure, double arcades built against the wall provided temporary shelter for Hindus who had migrated to India from Pakistan at partition in 1947.

When Shah Sher Sur defeated Humayun in 1540, he demolished everything within the walls of the citadel, replacing them with new structures designed in Indo-Afghan style. He also extended Dinapanah northward from the Purana Qila, re-naming the city Shergarh, and enclosing it with a wall. Shah Sher Sur died in 1545 and was replaced by his son, Islam, a much weaker ruler, who reigned for 9 years. Disputes on the succession gave Humayun his chance to return a year later and regain his empire for the Moguls. Once again, the palaces within the fortress were demolished. Even when known in advance, it still surprises visitors to discover that the extensive walls guard just two relatively small buildings set within an expanse of garden.

To the left is Sher Shah Sur's delightful **Qila-i-Khuna** mosque, built in 1541, and spared by Humayun on religious grounds. Although its builder was not a Mogul, the mosque is regarded as marking an important stage in the development of the Mogul style, its simplicity of form pointing to the forthcoming Akbar period. As is usual in Indian mosques, the screen is of greatest interest; pointed inner arches are recessed within outer arches, and typically Hindu sloping eaves extend protectively. White marble is combined with red sandstone, all enlivened by carving and exquisite mosaics. It appears that the design of the mosque was influenced by the Jamali Kamali Masjid, near the Qutb Minar, completed 5 years earlier. The domed interior may be entered to view its prayer wall, which retains much original decoration. Facing the mosque, the original paved courtyard, with a central ablutions tank, has been converted to a garden. To the south is the small octagonal pavilion, known as the Sher Mandal.

Shah Sher Sur built the **Sher Mandal** around 1541, presumably taking the air beneath its *chattri* on hot summer evenings. Humayun must have found the pavilion pleasing as, alone of the Purana Qila's secular buildings, he did not destroy it, but is believed to have installed his library within. By tradition, Humayun, a superstitious believer in astrology, was observing the planets when the muezzin called from the adjacent mosque; turning sharply to bow, he tripped on his robe, fell headlong down the steps, dying from his injuries 3 days later. He had only reconquered Delhi a few months previously, and apparently had not begun to rebuild the Purana Qila. Akbar, Humayun's teenage son, who succeeded his father, soon moved to Agra before building his new capital, Fatehpur Sikri. The citadel of Delhi's seventh city was henceforth deserted.

Most of the tower's white marble inlay has been lost, and the original delicacy of the pavilion thereby impaired. The building may no longer be entered, due to structural instability, and there is, therefore, no danger of visitors repeating Humayun's accident. Further south, the **Humayun Darwaza** provides the third entrance to the citadel. From this gate are gained distant views of Humayun's splendid tomb, possibly the reason why the gate is so named.

Returning to the main gate, to its left, a small **museum** exhibits archaeological discoveries made during excavations within the complex in 1955.

On the opposite side of Mathura Road to the Purana Qila stands the **Khair-ul-Manzil Masjid**, together with a religious college (madrasa), built for Maham Anga in 1561. She had been a wet-nurse to Akbar and maintained great influence over the Emperor throughout her life. An inscription above the central archway records the foundation. Unfortunately, the stone facing has been lost and the building now has a dilapidated appearance. From the roof of the madrasa, a would-be assassin fired an arrow at Akbar, but only grazed him: he was hacked down immediately. Adjacent to the mosque, the **Sher Shah Sur Gate** was an entrance in the city wall of Shergarh, which led to an important market.

Delhi's **Zoological Gardens** abut the south side of the Purana Qila, and may be entered either on foot or by car from Mathura Road. Enclosures are formed by canals, and the small, unhygienic cages, which are a sad feature of some of the regional zoos in India, are fortunately absent. As may be expected, native Indian species predominate, including a rare white tiger. Look out for an elephant playing the harmonica. The zoo specializes in parrots and minha birds which are able to speak in several languages. Birds migrating southward pause for a respite in the grounds every autumn, augmenting the permanent inhabitants.

Further south, on the east side of Mathura Road, and just north of the Dr Zakir Hussain Marg overpass, **Sundar Nagar** is a modern residential development. Its roadside market consists of a square, lined with establishments selling jewellery and crafts, mainly to tourists but at reasonable prices. There is also a vegetarian restaurant.

Mathura Road continues beneath the underpass, and a left turn leads in the direction of the Tomb of Humayun. In the centre of the roundabout stands **Sabz Burj** (Green Tower), the tomb of an anonymous Mogul dignitary. The glazed tiles are modern reproductions of the originals, and give an indication of the former splendour of Delhi's ancient domes, most of which have fallen into disrepair. Sabz Burj is unusual for a Mogul work in that no Hindu elements have been incorporated.

Tomb of Humayun

South of the main tomb's enclosure, a stone crenellated wall encloses the mosque and **Tomb of Isa Khan Niyazi**, a supporter of Sher Shah Sur. All was completed before Humayun's return, and therefore predates his tomb. It might be thought that the existence of a tomb and its accompanying mosque belonging to an enemy would have made the site unacceptable for Humayun's own mausoleum, but this was apparently not the case. Blue, yellow and green ceramic tiles enliven the mosque's triple-arch screen.

Of greater architectural interest than its mosque is the tomb, completed in 1547 but in the style of the previous century. A wide verandah is supported by angled buttresses at the corners of the octagonal structure. Above this, a terrace punctated by *chattris* surrounds the flattened dome. Battlemented tombs had been built in Delhi since the thirteenth century, but this is an example of a tomb within an enclosed, fortified area, and may have inspired the tomb-in-a-garden format adopted by many of the Great Moguls beginning with Humayun's.

Just before reaching the entrance to the main complex, a gateway in the wall, right, leads to the **Arab Sarai**, an enclosure built for masons working on the project. Originally, temporary covered accommodation would no doubt have been provided, but there are no traces of it. Afsarwala, one of the young Akbar's military leaders, commandeered this enclosure in 1566 for his own tomb and mosque, which stand in line sharing the same plinth. The buildings, although in need of restoration, are an harmonious pair, with their similar height, domes, and red and white colour schemes.

After the Red Fort and Qutb Minar, the Tomb of Humayun is Delhi's most popular tourist attraction, offering, as it does, a foretaste of Agra's Taj Mahal. The main approach was originally from the south, but this is now closed, and visitors must enter the enclosure from the west side. Tickets are obtained from within the gate to what remains of **Bu Halima Garden**. The origin of this garden, which provided the axis for the design of the entire complex, is unknown, but it was certainly laid out long before any of the tombs existed.

When built, it was usual for great mausoleums to be erected in advance of their occupant's demise, however, Humayun's fatal accident occurred so soon after his reconquest of Delhi that there had been no time to begin its preparation. Haji Begam, the Emperor's chief widow, commissioned an architect from Persia, Mirak Mirza Ghiyas, to design the great tomb. She had probably been made aware of his work during her sojourn in Persia, to which Humayun's court had been exiled. Work began in 1563, beginning with the enclosure's wall, and was completed in 1571.

For the first time in India, the Persian concept of a four-part formal garden (*charbagh*) was combined with a centrally-located tomb-raised on a high plinth. Work on the garden was completed in 1573, and it is the oldest formal Mogul example in Delhi to resemble, in essence, its original state. There are, however, fewer plants, and water no longer courses through the channels, which originally divided the area into thirty-two small lawns.

It is apparent that the Persian designer incorporated traditional Indian features in this tomb, which many consider to represent the first outstanding example of the Mogul style of architecture. Most of Humayun's own buildings, as has been noted, were demolished by Sher Shah Sur, and Babur, his father, spent his brief reign laying out gardens, rather than erecting notable structures. Babur lies in a simple grave in Kabul, at his own request. The Koran expressly forbids demonstrative tombs, and it is not clear why this injunction was so spectacularly ignored by India's Muslim rulers, particularly the Great Moguls, apart from Babur and, as might be expected, the pious hypocrite Aurangzeb, who similarly occupies an unadorned grave.

The most important feature of Humayun's tomb is its monumental scale and novel plan, rather than the introduction of new elements — all of which had appeared in India before. Resting on a broad, arched plinth, the octagonal, two-storey building is completely symmetrical, each of its four identical façades being dominated by central, high-arched *iwans*. *Chattris* surround the dome, which is of double construction, to permit greater external height without creating an unduly lofty interior. A similar device had been employed for the tomb of Sikandar Lodi, built in Delhi 50 years earlier; however, this method of dome construction had evolved in Persia much earlier. Sir Christopher Wren adopted the same principle when he designed the great dome of St Paul's Cathedral in London.

The flat surfaces of the side pavilions are panelled, and the whole unified by a parapet. Pink, white and cream stone is employed, and stars are outlined in green, all resulting in a vigorously decorated façade. Steps ascend to the terrace from the west and east bays; marble tombs set in the paving commemorate five men, believed to have been Persian supervisors that had worked on the great project.

The plan of the tomb comprises a domed, octagonal chamber, entered from the south side, to which are attached four smaller chambers at the corners, also octagonal. Light filters through the *jali* screens, illuminating Humayun's plain white marble cenotaph.

A writer records in 1611 that the chamber was carpeted, drapes formed a tent above the monument, and Humayun's sword, shoes and turban were exhibited. His remains lie in the grave chamber immediately below, which may be entered by descending steps from the south side of the terrace. This arrangement was common in Europe as well as in Asia during the sixteenth century; it seems that its main purpose was to make it impossible to walk directly over a grave.

After the failure of the Indian Mutiny, which he had supported, the venerable Bahadur Shah II, the last Mogul 'King of Delhi', who reigned between 1837 and 1858, took refuge in the complex and was arrested by Major Hodson. Dying at Rangoon, Burma, to where he had been exiled, Bahadur Shah's body was brought back to Delhi and he lies here, together with Emperors Farrukhsigar (1713-19), and Alamgir II (1754-59). Shah Jahan's eldest son Dara Shukoh, defeated in the fight for the succession by his brother Aurangzeb, also shares the tomb, along with Haji Begam, the widow of Humayun. The Moguls rarely identified the occupants of their tombs except by sex: a writing implement box indicated a man, and a writing slate a woman. For this reason, it is not certain exactly whose grave is where, but, by tradition, Haji Begam lies in the north-east chamber.

In the south-east corner of the garden is the domed **'Barber's Tomb'**. This was erected in 1590, but the identity of the occupant is unknown; its name suggests a well-loved manservant of Akbar.

A final tomb of importance, the **Nila Gumbad** (Blue Dome), built in 1625, stands just outside the east wall of the complex; it is reminiscent of the Sabz Burj, seen earlier, although in this case the ceramic tiles are original. Once again, the identity of the occupant is unknown. As with the Sabz Burj, there are no Hindu elements incorporated: both buildings might have come straight from Persia.

The terminal stage in the architectural development that resulted in the Taj Mahal is **Khan-i-Khanan's tomb**, which is reached by returning to the Sabz Burj roundabout and following Mathura Road southward. The massive red sandstone structure stands on the road's east side, at the entrance to the village of Nizamuddin East. Abdur Rahim Khan-i-Khanan was the son of Akbar's supporter Bairam Khan, who virtually served as Regent during the young Emperor's minority. Rahim fought both for Akbar and, later, his son Jahangir, by whom he was imprisoned for a short time following a misunderstanding. In addition, he was a man of great culture, writing poetry of some importance; Rahim died in 1626, and his tomb was completed the following year.

The layout of the structure is similar to that of Humayun's tomb, but it is square rather than octagonal, and the compact arrangement is more reminiscent of the Taj Mahal. There is no garden setting, but water channels run along the terrace itself. Prior to 1753, the tomb would have resembled the Taj Mahal even more but, in that year, the marble facing of its dome was removed and used as building material for the tomb of Safdarjang, then under construction. It must be hoped that, as with the nearby Sabz Burj, the authorities will be able to effect some restoration to this rapidly deteriorating, but architecturally important building.

Further south, a left turn leads to **Barapula Bridge**, built over a tributary of the Yamuna by Jahangir's chief eunuch Mihir Banu Agha in 1622. The name of the bridge refers to its twelve piers.

✳ Nizamuddin Basti

It is now quicker to double back to Mathura Road in order to reach the fascinating Nizamuddin Basti, situated to the west of the thoroughfare, its southern extremity facing Khan-i-Khanan's tomb.

The village is an ancient Sufi Muslim settlement, built up in the mid-fourteenth century around the shrine of Sheikh Nizam-ud-din Aulia (1236-1325), the fourth Chisti saint. Although geographically an enclave of New Delhi, Nizamuddin Basti, one of India's most picturesque villages, has a completely separate identity, and does not look as if it is connected with the city in any way. Narrow, winding alleyways can only be explored on foot, and a guide recruited on the spot for a few rupees will prove invaluable. Apart from the usual requirement that he speaks good English, the guide must be able to locate easily: Kalan Masjid (nearby, in the south-east corner of the village), Chaunsath Khamba, the Nizam-ud-din Aulia Dargah (shrine), Ataga Khan's tomb, Mirza Ghalib's tomb, Khan-i-Jahan Tilangani's tomb and Karim's restaurant.

A Hindu, Khan-i-Jahan Tilangani, Firoz Shah Tughlaq's chief minister, converted to Islam in the fourteenth century, and built seven mosques in Delhi, including the **Kalan Masjid** which, despite its dilapidated state, is still imposing. The mosque was built in 1373, and its arcaded courtyards were originally covered, one of only two such examples in north India; the second, South Delhi's Khirki Masjid, remains partly covered.

Winding streets lead to the centre of the village, and the **Chaunsath Khamba** (sixty-four columns), the mausoleum of the sons and brothers of Ataga Khan. It was erected in 1623, towards the end of Jahangir's reign, and was the first structure to be completed in India entirely built of marble. Apart from floral decoration, the building is plain, with simple pointed arches divided by columns, sixty-four in number, which gave the mausoleum its name. *Jali* screens are in Gujarat style. Unfortunately, the building is frequently shut. Within, amongst several tombs, is that of its builder, Mirza Aziz Kokaltash, dated 1624-25.

There are several entrances to the enclosed area containing the Saint's *dargah* (shrine), which is located towards the western edge of Nizamuddin basti; shoes must be removed at all of them. The *dargah* complex is made up of small courtyards, mosques, the shrine itself, various other tombs and graves and a large tank: all combine to give the appearance of a tiny, exotic village-within-a-village.

An outer courtyard, seen first, is known as the Chabutra-i-Yaran (Seat of the Friends), where Nizam-ud-din-Aulia would debate with his followers. Buried here is Amir Khusro (died 1325), an intimate friend and disciple of the Saint, whom he outlived by just 6 months. His present **tomb**, surrounded by pierced screens, is seventeenth-century work. An inscription refers to the 'sweet tongued parrot', a complimentary reference to Amir Khusro's literary skills.

Steps descend to the main courtyard of the mosque. Sited from left to right are the **grave of Jahanara**, the daughter of Shah Jahan who devotedly shared his confinement at Agra, and the tombs of **Emperor Muhammad Shah** (reigned 1719-48) and **Jahangir** the son of Akbar II. Jahanara's marble-screened grave is covered 'only with grass', at the princess's request, as recorded on the stone.

In the centre of the courtyard is the **Dargah of Nizam-ud-din Aulia**, who died in 1325 at the age of 92. Venerated as a saint in his own lifetime, he was a member of the Chishtiyah Order of Muslims, which was founded at a village of the same name in Afghanistan. The sect came to India in the twelfth century; its members were mystic ascetics, who lived solely for Allah, rejected personal possessions and shunned all forms of violence.

Firoz Shah Tughlaq erected the Saint's first shrine in the second half of the fourteenth century, but nothing remains of this as Akbar renewed the structure in 1562. Alterations and additions throughout the centuries have similarly eliminated most of Akbar's work, so that architecturally the white marble shrine offers little of historc interest. Mother-of-pearl is set in the tomb's canopy, and the structure is surmounted by a white marble dome inset with vertical stripes of black marble, built in 1823. Visitors are expected to make a small donation, and their names are then entered in a book: the money is spent on maintenance and further embellishments. Non-Muslims should not be persuaded to part with more than a few rupees.

Immediately west of the shrine is the prayer hall of the **Jama-at Khana Masjid**, built by Khizr Khan, a son of Ala-ud-din Khalji, in 1325. This possibly replaced an earlier mosque and, as the year of its construction coincided with that of Nizam-ud-din Aulia's death, it might be expected that Khizr Khan also created a tomb for the Saint, probably on the site of the present shrine. Built of red sandstone, the mosque, refreshingly for the *dargah* enclosure, has escaped 'improvement' and retains its fourteenth-century appearance. A resemblance to the Khalji period Quwat-ul-Islam mosque in South Delhi is apparent. The detail of greatest interest is the lotus-bud fringe to the arched entrances, a feature repeated on the Alai Darwaza gateway, within South Delhi's Qutb Minar complex.

North of the mosque's courtyard is the great *baoli* tank, named Dilkusha, an important feature of all Chishti mosques. Washing of clothes as well as bodies takes place in the water, which is regarded as sacred. By tradition, Nizam-ud-din Aulia commissioned the tank to be constructed at the same time as Ghiyas-ud-din Tughlaq was frenetically building his city of Tughlaqabad. The Sultan ordered the Saint's workmen to transfer to his project, but at night they returned to complete the tank by the aid of oil lamps. Furious, the Sultan forbade oil to be provided for Nizam-ud-din, but miraculously the water already in the tank was turned to oil. The Sultan cursed the oil and the Saint cursed the Sultan, who threatened retribution. Warned of this, Nizam-ud-din placidly remarked 'Delhi hanoz door ast' (Delhi is still far away), a phrase that may be heard to this day throughout India, indicating that it is too soon to foretell the outcome of events. In this instance, the Saint was proved right, the Sultan being killed in an accident probably engineered by his son and successor. However, the year was 1325, and the venerable Saint had only a short time to live. It must be hoped that he saw the completion of his tank.

If footwear has been carried, the complex may be left from the exit ahead. A return to the shrine around 8pm on any day is recommended to hear the Muslims singing after prayer.

A short distance away, but very hard to find, is the exquisite, 'jewel-casket', **tomb of Ataga Khan**. It now literally overlooks a villager's backyard, and must usually be viewed through lines of washing. Intricate geometric patterns of mosaics and inlaid marble cover almost all the surfaces, except the dome, which is of plain white marble, in apparent imitation of Humayun's tomb. Ataga (or Azam) Khan married a former wet-nurse of Akbar and served as a general for both Humayun, whom he served at Kanauj in 1540, and Akbar. He was murdered at Agra in 1562 by his jealous rival Adham Khan. An inscription above the arch on the south side records that the tomb was erected by Akbar 1566-67 (the same year in which he rebuilt Nizam-ud-din's shrine nearby).

A short distance north-east of the *dargah*, the **grave of Mirza Asadullah Khan Ghalib** has recently been enclosed and protected by a marble structure. Ghalib, 1796-1868, was a renowned poet, who wrote in Persian most of his life, before adopting Urdu in old age for the work which made him famous.

Admittedly unprepossessing in appearance, due to dilapidation, the **Tomb of Khan-i-Jahan Tilangani** is of great historical importance, as it was the first octagonal tomb to be built in Delhi. It lies in the north-west corner of Nizamuddin village, and is mid-fourteenth century work. Khan-i-Jahan Tilangani died in 1369, but the precise date of his tomb is uncertain. Mausoleums designed by the Sayyid and Lodi dynasties, which followed, appear to have been influenced by this domed building, with its cupolas and terrace.

Near Lodi Road, but still within Nizamuddin village, is the upmarket branch of Karim's, the famous Old Delhi restaurant. It is one of the smartest eating places to be found in Delhi outside the large hotels. The succulent lamb kebabs are unbeatable.

NEW DELHI

Indians first heard about the creation of New Delhi, and the transfer of the capital from Calcutta to it, when George V made the suprise announcement at the 1911 Coronation Durbar in Delhi.

How the secret had been kept, in a country so fond of rumours, has never been explained. It appears that Sir Guy Fleetwood-Wilson, financial advisor to Viceroy Lord Hardinge, had been responsible for suggesting the project, which would take 20 years to complete. Both Gandhi and Nehru complained to its architect, Lutyens, about the cost of building New Delhi, which amounted to £15 million, but Lutyens retorted that it was no more expensive than adding two battleships to the British fleet.

Sir Edwin Lutyens planned New Delhi as a garden city, and a green, open character still prevails, even though there are now seven million, rather than the 70,000 inhabitants originally planned for. Of greatest interest to visitors is Raj Path, which is the east/west imperial axis of the city, the Connaught Place commercial area, and the museums, including the houses in the gardens of which Mahatma Gandhi and Mrs Indira Gandhi were assassinated. It is better to make arrangements well in advance to visit the presidential palace Rashtrapati Bhavan, the Secretariat and Parliament House, all of which are grouped together at the west end of Raj Path.

Some may prefer to incorporate within this route the Lodi tombs and the Tomb of Safdarjang, which technically fall within the New Delhi area but are described in the South Delhi route.

Gandhi Balidan Stal, formerly a private house in the grounds of which Mahatma Gandhi was assassinated, has been converted to a museum. Located at 5 Tees January Road, it is within easy walking distance of Claridges Hotel. From 1939, Gandhi often stayed in what was then Birla House, as a guest of the wealthy Birla family. The

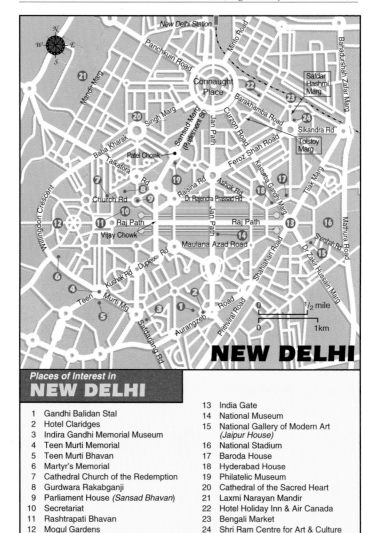

Places of Interest in

NEW DELHI

1   Gandhi Balidan Stal
2   Hotel Claridges
3   Indira Gandhi Memorial Museum
4   Teen Murti Memorial
5   Teen Murti Bhavan
6   Martyr's Memorial
7   Cathedral Church of the Redemption
8   Gurdwara Rakabganji
9   Parliament House (Sansad Bhavan)
10 Secretariat
11 Rashtrapati Bhavan
12 Mogul Gardens
13 India Gate
14 National Museum
15 National Gallery of Modern Art
    (Jaipur House)
16 National Stadium
17 Baroda House
18 Hyderabad House
19 Philatelic Museum
20 Cathedral of the Sacred Heart
21 Laxmi Narayan Mandir
22 Hotel Holiday Inn & Air Canada
23 Bengali Market
24 Shri Ram Centre for Art & Culture

Mahatma's bedroom may be seen as he left it on the fateful evening
when he stepped out of its door to the prayer ground, at the rear of
the garden. Red-painted footstep shapes have been inserted in the
ground, macabrely following his last walk; they end at the Martyrs
Column, erected to mark his final step before the bullet was fired. As

Gandhi fell dying he magnanimously made obeisance to his killer, a Hindu fanatic, who was infuriated by the Mahatma's attempts to unify Muslims and Hindus. Pilgrims visit the garden daily, many of them placing garlands of flowers around the column. A special prayer meeting is held in the grounds (also at Raj Ghat, where Gandhi was cremated) every 30 January, which has been designated Martyr's Day. In commemoration, the thoroughfare in which the house stands has been renamed Tees (30th) January Road.

At the north end of Safdarjang Road (number 1), which leads to the Tomb of Sardarjang, stands the **Indira Gandhi Memorial Museum**, where, by tragic coincidence, India's Prime Minister was, like Mahatma Gandhi, assassinated in the garden. Understandably some might feel, that a visit immediately following Gandhi Balidan Stal would prove too depressing, and prefer to return on another occasion.

Indira Gandhi (1917 to 1984), widow of Feroze Gandhi, and, as has been said earlier, not related to the Mahatma, occupied this bungalow during various periods from 1964 until her assassination in its grounds on the morning of 31 October 1984. During that time, she served as India's Prime Minister for three consecutive terms (1966-77), and again from 1980-84. A plaque in the garden marks the spot where Mrs Gandhi was shot dead by two of her Sikh guards in retribution for sending troops to quell the riot in the Golden Temple at Amritsar, the most holy of Sikh shrines.

A permanent exhibition includes photographs of Indira with Mahatma Gandhi, her father Pandit Nehru, and her sons. Of poignant interest is the timetable of events planned for Mrs Gandhi's last day, displayed within a frame in her study. It was very full, including tea with James Callaghan the then British Prime Minister, and dinner with Princess Anne. Neither of these events took place, however, as that morning, on her way to her first appointment — an interview with the BBC — Mrs Gandhi was assassinated.

Standing in the centre of the roundabout formed by the intersection of Teen Murti Marg and Willingdon Crescent is the **Teen Murti** (Three Soldiers) **Memorial**, commemorating members of the 15th Imperial Cavalry Brigade who fell in World War I.

The memorial faces **Teen Murti Bhavan**, the former residence of Jawaharlal Nehru (1889-1964) who lived here from 1948 until his death, this time, thankfully, from natural causes. Throughout his residency, Nehru served as India's Prime Minister.

Coming from a wealthy Hindu family, he was educated in England at Harrow, before graduating from Cambridge University and qualifying as a barrister at London's Inner Temple. Nehru, known as Pandit (Teacher), was frequently imprisoned by the British for vigorously espousing the cause of Indian independence, and spent much of his time in jail writing books, which included an early autobiography. Although a great admirer of Gandhi, 20 years older than himself, whom he regarded as his guru, Nehru found the Mahatma less than pragmatic, disagreeing profoundly with his complete renunciation of force, and eventually, albeit reluctantly, his opposition to partition. Nehru is blamed in some quarters for not doing more to prevent the bloodshed which occurred between Hindus and Muslims at the time of partition. Many also believe that, as Prime Minister, he should have promoted birth control, thus avoiding his country's disastrous population explosion. Nehru's hypocritical refusal to condemn Russia's invasion of Hungary greatly diminished his position as a world statesman. Nevertheless, Pandit Nehru must take much of the credit for India successfully walking the tightrope between the great powers during the cold war, and establishing his country as the largest of the world's democracies. Nehru has been described as a democratic socialist influenced by Marxist theory.

The house was designed in colonial style by Robert Tor Russell as the residence of the Commander in Chief of India, who acted as deputy for the viceroy. Completed in 1930, this building was converted to the Jawaharlal Nehru Museum following Nehru's death. Arrows mark the suggested route to be followed, which passes through the garden before the upper floor is reached. Nehru's reception room, study and bedroom have been preserved, as has the modest bedroom of his only child Indira (Gandhi). Most of the furniture is original and includes a superb Art-Deco desk. Panels of text and photographs in the hallways and rooms relate events in the life of Nehru, and India's long struggle for independence.

The lawned grounds are beautifully maintained. From its rose garden, Nehru would pluck a bloom each day for his buttonhole. The rear façade of the house incorporates three loggias, their columns designed in the Ionic order, which was almost exclusively favoured by the British architects of New Delhi. Facing the south-east corner, three flames burn continuously from a *Jawahar Joyti* in Nehru's memory. Last seen, on the upper floor, is the bedroom in which the Prime Minister died.

Willingdon Crescent stretches diagonally north-westward, and is laid out with bungalows and staff quarters. Lutyens, the planning supremo of New Delhi, lodged at number one during his supervisory visits between 1923 and 1928.

At the far end, on the right, within the grounds of Budha Jayanti Park, the **Martyr's Memorial**, designed by D.P. Chowdlay, overlooks the road. Cast in bronze, Mahatma Gandhi is dominant among the figures of eleven Indians who struggled for their country's independence.

Church Road branches right, as Willingdon Crescent begins to curve gently eastward. Just over half way along, on the left hand side, rises the **Cathedral Church of the Redemption**, Delhi's most important Anglican building, constructed between 1931 and 1935. Like Lord Hardinge, his predecessor as viceroy, Lord Irwin and his wife, both devoutly religious, survived an assassination attempt and, in gratitude, raised money for a new cathedral. Lutyens was asked to design the building, but his plans were considered too extravagant, and an architectural competition was held: it was felt only right that this should be judged by Lutyens; a neo-Classical design by Henry Medd, a protégé of Lutyens, was the winner. To commemorate the thirteenth centenary of York Minster, the Dean and Chapter of York were persuaded to donate the altar, and Lord and Lady Irwin presented the painting for the chancel. Irwin later became Lord Halifax and, as Neville Chamberlain's Foreign Secretary, is best remembered outside India for his part in the Munich crisis of 1938.

Further eastward, on the same side of Church Road, the **Gurdwara Rakabganji** was built to commemorate the traditional cremation on the site, in 1675, of the ninth Sikh guru, Teg Bahadur, who had been executed in Chandni Chowk by Aurangzeb. Both Hindu and Islamic features have been incorporated in this white marble shrine.

Ahead, surrounded by its 310 acres (124 hectares) of grounds, lies **Parliament House** (Sansad Bhavan). Herbert Baker, who designed the building, obeyed the stipulation of Lutyens that it should be circular in plan. The Duke of Connaught laid the foundation stone in 1921, and the building was opened by Lord Irwin 6 years later. Red and cream sandstone were employed for the lower stages, but the upper floor is of plastered brickwork, suggesting that economies had to be made, probably at the insistence of the frugal Lord Hardinge. A colonnade encircles the structure, which is surmounted by a shallow dome, invisible from ground level; a modern extension has been added.

Directly beneath the dome, the circular **Princes Hall** was built for ceremonial occasions and decorated with the crests of the princely states. It was here that the Indian constitution was drafted and the country's independence proclaimed by a bugler blowing through a conch shell. The oak-panelled hall has been converted to house one of the finest libraries in Asia.

Semi-circular chambers surrounding the library accommodate the legislative assemblies of India's parliament, which is based on the British system of upper and lower houses, although there are no hereditary seats, all members being elected. **The Lok Sabha** (House

Mahatma Gandhi

Mohandas Karamchand Gandhi was born at Porbandar, in the state of Gujarat, 2 October 1869. To the world, he is known as the Mahatma (Great Souled), and to Indians, Bapu (Father of the Country).

Gandhi's parents were strict Hindus, although there seems to have been an element of Jainism incorporated in their religion. Certainly, they instilled in their son, at an early age, respect for all life, self-purification through fasting, and tolerance of other religions. Nevertheless, the adolescent Gandhi, who married at 13, rebelled against many sacrosanct edicts for a short period: he smoked, ate meat and became an atheist, much to his parents' distress. It seems likely, however, that the motivation for Gandhi's behaviour was empiricism rather than mutiny; throughout his life he wanted to understand worldly temptations and prove that he could resist them.

Gandhi's native language was Gujarat, and he had some difficulty in matriculating at Bombay University, as all lectures there were in English.

In spite of the fact that his father was dead, his brother raised enough money to send the shy 19 year old to London in 1888, where he studied law for 3 years at the Inner Temple. While in England, Gandhi joined the London Vegetarian Society, indicating that his philosophy at least in part, had returned to that of the Hindu religion. After a brief sojourn in India, Gandhi took a one year contract with an Indian company in South Africa, where he worked as a clerk. Appalled at the government's racial discrimination, he lost his shyness for good and protested vehemently; for the first of many times he was sent to gaol. During his 21 years in South Africa, where he was joined by his wife, Gandhi legally represented ethnic Indians as their advocate, particularly in cases which had a racist element.

Although Gandhi's philosophy was always inspired by religious teaching, he entered politics in 1919, 5 years after returning to India, and led the National Congress in its struggle against British rule. As always, Gandhi insisted that opposition should be non-violent, whatever the provocation — but he was imprisoned for sedition (1922-24), being released after a 3-week fast. Sometimes, Gandhi was spectacularly successful, one instance being the march to the sea, which he led in 1930 as a protest against the recently introduced tax on salt, and the debilitating effect that it had on the poor: making salt for personal use, free of tax, was permitted the following year. A few months later, Gandhi returned to London, this time representing the Indian National Congress at a conference. It was not long, however, before he was imprisoned once more, his relationship with the new viceroy, Lord Willingdon, an unsympathetic imperialist, proving impossible. From gaol, Gandhi protested against new British legislation discriminating against the untouchables, whom he named Harijans (Children of God). After his release, Gandhi discovered that although members of the National Congress professed non-violence, it was not a heartfelt belief, and he resigned from the party in 1934.

During World War II, Gandhi and Nehru pledged support for the British war effort, but only in return for the promise of independence. The British would not budge and, in 1942, both were imprisoned, together with all leaders of the National Congress. The post-war labour government of the United Kingdom, which took over from Churchill in 1945, decided to give India its independence as soon as possible, and a new viceroy, Mountbatten, was sent to the country to plan the details and supervise the transition period. Gandhi played an important part in the negotiations, insisting that all Indians were the same people whatever their beliefs, and that partition on religious grounds would be wrong. Nehru, pragmatic as ever, was equally certain that the division of the sub-continent to provide separate Hindu and Muslim states was inevitable; Muslim leaders fervently agreed, and plans for partition were laid — Gandhi had lost his greatest battle.

सूचना

महात्मा गांधी की जीवन यात्रा 30 जनवरी 1948 को समाप्त हुई। दूसरे दिन यहाँ यमुना के किनारे उनके पार्थिव शरीर का दाह संस्कार किया गया उनकी अस्थियाँ समुद्री और सभी प्रमुख नदियों में प्रवाहित की गयीं स्थित, जल, पावक, ग्लान समीर से गांधी जी का सौंदर्य या। इस समाधि की निर्माण शैली की उनकी गौण्य सादगी की परिचायक है। यहाँ से पश्चिम में उस पार गांधी स्मारक संग्रहालय है। यहाँ महात्मा गांधी की कुछ निजी वस्तुएँ प्रदर्शन के लिए रखी हुई हैं। और गांधी साहित्य का पुस्तकालय है। दाहिनी ओर गांधी दर्शन है। जिसमें गांधी जी के जीवन और संदेशों का चित्रात्मक वर्णन किया गया है। यहाँ से आठ किलोमीटर दूर तीस जनवरी मार्ग पर रूक दूसरा तीर्थ स्थान है गांधी स्मृति जहाँ महात्मा गांधी ने अपने जीवन के अंतिम एक सौ चौवालीस दिन बिताए और मृत्यु का आलिंगन किया।

NOTICE

MAHATMA GANDHI'S EARTHLY JOURNEY CAME TO END ON JANUARY 30, 1948. THE BODY WAS CREMATED THE FOLLOWING DAY HERE ON THE BANK OF THE YAMUNA. THE ASHES WERE STREWN IN THE SEAS AND ALL THE PRINCIPAL RIVERS. GANDHI JI WAS IN HARMONY WITH THE ELEMENTS OF NATURE THE STRUCTURE OF THE SAMADHI REFLECTS HIS CERAMIC SIMPLICITY DIAGONALLY CROSSES FROM HERE IS THE GANDHI SMARK SANGRAHALAY WHERE A FEW PERSONAL BELONGINGS OF MAHATMA GANDHI ARE ON DISPLAY THE SANGRAHALAY ALSO HOUSES A LIBRARY ON BOOKS ON THE MAHATMA JI TO THE RIGHT IS THE GANDHI DARSHAN WHICH PORTRAYS GANDHI JI'S LIFE & MESSAGE IN WORDS & PICTURES EIGHT KILOMETERS FROM HERE ON TEES JANUARY MARG IS ANOTHER PLACE OF PILGRIMAGE THE GANDHI SMRITI, WHERE MAHATMA GANDHI SPENT THE LAST ONE HUNDRED FORTY FOUR DAYS OF HIS LIFE TO KEPT HIS APPOINTMENT WITH DEATH.

Whatever the merits of partition, the speed with which it was put into effect, without the supervision of the British, who had washed their hands of the affair and departed virtually overnight, led to appalling bloodshed. Muslims migrating from India to Pakistan, and Hindus migrating from Pakistan to India, were slaughtered in thousands by extremists on both sides.

Distraught, Gandhi pleaded for the carnage to stop, two lengthy fasts persuading combatants to call a truce in Calcutta and Delhi. For his pains, a young Hindu fanatic, Nathuram Godse, shot dead the 79 year-old Mahatma in the grounds of Birla House, New Delhi, 30 January 1948. Poignant memories of the great man abound at Birla House, Raj Ghat and the Gandhi Memorial Museum.

of the People) is the administrative house, its 544 members including the Prime Minister and his cabinet. Forming the upper house, the **Rajya Sabha** (Council of States), has 244 members, one-third of whom must be replaced every 2 years. In addition, 340 committee rooms and offices are spread over the ground and first floors and the annexe.

Bisected by Raj Path, **Vijay Chowk**, a grand circus covering 26 acres (10 hectares), and embellished with six fountains, lies due south of Parliament House. It originally functioned as a mason's yard, stone being deposited here by trains running a shuttle service between Delhi and the quarries on a temporary track. More than 30,000 men and women migrated to the city to work on the construction of New Delhi.

Important roads radiate from the circus, which was formerly called Prince Edward Place, commemorating George V's son, the Prince of Wales, later to become, briefly, Edward VIII, and later the Duke of Windsor. At dusk on 29 January, Beating the Retreat takes place at Vijay Chowk, military bands parading to mark the end of the annual Republic Day celebrations. Rising gradually from Vijay Chowk is Raisina Hill, on which the outline of the Secretariat and Rashtrapati Bhavan are illuminated for the event, providing a fairy-tale effect. A lone piper movingly terminates the proceedings.

An important part of Lutyens's brief in designing New Delhi was to incorporate established Indian architectural features, and he toured north and west India with his assistant, Herbert Baker, searching for inspiration. Both were equally unimpressed by most of what they saw, and Lutyens decided to adopt an idiosyncratic 'Imperial' style, neither Indian, nor English, nor Roman. 'An Englishman dressed for the tropics' was how he described his intentions. The result was that, apart from a scattering of Hindu kiosks (*chattris*) and deep, sloping eaves (*chajjas*), the architecture of the British Raj in New Delhi would not look out of place in any Western European city of importance. Visitors should not expect to see anything designed by the British in New Delhi that is remotely comparable with the Mogul pastiche Royal Pavilion, built by John Nash at Brighton a century earlier.

⌂ Rashtrapati Bhavan and the Secretariat

It must be said that the complex of buildings on Raisina Hill is magisterial, even though its domed centrepiece, Rashtrapati Bhavan, does not dominate completely, in the way that Lutyens had intended. Baker, who was responsible for designing both the flanking blocks of the Secretariat, felt that his buildings also warranted a hilltop position, and laid them out in such a way that Lutyens's building was pushed fractionally over the brow of the hill. Lutyens, of course, had to approve the amendment, and did so, little realising that a strange 'conjuring trick' would result: the dome of the Rashtrapati Bhavan, visible from most of Raj Path, appears to sink from view as Raisina Hill is reached, only to rise again as the building is approached more closely. Furious, Lutyens stormed 'I have met my Bakerloo': never again would the architects be on amicable terms.

The buildings of the Secretariat, opened in 1926, are now defined as **North Block** and **South Block**, only the Palladian loggias offering much relief from the rather cold severity of their appearance. Over 1,000 rooms and 10 miles (16km) of corridors are incorporated, including the Prime Minister's suite, which occupies the west end of the North Block.

Inserted in the east walls of both blocks are the foundation stones of New Delhi, laid, respectively, by King George V and Queen Mary at the Coronation Durbar in 1911. Originally sited in North Delhi, the stones were surreptitiously dug up and transferred here in 1913 (on a bullock cart, so it is said), after the new site for the city had been chosen.

'Dominion' columns, at the main entrances, were presented by Australia, Canada, New Zealand and South Africa. Each is surmounted by a gilded bronze sailing ship on a globe. The respective arms of the countries are depicted on their bases.

Viceroy Lord Hardinge personally selected the site for Viceroy's House, now Rashtrapati Bhavan, after admiring the extensive views from the top of Raisina Hill, but it was not ready for occupancy until 1931. The building has been the official residence of the President of India since independence. Rashtrapati Bhavan comprises 340 rooms, which include 54 bedrooms, and its area of 200,000sq ft (19,000sq m) exceeds that of the Palace of Versailles. In the days of the Raj, 2,000 staff cared for the palace, its grounds and its inhabitants.

The dome, unusually in India, is clad with copper rather than marble. Lutyens was apparently much more impressed by the Buddhist complex of buildings at Sanchi, near Bhopal in western India, than he was by any Hindu or Mogul work, and the form of this dome is reminiscent of the stupas which he had seen there. Lutyens set fountains on the flat roof, but these have not been operational for some years, due to a series of droughts.

Carved elephants decorate the gateposts set in the courtyard's elegant grille. In the centre of the courtyard stands the **Jaipur Column**, designed by Lutyens and paid for by Maharaja Madho Singh of Jaipur, who presented it to commemorate the building of

New Delhi. One face of its plinth depicts a subsequently altered plan for the city. Also inscribed is the rather banal composition of Lutyens: 'In thought faith; in word wisdom; in deed courage; in life service. So may India be great' — and they could have had Kipling! Very English oak leaves are carved on the column, the finial of which is in the form of a lotus blossom supporting a crystal star.

First seen within is the **Durbar Hall**, designed for formal occasions, and where Viceroy Lord Mountbatten, on behalf of King George VI, surrendered British rule over India to the new nation state. Situated directly beneath the dome, the hall is circular, and its surfaces are faced with marble. A statue of Buddha, standing rather than seated cross-legged as is more common, is a novel feature. In addition to his architectural responsibilities, Lutyens emulated the eighteenth-century British architect, Robert Adam, by personally designing most of the fixtures and fittings.

Other rooms, ranged around the hall, are: the **State Library**; the **Ashoka Hall**, with its painted ceiling and large Persian carpet; the **Ballroom**; and the **State Dining Room**, which boasts a musicians gallery, wood-panelling and portraits of viceroys. Marble stairways lead to the private apartments.

At the rear of the building, the **Mogul Gardens** were laid out by Lutyens in *charbagh* style, said to have been inspired by examples in Kashmir. From the water gardens, the long walk leads to a circular garden, where the blooms of a multitude of flowers, all of which may be seen in England, are at their best during the short Delhi spring (February).

Soon after moving into Viceroy's House as vicereine, the 'vivacious but vulgar' Lady Willingdon began to impose her idiosyncratic taste on the building and its grounds, redecorating many of the rooms in her favourite mauve colour; the ballroom was given Mogul motifs, chintzy flowers, and arabesques. In the garden, many of Lutyens's fruit trees were ripped up and replaced with unsuitable cypresses; for good measure, Lady Willingdon removed the stone elephants from the forecourt's gateposts to the garden, where they served as ornaments. Back in England, Lutyens, on learning of this vandalism, complained to Queen Mary, who wrote Lady Willingdon a letter of reproval but to no effect. In 1934, Lutyens met his bête noir, who was then in London on leave, and ironically remarked to her that if she owned the Parthenon, she would add bay windows to it. Her ladyship's bland response was that she did not like the Parthenon. Subsequently, all ended happily for Lutyens at Viceroy's House, as Lord Linlithgow, the next viceroy, commissioned him to put right Lady Willingdon's 'vagarious vagaries'.

The gates of Rashtrapati Bhavan, New Delhi

Raj Path, originally called Kingsway, runs precisely west to east, linking Rashtrapati Bhavan with India Gate. Every 26 January, the Republic Day parade takes place on this processional route, when temporary stands are erected for much of its length. Lutyens was almost certainly influenced in his plan by Sir Aston Webb's scheme of 1910 for the Mall in London, which similarly links the country's most important palace with a triumphal archway, and is also tree-lined. However, those considering a promenade from end to end of Raj Path should bear in mind that it is 1½ miles (2½km) long, whereas the Mall only stretches ½ mile (1km). A taxi ride the length of Raj Path (in both directions) will enable visitors to appreciate its grandeur without suffering undue fatigue.

A right turn at Jan Path, the next crossing, leads to the **National Museum**, on the left hand side. The Royal Academy's winter exhibition at Burlington House, London (1947-48), was the inspiration for India's National Museum, which opened on its present site in 1960. There are three floors: sculptures and prehistoric artefacts on the ground floor; manuscripts, miniature paintings and antiquities on the first floor; and, a surprise, pre-Columbian art from America, and a musical instrument collection on the second floor. Most groups of exhibits are arranged chronologically.

Particular interests will dictate what are the 'outstanding' items, but look out for: a massive carved elephant from the Sunga period; the Buddhist Gallery, opened in 1990, with relics of the Buddha which were discovered only in 1972; a bust of Vishnu found at Lal Kot (the first Delhi); the Babur Nama manuscript, written by the first Mogul emperor himself; the memoirs of Jahangir; an illuminated Mahabharata; the collection of miniature paintings, particularly the jewel-like examples from the Mogul period; Mayan terracottas from Mexico; and Inca metalwork from Peru. Not to be missed, displayed in a ground floor corridor, is an allegorical painting of Edward VII (when Prince of Wales), accompanied by an Indian-looking consort who is definitely not Queen Alexandra.

At the east end of Raj Path stands the all India War Memorial, now known as **India Gate**, which was designed by Lutyens who also had recently designed London's Cenotaph in Whitehall. Lord Hardinge paid for the memorial, the foundation stone was laid by the Duke of Connaught in 1921, and the archway dedicated by Lord Irwin in 1931. The memorial is reminiscent of the Menin Gate in Belgium, apparently, Lutyens's inspiration for the work. It is surmounted by a bowl from which flames rise on special occasions. Lutyens wanted the flames to appear every night and a column of smoke every day, but was overruled. Inscribed on both sides of the arch is 'India', flanked by 'MCMXV' (1915) and 'MCMXX' (1920). Within the arch are the names of 13,516 soldiers who died in World War I, the North West Frontier campaign and the Afghan campaign.

In 1972, as a memorial to Indians killed in the war with Pakistan, a rifle supporting a helmet was erected to mark the grave of an 'immortal soldier'. The surrounding flames are continuous, and each evening, at 5pm, the Last Post is sounded. The entire group of monuments and fountains is illuminated nightly.

Immediately east of the arch is a delicate sandstone canopy designed by Lutyens as a baldachino for the white marble statue of King George V, which stood beneath it from 1936 until removed to Coronation Park in North Delhi. It was once thought that an Indian hero would replace the King but, apparently, this is now considered inappropriate.

The India Gate stands within the hexagonal Fifteenth August Maidan, formerly Princes Place, around which residences for India's royal princes were originally planned to be built. In the event, only a handful were completed, the concept being ridiculously extravagant, as the occupants would only be in residence for the annual gathering of princes and the short Delhi 'season', which followed it. Houses were allocated to the princes of greatest importance, as long as they exhibited firm allegiance to the Crown. Once again, few indigenous architectural features were incorporated in the design of these houses, although most are given carved *jali* screens.

Jaipur House, which stands between Dr Zakir Hussain Marg and Sher Shah Road, on the south-east side, was built for the Maharajas of Jaipur, and has since been converted to accommodate the **National Gallery of Modern Art**. Exhibits, on two floors, are primarily by Indian artists, or foreigners who have worked in India, such as Thomas and William Daniell. Influences from other countries are apparent, but no specifically Indian style has yet emerged, and few Western visitors will find the museum of overwhelming interest.

Facing the east side of India Gate is the **National Stadium**, possibly the most unattractive and ill-sited structure erected by the British in New Delhi. It is the work of Robert Tor Russell, and was begun in 1931, much to the justified annoyance of Lutyens. Prior to the stadium's construction, the picturesque ruins of Purana Qila, which lie behind it, provided the terminal eastern viewpoint from Raj Path, as had been intended. Lutyens now saw this replaced by a hideous expanse of concrete, which spoiled the eastern vista from Raj Path even more than Baker's modifications to the siting of Rashtrapati Bhavan had spoiled the planned western vista. It is said that the location of the stadium was suggested to her husband by Lady Willingdon: a final gesture of iconoclasm, which, unfortunately, could not be remedied.

The Gujarat Market, just off Jan Path, is Delhi's most colourful

opposite; India Gate, New Delhi

By following Fifteenth August Maidan anti-clockwise, two further houses built for Indian royalty are passed on the north-west side. **Baroda House**, designed by Lutyens, can now be entered, as much of the interior has been converted to a booking office for Indian Railways. On the west side of Kasturba Gandhi Marg, **Hyderabad House**, also by Lutyens, was built for the Grand Nizzam of Hyderabad, who was reputedly, at the time, the richest man in the world.

Ashok Road, the next turning right, intersects with **Jan Path** (People's Road), which links Raj Path with Connaught Place. Originally called Queensway, Lutyens intended that both sides of the street should be lined with museums, however, only the National Archives and East and West Courts were built in his time, although the National Museum was added after independence. Just before the Imperial Hotel is reached, but on the opposite (east) side of Jan Path, is Chandralok Building, within which the **Rajasthan State Tourist Office** is situated. Those who plan to visit Rajasthan may wish to obtain up-to-date information and travel literature here. For shoppers, however, the most interesting part of Jan Path, which should be explored on foot, is the stretch between Hotel Imperial and Connaught Place, where the thoroughfare is designated Radial Road 8.

The **Hotel Imperial** was built by Bloomfield in 1935, and retains some contemporary interiors. Its swimming pool may be used by non-residents for a small fee, and the lawned grounds are still a popular venue for tea in the winter — a legacy from the Raj; **Thomas Cooks** have an office in the hotel. Robert Lutyens, the son of Sir Edwin, described the Imperial as 'jerry-built, patronized by Lady Willingdon, and frightful': the Lutyens/Lady Willingdon feud had passed to another generation! Outside the Imperial is the **Tibetan Market**, where most stallholders and artefacts actually do come from Tibet, however, few of the 'antiques' are genuine.

For some reason, the trees at this end of Jan Path attract fruit bats; their strange black bodies hang upside down from so many branches that the creatures themselves look like unappetizing fruit.

Tolstoy Marg crosses Jan Path and, on the north-east corner, the **Royal Nepal Airlines** office may be of interest to those who intend to visit Kathmandu. Almost opposite, on the west side of Jan Path, Jan Path Lane has been commandeered by Gujaratis, whose stalls overflow with brilliantly-coloured fabrics from their state. As the stallholders' own apparel is equally ravishing, this is one of the most picturesque of Delhi's markets. At number 88 Jan Path, the **Government of India Tourist Office** is particularly useful for supplying passes and tickets for government buildings.

Laying back from the west side of the main road is the renowned **Central Cottage Industries Emporium**. This is run by the government, prices are fixed, and high quality assured. It is virtually a department store, many of the departments representing, and run by, individual states. Superb silk clothing and leather goods are great bargains for Western visitors. After the Connaught Lane junction has been passed, the first of the three circular thoroughfares, which together form Connaught Place, is approached.

※ Connaught Place

Connaught Place comprises Connaught Circus, Inner Circle and Outer Circle, laid out in concentric circles and intersected by eight radial roads, numbered one to eight like spokes in a wheel. Parliament Street, the next radial road to the west, begins the clockwise numbering system as Radial Road 1. Blocks between the roads are identified by letters A to N, beginning on the west side of Connaught Circus. All this sounds very efficient, but, unfortunately, neither the roads nor the blocks are clearly named, and it is difficult for a stranger to locate a specific address. Most first-time visitors will find it simpler to begin at the centre and proceed clockwise until interest wanes or exhaustion sets in.

Lutyens planned Connaught Place, named after an uncle of George V, as the commercial hub of New Delhi. It forms the apex of the triangle encompassing New Delhi's area, and provides its link with Old Delhi. The colonnaded blocks were designed by Robert Tor Russell and, in spite of their uniformity, are rather more acceptable architecturally than his National Stadium. Initially, the development was not a commercial success, and prices had to be reduced drastically to sell plots: now, units are snapped up as they are vacated. The first shops to open were very genteel, selling goods only to British residents and the few Indians who could afford their prices; most provisions were imported from England, and the interiors of the shops, panelled in hardwoods, resembled European models of the period. What a change! It is now primarily Indians who are catered for, apart from those retailers who concentrate on the needs of tourists, and few window displays or shop interiors could be described as compelling. Nevertheless, with the favourable exchange rates and low Indian labour costs, bargains are a-plenty, and quality is usually high. Clothing of all kinds, particularly bespoke, is probably the best buy. Most establishments open Monday to Saturday from 10am to 7pm, which is a good reason for staying in a hotel nearby, bearing in mind Delhi's lack of 'night life'.

Immediately right is N Block, where several shops specializing in English language books are to be found. Here also is **South India Boarding House**, where a genuine Madras fish curry is offered, **Charisma** (9) Ladies fashions, and **Banaras House** (13) silks.

Returning to Jan Path (now Radial Road 8), steps, left, lead to a subterannean, air-conditioned shopping mall, **Palika Bazar**, a warren of passages with several entrances. Although the bazar is unkempt, crowded, and caters primarily for youngsters, some shops of interest can be found. In the central, circular hall, **Tandon** (20) sell chikan white muslin, delicately embroidered in the form of bed linen and tablecloths, all made at the family workshops in Lucknow. Nearby, **Jewel Mine** (12a), specializes in silverware and jewellery. Ask directions for the Central Park exit from the bazar.

All Connaught Place revolves around its pleasant **Central Park**, with many seats from which the colours of the ladies' sarees, in addition to the flowers and fountains, may be admired. From here it can be observed that the low-rise character of the area is gradually changing as tower blocks rear up to the south. Most of the white colonnades of the buildings are in need of a coat of paint, but the main cause of their tawdry appearance is flyposting: layers of obsolete posters obscure the columns at lower level, including, in 1994, some years after his assassination, an election message from Rajiv Gandhi!

Tourists must expect a degree of hassle in Connaught Place from shoe-shine boys, ear-cleaners (wielding fearsome metal prongs), and, particularly if alone, suppliers of even more personal services. It is prudent to avoid the gardens after dark.

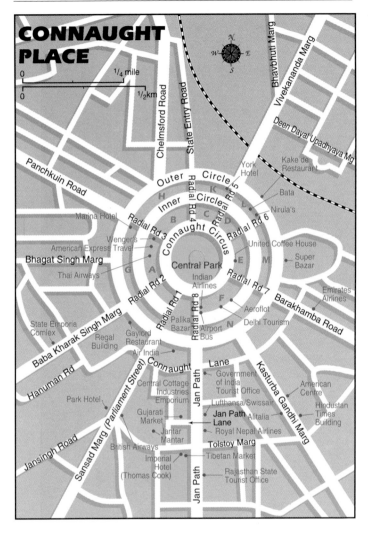

Most international airlines have their offices in or around Connaught Place, and it is convenient for individual tourists to confirm their international return flights while in the area: telephone connections in India can be extremely difficult, and non-confirmation may well result in a 'flight full' confrontation at the airport — usually in the middle of the night, which is not to be recommended.

A good point to begin an ambulation is the **American Express Travel** offices in A Block. **Handloom House** (9) is government-run and excellent for fabrics, particularly vibrant silks. On the corner is **Wenger's**, generally regarded as Delhi's best European-style cake shop. **Volga** restaurant is in B Block, and the economical **Embassy** restaurant in D Block (11). Also in D Block is **Bata** (4), Delhi's main branch of the footwear chain. **Kemp & Co**, reliable chemists, are nearby.

E Block accommodates the **United Coffee House**, good for a break, and the outstanding **Bharat Leather Emporium**. Excellent men's tailoring is found at **Style** (13). **Bercos** restaurant (8) offers

The extraordinary Jantar Mantar observatory, New Delhi

Japanese, Chinese and Indian cuisines. The airport bus leaves from the south-west corner of F Block.

For some reason, there is a break in the Inner Circle road at this point, and to continue westward it is first necessary to proceed southward and then follow Outer Circle, first right. Regal Building (named after its cinema) occupies the entire block, left, which has not been given an identifying letter. Restaurants include: on the Parliament Street side, **Kwality** (7), famous for its dish of chick peas and fried bread (*chhole batura*), **El Arab**, and **Degchi** on the Regent Cinema corner, **Gaylord** (16), of a higher standard, faces the Outer Circle. Shops of interest are **The Shop** (beside Kwality), good for linen and pottery. **Khadi Gramodyog Bhandar** stocks the rough, hand-woven cloth made famous by Mahatma Gandhi, and known as *khadi*; Indian honey is another of the shop's specialities. Annually, in October, this shop holds a sale, and genuine bargains are available.

Baba Kharak Singh Marg skirts the north side of Regal Building. Here, all in a row on the north side, are the individual emporia of the State Emporia Complex, each one officially controlled and with fixed prices. They are open Monday to Saturday 10am-5pm, but close for lunch 1.30 to 2.30pm.

As there is not a great deal of interest for tourists in G or H Blocks it is advisable to take an auto-rickshaw clockwise around the Outer Circle to the **York Hotel** on the north-east corner of K Block. The hotel's restaurant is popular, as are other restaurants in K Block, such as **Ginza**, **Darbar** and **Minar**.

The Outer Circle at this point offers probably the greatest concentration of restaurants in the capital. All offer good value for the handful of rupees demanded; try not to be put off by the spartan nature of their dining rooms. Particularly economical is the **National Restaurant** on the far side of the road. **Kake de Restaurant's** speciality is butter chicken, in half or whole portions; many rate it the best in Delhi. The chicken is served with an extremely viscous, tomato-based sauce, and it is essential that diners bring with them either a quantity of paper napkins or a good quality toilet roll for mopping-up afterwards.

On the corner of Outer Circle and Radial Road 6 is the **Nirula** complex, a must for all visitors to Delhi. This comprises a medium-grade and modestly-priced hotel, two self-service (stand up to eat) fast food outlets, an ice cream parlour, undoubtedly north India's finest, the **Pot-Pourri** international restaurant, and the **Chinese Room**, Delhi's first oriental restaurant, and still one of its best. The Nirula complex is unique in that it offers Western-style quality and decor, neatly fitting between grand hotel luxury and the more basic establishments. Nirula's first floor bar is the closest to an ordinary European bar that can be found in Delhi, and prices are much lower than those demanded in the leading hotels. Block M accommodates the **Mughlai** and **Dynasty** (Chinese) restaurants, and a competent photographic shop **Mahatta**, where camera repairs are efficient.

On the east side of the Outer Circle, **New Kerala** specializes in food from India's most southerly state. **Super Bazar**, further along, is large but of no particular interest to non-Indians. Behind this, however, a road leads eastward towards the **Holiday Inn Hotel** and the **Bengali Market**. In the centre of the latter is **Nathu's sweet shop**, a Delhi legend, open daily 7am-11pm. Here, seventy chefs produce gourmet versions of north Indian, milk-based sweetmeats. Most are incredibly sweet and extremely filling: the calorie count should not be thought about. Ask for the least sweet varieties (these will still be very sweet), which should include *Pista barfi*, green in colour and made from pistachio nuts, and *Gulab jaman*, soaked in an unctuous syrup. After the first tentative bites, which will seek out any dental failings, the sweetness becomes less cloying. At the rear is a popular vegetarian café, with excellent *dosas* and *lassi* (insist firmly, when ordering, that no ice is put in, as this appears to be the habitual practise at Nathu's).

South of the Bengali Market, centred on Barakhamba Road, is Delhi's cultural campus. The **Shri Ram Centre for Art and Culture**, 4 Safdar Hashmi Marg, occupies a building designed in 1966 by Shivnath Prasad. It is one of the city's most highly regarded examples of modern architecture, and incorporates three auditoriums. A national festival of drama and Ramlila ballet takes place every October; there are also regular readings of poetry and monthly concerts of classical Indian music. On Saturdays and Sundays, the Sutradhar Puppet Theatre gives performances.

Nearby, to the south, **Rabindra Bhavan**, at the north end of Copernicus Marg, was built by Habib Rahman, (1959-61), and houses the national literature, fine arts, sculpture and performing arts academies. **Triveni Kala Sangam**, 205 Tansen Marg, is a centre for studying painting, music and drawing. Incorporated are dance studios, an auditorium, art galleries and an open-air theatre.

Tolstoy Marg runs westward from Barakhamba Road. At its first junction, right, in Kasturba Gandhi Marg, the Hindustan Times Building (18-20) incorporates the **American Express** office that deals with claims for lost or stolen travellers cheques issued in their name. Almost next door, the **American Centre** (24) has a vast library, its technological section being particularly strong. Also available, on micro film, are copies of the *New York Times* from 1950 onwards (Open: Thursday to Monday 9.30am-6pm).

The British High Commission Building, in Kasturba Gandhi Marg, occupies one of Delhi's finest modern buildings, the work of Charles Correa, who also designed Delhi's Crafts Museum complex. Here also may be found the **British Council**, which possesses an extensive lending library and exhibition room.

Tolstoy Marg continues westward; overlooking the road just before its next junction, right, is the extraordinary **Jantar Mantar**

observatory, entered from Sansad Marg (Parliament Street). This collection of what appear to be modern sculptures painted a uniform salmon-pink, was built of plastered brick by the astronomer Jantar Mantar in 1725, although his work was much restored by the British in 1910. The observatory was commissioned by Maharaja Sawai Jai

Modern Hindu exoticism overwhelms the Laxmi Narayan Temple. This was built by the wealthy industrialist Raja Baldev Birla in New Delhi, and inaugurated by Mahatma Gandhi in 1939

Singh II of Jaipur, encouraged by the Mogul emperor Muhammad Shah. The Maharaja commissioned five observatories of this type, including one at Jaipur, but this was the first. At the time, astronomical omens were taken very seriously indeed, in Europe as well as Asia.

The strange shapes are, in fact, giant versions of contemporary astronomical instruments. In the centre, the Samrat Yantra, in the form of a great triangular gnomen, measures time to an accuracy of 0.5 seconds. The huge sundial's name, meaning Prince of Dials, was chosen by the Maharaja. To the south, the varying positions of the stars are indicated on two indented circles.

Parliament Street continues southward to the Patel Chowk roundabout where, on the south side, is the Head Post Office. Passes to visit the **Philatelic Museum** may be obtained at basement level. The museum, in Dak Tar Bhavan, is adjacent. Philatelists will delight in early Indian stamps and those issued by the individual princely states; there are also specimens of the British Penny Black, the world's first postage stamp.

From Patel Chowk, Ashok Road continues north-westward to Ashok Place. Delhi's Roman Catholic **Cathedral of the Sacred Heart** stands on the north side. Like the Anglican Cathedral, it is the work of Henry Medd, but this example is much more flamboyant. Built in baroque style in 1934, the russet and ochre colour scheme, a compliment to Hindu taste, is also reminiscent of Seville. Internally, all is surprisingly restrained, with fan decoration to the aisle's columns, and a 'Last Supper' painting in the sanctuary providing the few points of particular interest.

A much more exuberant religious building is reached by continuing north-westward to Mandir Marg, where a right turn leads to the theatrical **Laxmi Narayan Mandir**, a Hindu temple dedicated to Vishnu (Narayan) and his consort Laxmi. The wealthy industrialist Raja Baldev Birla, in whose private ground Mahatma Gandhi was assassinated, commissioned this temple for worship by all Hindus (including the untouchables), Jains and Buddhists. Gandhi inaugurated the temple in 1939. Foreigners must leave their shoes right of the entrance, above which is inscribed 'This temple is open to all Hindus subject to prescribed conditions of cleanliness, full faith and sincere devotion.'

The temple traditionally incorporates red and cream sandstone and white marble. Approached from a central courtyard are the shrines of Vishnu, Laxmi, Shiva, and his consort Durga. It is interesting to note within that the Hindu swastika is depicted at an angle inside a circle, exactly as on the German flag displayed at the time. One wonders if, on this occasion, the architect of the temple had been influenced by the Germans, thus bringing the iconographic process full circle. Only rarely in India is the swastika represented in its reverse form.

To visit the delightful rear garden it is necessary to collect one's shoes, turn left, and left again through the gate. A statue of Birla stands in the grounds.

❋ SOUTH DELHI

Delhi originated well to the south of its present centre, the first five cities, Lalkot, Qila Rai Pithora, Siri, Tughlaqabad and Jahanpanah all being built within a few miles of each other. Numerous mosques, mausoleums and stretches of ancient walls survive. The complexes of Hauz Khas and Qutb Minar are two of Delhi's most important sites and should not be missed. To see everything would involve an entire day, and many will prefer to see the three locations which begin the route, on another occasion, in order to reduce pressure of time. There are, of course, buses and excursions to the Qutb Minar, but it is far better to hire a taxi for the day if funds permit, otherwise, little more than the Qutb Minar will be seen.

❋ Lodi Gardens

Lady Willingdon's iconoclasm at Viceroy's House has already been described but, in fairness, she did make some amends by creating a park around the tombs of the Sayyid and Lodi dynasties. They fell within the New Delhi area and were apparently at some risk of being swallowed up by development. Originally known as Lady Willingdon Park, the lawned grounds, now called Lodi Gardens, are extremely popular with Indian families, particularly at weekends and on public holidays, when every other little boy seems to be swinging a cricket bat or bowling a tennis ball. A number of small mausoleums are set in clusters, but the occupants of only two of them are known for certain.

Set in the south-west corner is the mausoleum of the third Sayyid Sultan of Delhi, **Muhammad Shah**. The structure was built in 1445, 5 years before its occupant's death, and the octagonal, domed format appears to have served as a prototype for the tombs of the Moguls, begining with Humayun a century later.

In the centre of the park, facing the east gate, is the square **Bara Gumbad** (Big Dome), built in 1494, apparently as a monumental gateway to the mosque which it faces; no traces of tombs have been discovered within. The ablutions tank of the courtyard has been filled. Alternating rounded and pointed fluting to the columns of the prayer hall are similar to that of the lower stage of the Qutb Minar.

Directly ahead, the **Shish Gumbad** (Glass Dome), also square, was originally clad with blue enamelled tiles, but only a few have survived. From the exterior, this Lodi building appears to comprise two storeys but, on entering the building, it is apparent that there is just one. Some decorative stucco and paintwork survive internally. Although the building is primarily a mausoleum, it also formed part of a mosque. An occupant of one of the tombs may be Ibrahim Lodi killed in battle by the forces of Babur.

At the north end of the park is the **Tomb of Sikandar Lodi**, the second of the dynasty's rulers (1489-1516). It was built in 1518 by Ibrahim Lodi, his son. The tomb lies within a fortified enclosure and is octagonal in plan. Its Persian-style double dome served as the model for that of Humayun's tomb. Forming the north-east entrance to the park, the **Athpula** (Eight pier bridge) was built in the sixteenth century by a nobleman, Nawab Bahadur.

Tomb of Safdarjang

A short distance west of the Lodi Gardens, Lodi Road joins Aurobindo Marg; ahead lies the enclosure to the Tomb of Safdarjang, 'the last flicker of the lamp of Mogul architecture'. Safdarjang was the title given to 'Mirza Muqim' Abul Mansur Khan, Nawab (Governor) of Oudh and later, prime minister to the late-Mogul emperor Ahmad Shah. In 1753, Safdarjang fell out with the emperor and was forcibly deposed, dying within a few months. His son Shujah-ud-Daulah commissioned the tomb immediately and work continued for many years but was never completely finished. A small mosque is situated within the grounds, and the tomb lies, as usual, on a direct axis with its main gate. The water channel survives in the grounds but is now empty.

Not only was Safdarjang's Tomb the last major construction project in Delhi before the British took over in 1803, it was also the last Mogul project of any importance to be built in India. Similarities with the earlier Mogul mausoleums are apparent, but the building is set on a platform which is too shallow, and its plan is square rather than octagonal. Chamfered corners are replaced by polygonal towers surmounted by *chattris*, and the arches throughout, like the general decoration, are fussy. As has been noted, marble for the dome, and other stonework was taken from Khan-i-Khanan's tomb at Nizamuddin East to reduce construction costs.

Vaulting of the central chamber is decorated with superb plasterwork, and the cenotaph itself is well carved. Safdarjang lies in

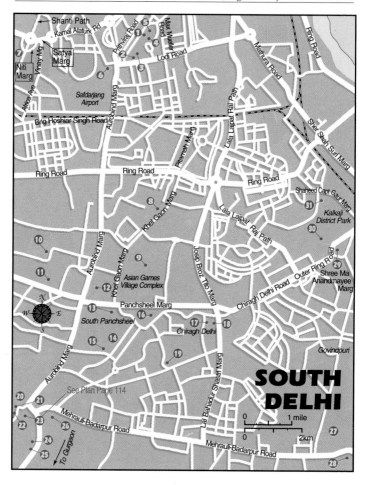

a small chamber below. Shuja-ud-Daula succeeded his father as Nawab of Oudh, and it is said that he lodged in the tomb's pavilions during his visits to Delhi.

Fine views from the terraces include, immediately to the south, Safdarjang Airport, part of the site of the battlefield where Timur, ancestor of the Moguls, defeated Nasir-ud-din Muhammad Tughlaq in 1398. It was at Safdarjang Airport that tragedy first struck the family of Prime Minister Indira Gandhi when, in 1980, her younger son Sanjay was killed as his private plane crash-landed.

Places of Interest in
SOUTH DELHI

1 Lodi Gardens
2 Tomb of Muhammad Shah
3 Bara Gumbad
4 Shish Gumbad
5 Tomb of Sikandar Lodi
6 Tomb of Safdarjang
7 Rail Transport Museum
8 Moth-ki-Masjid
9 Siri (walls & site)
10 Hauz Khas Village
11 Hauz Khas
12 Chor Minar
13 Bijai Mandal
14 Jahanpanah (site)
15 Begampuri Masjid
16 Lal Gumbad
17 Dargah of Nasir-ud-din Muhammad
18 Tomb of Bahlol Lodi
19 Khirki Masjid
20 Lal Kot (walls & site)
21 Jogmaya Temple
22 Tomb of Adham Khan
23 Qutb Minar
24 Tomb of Jamali Kamali
25 Madhi Masjid
26 Tomb of Balban (ruins)
27 Tughlaqabad (ruins)
28 Tomb of Ghiyas-ud-din Tughlaq
29 Kalkaji Temple
30 Baha'i Temple
31 Ashokan Rock Edict

Built in the mid-eighteenth century, the Tomb of Safdarjang, in South Delhi, is regarded as 'the last flicker of Mogul architecture'

At this stage (but not on Mondays), vintage train enthusiasts may wish to visit the **Rail Transport Museum**, 2 miles (3km) to the west, in the suburb of Chanakyapuri. However, this will almost certainly entail completing the South Delhi route on another occasion. The museum is reached by continuing southward on Aurobindo Marg and then taking Brig Hoshar Singh Road, first right, to Africa Avenue, first right. Satya Marg, the first turning left after passing beneath the railway bridge, leads to a roundabout and Niti Marg, first left, at the end of which, where it joins Shanti Path, the museum is located. Some visit India primarily to experience travelling on the country's vintage, steam-powered trains, which still operate in parts of the country; for those, and others of a nostalgic disposition, a visit to the Rail Transport Museum is a must. The museum, laid out to resemble a station yard, was opened in 1977, and occupies a 10 acre (4 hectare) site, which is toured by the non-stopping *Joy Express*, a miniature steam train, throughout the day (except 1-1.30pm).

India's first train departed from Bombay 16 April 1853, at a time when only eight other countries in the world had introduced a rail system. A network evolved very quickly, partly owned by individual states and partly by private companies. Even at the time of partition, forty-eight separate operators existed, but now the entire system is controlled by the national government.

Most exhibits, but not all, were made in the industrial centres of northern England and shipped to India in component parts for local assembly. *Fairy Queen* (Leeds), of 1855, is the oldest steam engine in India still in working order. Adjacent, the *Railbus*, was converted from a bus made by the American Dodge motor company. *Ramgotty* was built in Paris in 1877 to run on a unique 4 foot gauge track; its brakes are wooden. The Maharaja of Patiala commissioned this monorail train in 1907; initially, mules pulled the coaches, but were later replaced by four German steam engines. *Garratt*, weighing 253 tons, was the most powerful steam engine ever to operate in India.

Equally fascinating is the collection of beautifully restored coaches, owned by and luxuriously fitted-out for Indian princes. The white saloon was specially prepared for use by the Prince of Wales (later Edward VII) during his visit to India in 1876. The country's railway history is related in a permanent exhibition, housed in the octagonal building near the entrance. On display is the tuskless skull of an elephant that inadvisably charged a mail train in 1894 — and lost the confrontation.

After leaving the museum, return to Shanti Path and continue southward to the Ring Road, which should be followed eastward to the fifth main intersection to the south, Khel Gaon Marg.

For those who have not visited the Rail Transport Museum,

Aurobindo Marg passes the east side of Safdarjang's Tomb. Continue southward to Ring Road, which should be followed eastward to Khel Gaon Marg, right. Moth ki Masjid lies on the right hand side, in the district of Mujahidpur.

Acknowledged as the finest mosque built in the Lodi style, by tradition, the name of the **Moth-ki-Masjid** (Lentil Mosque) was chosen by its builder, Miyan Bhuwa. He was the minister of Sikandar Lodi, who presented him with a single lentil grain for planting; the ensuing crop earned sufficient to pay for the construction of the mosque, which was completed in 1505. This building, almost contemporary with the Bara Gumbad in the Lodi Gardens, is much more ambitious in scale. The prayer hall is lengthy enough to warrant a five-arched screen and three domes. Elegant towers and turrets result in a pleasing delicacy externally, and the plasterwork remains in good order within, although most of its decoration has disappeared. It is interesting to note that only the central chamber is domed, the flanking ceilings being vaulted, and decorated with central pendants.

Half a mile (1km) to the south, on the left hand side of Khel Gaon Marg, may be glimpsed the remains of the citadel of **Siri**, Delhi's third city, built by Ala-ud-din-Khalji (reigned 1296-1316). To approach them further it is necessary to proceed to Shahpur, which has been built within the walls. However, not a great deal of interest remains, and the chief appeal is to historians and archaeologists.

The next turn right off Khel Gaon Marg connects with Aurobindo Marg. Turn right and then first left to **Hauz Khas Village**. The 'village' has been set up as a collection of boutiques and craft galleries for the many tourists who come to visit the nearby tank and its complex of fourteenth-century buildings. Many of the items sold are made by artists who live and work at the back of the shops.

Hauz Khas ⁂

The main street continues to Hauz Khas, a great tank excavated by Ala-ud-din Tughlaq in the early years of the fourteenth century to provide a water supply for Siri. Firoz Shah Tughlaq restored the tank, which had silted up, in 1354, and built a madrasa on its banks, with a small mosque to the north. The madrasa has two storeys on the tank side, but only a single storey behind; colonnades still link the square, domed halls. Steps lead to the tank, which is now dry.

The domed tomb of Firoz Shah, who died in 1388, lies to the south. Undemonstrative in style, the building was restored by Sikandar Lodi in 1507. Timur's army rested at Hauz Khas after defeating Nasir-ud-din Muhammad, the last Tughlaq, in 1398.

Further south, Aurobindo Marg passes through the Hauz Khas Enclave residential development, which incorporates, on the east side, the **Chor Minar** (Thief's Tower), believed to date from the Khalji period. Heads of executed thieves are said to have been displayed in the indentations of the external walls. Also found within the Enclave are the **Idgah Masjid**, of 1405, and, to its north, the **Nili Masjid's** prayer hall, all that survives of the mosque built in 1506. Some original blue tiles remain on the façade.

Aurobindo Marg continues southward to the Qutb Minar, however, an interesting circular detour eastward can be made by those with sufficient time at their disposal.

Turn left at the first main intersection, Panchsheel Marg. Just ½ mile (1km) further on, south of Sarvapriya Vihar, lies the **Bijai Mandal** (Palace of Victory), a square tower with sloping walls and four entrances. It may have been a bastion in the wall of Jahanpanah, the fifth city of Delhi, built by Muhammad-bin-Tughlaq, 1325-51. Little else of his city remains, apart from ruined sections of wall, seen later.

Directly south of the tower stands the large **Begampuri Masjid**, dominating the village of the same name. This was one of the seven mosques built in the fourteenth century by Khan-i-Jahan Tilangani, chief minister to Firoz Shah. Another example, in Nizamuddin village, the Kalan Masjid, has already been described, while a third, the Khirki Masjid, will be visited later on this route. Cloisters around the courtyard flank the prayer hall, with its tapering minarets.

A return northward, in the direction of Panchsheel Marg, leads to the district of Panchsheel South, and the **Lal Gumbad** (Red Dome), shrine of Kabir-ud-din Aulia, a Chisti saint. Fixed to the face of the building's west wall are iron rings, said to have been inserted by thieves when they scaled the building to remove a gold finial from the top of its dome: hence the tomb's alternative name, Rakabwalla Gumbad (Iron Ring Dome).

Continue to Panchsheel Marg, right, which leads to the Chiragh Delhi district, where there is a shrine to another Chisti saint, **Nasir-ud-din-Muhammad**, successor to Nizam-ud-din Aulia, as the fifth and last saint of the Order. Highly revered, he gained the title Roshan Chiragh-i-Delhi (Illuminated Lamp of Delhi). As at Nizamuddin, the original tomb of the saint, who died in 1356, has been much rebuilt and extended, and a madrasa now forms part of the complex. The village grew up around the shrine and now forms the core of a modern residential suburb of New Delhi. Also at Chiragh Delhi is the plain, dilapidated **Tomb of Bahlol Lodi**, founder of the dynasty of Delhi sultans, who died in 1489.

Lal Bahadur Shastri Marg sweeps southward, passing the eastern edge of Chiragh Delhi. Take the first right turn, in the direction of the Qutb Minar. Approximately 1½ miles (2½km) to the west, a minor road, right, leads to **Khirki Masjid** (Windows Mosque), the most interesting of the set of mosques built by Jahan Khan in the fourteenth century. Completed in 1380, it is one of only two examples to survive in north India, and resembles the original appearance of the Kalan Masjid at Nizamuddin. The building apparently gained its name from the *khirkis* (windows) to the upper storeys. Bastions at each corner evoke a fortress rather than a mosque. The partly-covered courtyard is divided into four square sections. Attached to the east side of the building is a sluice, which seems to be contemporary with it. Return to the main road and continue westward, following, on the left hand side, the route of the south wall of **Jahanpanah**. The western section of this wall, ahead, is formed by the reused twelfth century north wall of **Qila Rai Pithora** the second Delhi.

Turn left at Aurobindo Marg but, before entering the Qutb Minar enclosure, take the road which skirts it, right. The area of the former **Lal Kot** citadel, the first Delhi, has now been entered, and remains of its west wall may be seen.

On the right stands the nineteenth-century **Jogmaya Temple**, its name commemorating an earlier building on the site, in which female deities, known as *yogins*, were worshipped: Yoginpura is an alternative name for Delhi.

The water tank, which supplied Lal Kot, lies to the north, but in a ruined state. It was allegedly built by Anangpar Tomar, a Rajput prince, and is known as the Anang Tal.

The exquisite Tomb of Ataga Khan, at Nizamuddin, has been described and a short distance to the south stands the much larger tomb of his murderer, **Muhammad Adham Khan**, also a half-brother of Akbar. Adham Khan's mother Maham Anga had been a wet-nurse to Akbar, as had the wife of Ataga Khan; both were therefore regarded as foster-brothers of the Emperor and treated as members of the royal family. Akbar appointed Ataga Khan his chief minister, and the much younger but jealous Adham Khan slew him at Agra Fort in 1526, following a dispute. Furious, Akbar felled his foster-brother with a single blow and ordered that his body should be thrown from the ramparts. It is recorded that Adham Khan had to be thrown again before finally expiring. His grieving mother died 5 days later, allegedly of a broken heart, and Akbar, who had retained great affection for her, appears to have shown remorse, commissioning this mausoleum as the last resting place of both Adham Khan and Maham Anga. This, the last octagonal tomb to be built in Delhi, is said to have been inspired by Jerusalem's Dome of the Rock. It is sometimes called the Bhul Bhulaiyan (labyrinth), as a network of interconnecting passages and chambers snake within its thick walls. Surprisingly, this tomb served as the summer residence of the British Resident in Delhi, 1835-53.

Return to the Qutb Minar enclosure.

✳ **Qutb Minar**

The Qutb Minar complex lies within the east wall of the Lal Kot citadel; it incorporates some of India's most famous and ancient structures, all of which contribute to the **Quwwat-ul-Islam Masjid** (Might of Islam Mosque). Begun in 1193, this was Delhi's first Muslim building, although mosques had been constructed in India 33 years earlier. It is said that the main temple of Qila Rai Pithora originally occupied the site of the mosque, and remains of it still lie below ground. Entry is via the east gate, one of three built by Ala-ud-din-Khalji as part of his early thirteenth-century extensions. Within its inner archway, a Persian inscription, allegedly composed by the creator of the mosque, Qutb-ud-din Aibak, records that it was constructed from materials obtained by dismantling twenty-seven 'idolatrous' temples.

In order to comprehend more easily the chronology of the mosque's development, it is advisable to proceed directly to the **Iron Pillar**, at its core. Forming the axis of the entire scheme is a slender, 22ft (7m) high pillar of wrought-iron, which faces the ruined screen of the mosque. It is not completely certain when the pillar was made, where it first stood, or when it was brought here. The six-line Sanskrit inscription is eastern Gupta work, praising a victorious king named Chandra, who had recently died, and proclaiming that the pillar, a standard of the Lord Vishnu, was erected in his memory on 'the mountain called Vishnupada'. From this, it has been surmised that the pillar originally stood outside a Vishnu temple sited on a hilltop, probably in Bihar. If so, it would almost certainly have been sur-mounted by a Garuda, the man/bird vehicle of Vishnu. The King Chandra referred to is likely to have been either Chandra-Gupta Vikramaditya (reigned 375-413) or Chandravarman (326-375), which means that the pillar is fourth- or fifth-century work. It is said that Anang Pal, founder of the Tamar dynasty, dug the pillar out of the ground to discover if the tradition that it rested on the head of a giant snake was true — it was not. As the name of Anang Pal, followed by the date 1109, is also inscribed on the pillar, it seems likely that he was responsible for transferring this strange antiquity to its present position, which now faces a mosque rather than a Hindu temple. A dent approximately 4ft (1m) above the inscription is said to have been made by a cannon ball fired by the troops of the Maharaja of Bharatpur.

In spite of its great age, the 15ft (4m) wrought-iron shaft shows no sign of rusting; modern analysis has discovered that the sulphur content is negligible and there is, unusually, no manganese in its composition. It may be that the Muslim conquerors were so impressed by the purity of the iron that they believed the pillar to have mystic qualities, and therefore decided to retain it as the centrepiece of their mosque. Many visitors will be seen standing with their backs to the pillar, attempting to encircle it with their arms behind them. To accomplish this is regarded as an omen of good fortune — at any rate it makes a good photo for the family album.

A further example of native influence can be seen in the ruined five-arched **screen** to the prayer hall of the mosque, which was completed by Qutb-ud-din Aibak in 1199, and incorporates, on its inner side, floral carving that is Hindu in style. Obviously the work of Hindu craftsmen, and apparently inspired by the columns of the cloister, the combination of a filigree background with arabesques and tracts from the Koran results in some of the finest caligraphic relief work in all Islam. It is interesting to note that the lower curves of the arches have been formed by the Hindu method of overlapping one stone with another and then removing the overlap, rather than by the established Islamic method of curving the stones as they ascend. Major restoration of the entire complex took place between 1912 and 1916, but it was too late to save much of Qutb-ud-din Aibak's **prayer hall**, begun in 1193.

Outside the south-east corner of the courtyard, Qutb-ud-din Aibak built his tower of victory, in the form of a great minar (a large version of a minaret). It seems likely that the muezzin would have called the faithful to prayer from one of its lower balconies, as he could not possibly have been heard from the top. *Qutb* means a rod or tower, and the conqueror of Qila Rai Pithora decided to commemorate himself by giving the great structure his own appellation: hence **Qutb Minar**. Inscribed on the lower level are the names of Qutb-ud-din-Aibak, and Muhammad-bin-Sam (Shahab-ud-din-Ghori), whose army had been victorious under the former's leadership.

The minar tapers gradually, and its lower three stages are fluted, measures obviously designed to give the appearance of even greater height than the 238ft (72m) that it posesses. On the lower stage, the fluting is alternately rounded and angular, on the second stage rounded, and on the third stage angular; the two upper storeys, later replacements, are smooth. Passages from the Koran are incised in bands around the minar, and balconies extend between each of its

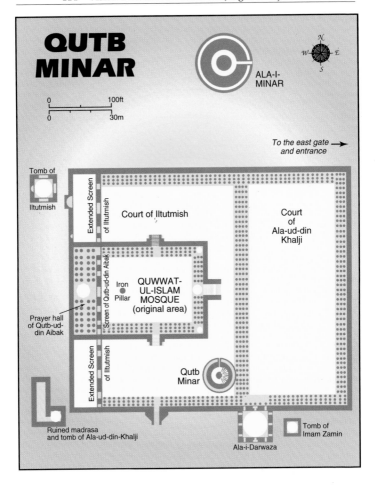

four stages, supported by honeycomb corbels. Qutb-ud-dinAibak only built the first stage, dying in 1210, but work was completed by his son-in-law and successor, Shams-ud-din-Iltutmish (or Altamish), who added three further stages, inscribing his name on each of them. It is said that the Qutb Minar was built to resemble a vertical alif: the initial letter of both the Arabic alphabet and the name of Allah.

An earthquake in 1368 badly damaged the upper stage and, after further destruction had been caused by lightning, Firoz Shah rebuilt

One of Delhi's most famous sights, the Qutb Minar tower, is the tallest stone structure of its type in India

it. However, he created two stages rather than one, increased the overall height, reduced the degree of tapering, and omitted fluting. In addition, white marble was incorporated in the red sandstone structure for the first time, and a cupola placed on top. Another earthquake occurred in 1803 (an ominous greeting to the British invaders), in which the cupola fell. General restoration in 1829 included the replacement of the original castellation to the balconies by the present balustrades. A new cupola was made, but did not meet with favour; it now serves as a decorative feature in the garden.

The present slight tilt to the Qutb Minar may be the result of the earthquakes, nevertheless, the building has been pronounced safe.

A fifteenth-century inscription by Sikandar Lodi may be seen at the entrance door. It is extraordinary how, in spite of three separate construction periods, the Qutb Minar, still the highest stone tower in India, has achieved such a pleasing homogeneity.

Formerly the 376 steps to the top could be ascended by visitor's but an accident, in which several were crushed to death, has lead to the closure of the tower.

Soon after Qila Rai Pithora was captured, all its religious buildings were demolished, however, material from the twenty-seven temples, as referred to on the gate, was reused to form a colonnade around the mosque's courtyard. The reused columns (now mostly lost on the south side) were considered too short, and pairs were therefore selected, one being placed on top of the other; much of their original decorative carving was spared. The style of this carving indicates that the columns came from both Jain and Hindu temples. Historians have noted that the incorporation of native Indian work in a Muslim building at this early period, even though on the grounds of economy, was remarkably prescient, and appears to have set the stage for the subsequent wholesale adoption of Hindu architectural elements, which reached its peak in the Mogul period.

Apart from the ruined walls of Lal Kot/Qila Rai Pithora, these columns are the only ancient structures built by Hindus to have survived in Delhi. From Aibak's victory until the British arrival in 1803, Delhi would be under Muslim rule, a period of just over 600 years.

Iltutmish decided to enlarge what was still a relatively small mosque in 1230, doubling its area by creating a new courtyard around the original, which would be similarly enclosed with cloisters; by this means, the Qutb Minar was now located within the area of the mosque. Iltutmish also extended the screen of the prayer hall to the north and south. In his new cloister, architectural good manners prevailed in an extraordinary way, the columns, although newly commissioned, imitating the style of the re-used Hindu/Jain examples of the earlier courtyard, even repeating their arrangement of pairs placed one above the other. The decorative carving, however, is much less ambitious.

Behind the north end of his screen extension is the **Tomb of Iltutmish**, which was completed shortly before his death in 1235; it is the oldest of all Delhi's Muslim tombs. The roof, probably once domed, has been lost, but much of the opulent carving of the walls at lower level is well-preserved. Bells on chains and lotus blooms, typical Hindu themes, have been incorporated in the basically

Saracenic design. Although the Sultan's sarcophagus rests on a plinth, his grave lies in the chamber below. The west wall of the chamber is in the form of a marble qibla, its mihrabs profusely decorated.

Ala-ud-din-Khalji, builder of Siri, was the next to make his mark on the mosque. Located directly to the south, outside the south-west corner of the extended courtyard, is what is believed to have been his tomb. Excavations in 1914 discovered an unfinished grave on the south side of the group of L-shaped ruins, and there was some evidence that it belonged to the Sultan. Attached to the shrine is the ruined madrasa, built at the same time.

Ala-ud-din-Khalji planned an even grander mosque, creating a new courtyard to the east, and building the present gateways. Much of his south cloister survives, but it seems that the north and east sides were never completed, nor did he double the length of the prayer hall's screen as planned. Once again, the style of the original courtyard's columns was followed.

Known as the **Ala-i-Darwaza**, the domed south gate, no longer used as an entrance, is a delightful structure. It was completed in 1310 as the main gateway to the mosque. Pointed arches, slightly horseshoe-shaped, are given a lotus-bud fringe, typical of the Khalji period. They are flanked by pairs of lower-level windows with marble screens, which are matched by blind rectangular recesses above, resembling false windows; the resulting symmetrical ensemble is satisfyingly harmonious. Above the arches, inscriptions in Arabic immodestly refer to Ala-ud-din-Khalji as Sikandar Sani — the second Alexander (the first being Alexander the Great). It is believed that this was the first building in India to combine white marble with red sandstone on its façade.

Immediately east of the gate is the **Tomb of Imam Zamin** (or Muhammad Ali), built in the lifetime of this Muslim saint, who came to India from Turkestan in 1500 and died in 1539. The structure looks as if it incorporates marble, but this is, in fact, a glossy plaster, known as chunam. Although square in plan, the chamber appears octagonal, as beams have been erected diagonally at the corners to support the dome. Delightful *jalis* screen the area.

The stump of the **Ala-i-Minar**, to the left of the exit from the complex, is all that was ever built of a structure which, if completed, would have dwarfed the Qutb Minar. Set on a plinth, it rises 87ft (26m) above ground level, but was intended to reach 500ft (152m), twice the height of its rival. The bulk would have been equally impressive, as the diameter of the existing base measures two and a half times that of the Qutb Minar. Although the stump is built of rubble, ridges have been cut in preparation for facing with sandstone.

The iron pillar within the Qutb Minar complex is Delhi's oldest monument.
Those who can encircle the pillar with both hands are deemed to be fortunate

Ibn Batuta, the great Arab explorer, visited the Quwwat-ul-Islam mosque in the mid-fourteenth century, recording that it was un-equalled in beauty and extent. The mosque's enclosure became a place of refuge for many citizens of Firozabad, when Timur sacked the city in 1398. But to no avail, all were slaughtered by his rampaging troops.

From the Qutb Minar, the main road forks right towards Gurgaon. The **Tomb of Jamali Kamali** and its **mosque** (built 1529-35) stand on the west side, rare examples of architecture from the early Mogul period. This mosque marks the transition in style between Sikandar Lodi's Moth ki Masjid and the Purana Qila's mosque, and it is interesting to note that the white marble/red sandstone scheme, dispensed with by the immediate predecessors of the Moguls, has been revived. Boldly carved rosettes within roundels, and blind arches set in the pillars, are the main decorative features of the prayer hall's **screen**. Jamali was the pseudonym of a Muslim saint, Sheikh Fazululla, who built the mosque during his lifetime. As was usual, he also built his tomb adjacent to it. A renowned poet, Jamali composed the verse which is incorporated in the design of the ceramics within the tomb chamber. The identity of Kamali, whose grave shares the Saint's mausoleum, is unknown.

Also probably dating from the early-Mogul period is the **Madhi Masjid**, which lies a short distance to the south. It is enclosed by a wall with bastions at each corner and an imposing gateway, reminiscent of Lodi period buildings. The prayer hall's screen is enlivened with blue tiles; uniquely, its central chamber has always been roofless.

Return northward to the Mehrauli-Badarpur Road, and turn right. On the south side, a short distance ahead, is the **Tomb of Balban**. This is historically interesting in the development of Indian architecture, in spite of its ruined state, as, for the first time, an arch has been created by superimposing curved stones (the Muslim method), rather than carving the overlaps of flat stones (the Hindu method). Its occupant, Ulag Khan Balban, (1265-87), a former slave of Iltutmish, eventually became Sultan of Delhi.

Tughlaqabad   ✳

Of all Delhi's early cities, the formidable walls of Tughlaqabad are the most impressive to survive. They are reached by following Mehrauli-Badarpur Road eastward for 6 miles (10km). On route, after 1 mile (2km), the road bisects a good stretch of the east wall of Qila Rai Pithora. The massive walls of Tughlaqabad, forming a circuit of about 4 miles (6km), suddenly appear ahead, imperceptibly merging with the rocky hill on which they stand. Steps ascend to the complex, which comprises: the octagonal citadel, palaces, a mosque and the grid plan of the city's streets. Amateur guides insist on providing visitors with information which is not, generally, of great assistance — but they mean no harm.

Ghiyas-ud-din Tughlaq began constructing this city at the beginning of his reign in 1320, and all was completed in just 2 years. It has been suggested that problems arose with Tughlaqabad's water supply and, on his succession, the new Sultan, having adopted the name of Muhammad, began to build Jahanpanah (Refuge from the World) to the north-west. Wishing to create a more centrally located capital for his greatly increased territory, the area was almost completely evacuated by Muhammad in 1327, its citizens being forcibly transferred to Daulatabad, about 1,000 miles (1,610km) away in the Deccan. Within 4 years, however, they were forced back through famine, to become the first inhabitants of Jahanpanah which was now ready. Tughlaqabad was never to be occupied again, except by shepherds (and tribes of monkeys), thus fulfilling the curse that Nizam-ud-din Aulia had put on Ghiyas-ud-din Tughlaq's city: 'may it be inhabited by gujars (shepherds), or else deserted: the great size of many of the stones indicates that they were quarried on site one specimen weighs 6 tons. An archway forms the entrance, and below can be seen the largest of the city's **water tanks**. The enclosed **citadel**, right of the entrance, which takes up around 15 per cent of the entire area, was naturally built on the highest point, overlooking the city. Part of a **Bijai Mandal** (Palace of Victory) tower survives, and it is said that an underground passageway nearby leads to the Bijai Mandal at Jahanpanah. However, as that tower lies 6 miles (10km) distant, it would seem unlikely that the tradition is true. Sadly, very few 'secret passageway' legends anywhere in the world prove to be more than the products of romantic imaginations. A ruined **mosque** stands to the north below.

Similarly enclosed is the **palace area**, to the west, while ahead, ruined **houses** set on a grid pattern of streets mark the residential area of the city. A **subterranean passage**, with indications of name plates and niches for oil lamps, is believed to have been a shopping precinct.

Opposite the steps to Tughlaqabad, on the south side of the Mehrauli-Badarpur Road, stands the fortified **Tomb of Ghiyas-ud-din Tughlaq**, founder of the city. Erected by its occupant, the domed mausoleum, its thick walls built to lean inward, reinforces the impression of impregnable strength created by the ramparts of the city facing it. Originally, the tomb stood in the centre of an artificial lake, now filled, and it is still reached by part of the causeway that was constructed to give direct access to the fort from the city. Minimal use of white marble gives scant relief to the solidity of the structure, which has been extremely well-preserved.

Within the mausoleum, the three cenotaphs are believed to be those of Ghiyas-ud-din Tughlaq, his wife, and their murderous son Muhammad-bin Tughlaq, known as Sultan Khuni (Bloody), who died in 1351. He was succeeded by his cousin, Firoz Shah Tughlaq, who appears to have been worried by his predecessor's wrongdoings, as he paid the victims to record their forgiveness and then put their acquitals in a chest at the head of the Sultan's tomb, to assist his 'not guilty' plea on Judgement Day. What appear to be the graves Tughlaq's lie, not in a crypt beneath the cenotaph as was common, but in a separate, domed chamber set in the corner of the enclosure.

Return westward along Mehrauli-Badarpur Road, and take the first turning right, leading to Govindpuri. This road ends at its junction with Shree Ma Anandmayee Marg, which continues northward to Outer Ring Road, left. After a short distance, a minor road, right, leads to the Baha'i Temple. Just before this is reached, the **Kalkaji Temple** stands on the right. It was built in the eighteenth century to honour Kalki, Shiva's consort in her most violent form. By tradition, Kalki insisted that she should be worshipped here as a reward for slaying local demons. Every October, a festival at the temple is attended by many devotees of the goddess.

The recently completed **Baha'i Temple**, on its hilltop site, is the most impressive contemporary religious building in Delhi. It is the first temple to be erected in India by members of the Baha'i faith, which was brought to the country in 1872. Its founder was the prophet Baha'u'llah (the name Baha means light), whose aim was to create harmony between all the world's religions. Architect Fariburz Sabha has designed the building in the form of concrete lotus petals faced with white marble. The great amphitheatre seats 1,300, and all are welcome to pause for meditation and prayer. A feature of the temple is its grounds, which comprise 26 acres (10 hectare) of gardens, with ornamental pools and bridges. There are good views of the distant city.

Directly north of the temple may be seen the historic rock inscription, dating from the third century BC, known as the **Ashokan Rock Edict**. To reach this, it is necessary to proceed anti-clockwise around Kalkaji Park, which adjoins the Baha'i Temple grounds, following Shaheed Gaur Marg to Srinivaspuri. A left turn leads to the site. Only discovered in 1966, the faint, ten-line inscription records the Emperor Ashoka's satisfaction with his people's adherence to Buddhist teachings.

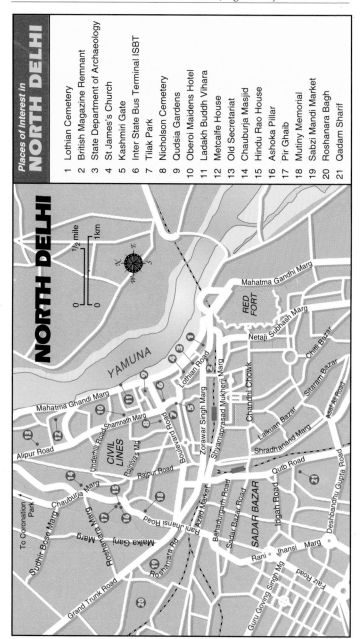

Places of Interest in
NORTH DELHI

1 Lothian Cemetery
2 British Magazine Remnant
3 State Department of Archaeology
4 St James's Church
5 Kashmiri Gate
6 Inter State Bus Terminal ISBT
7 Tilak Park
8 Nicholson Cemetery
9 Qudsia Gardens
10 Oberoi Maidens Hotel
11 Ladakh Buddh Vihara
12 Metcalfe House
13 Old Secretariat
14 Chauburja Masjid
15 Hindu Rao House
16 Ashoka Pillar
17 Pir Ghaib
18 Mutiny Memorial
19 Sabzi Mandi Market
20 Roshanara Bagh
21 Qadam Sharif

NORTH DELHI ✳

North Delhi, that is to say the area that lies immediately north of Shahjahanabad (Old Delhi), is chiefly of interest to British visitors, with its reminders of the British presence in Delhi prior to the construction of New Delhi, and its memorials to the bravery of soldiers on both sides during the Indian Mutiny. The route begins just within the Kashmiri Gate of Shahjahanabad and continues as far north as Coronation Park, the site of the 1911 Coronation Durbar of King George V. Everything can be seen in half a day and, as no lengthy stops are entailed, it is worth hiring the services of one, knowledgable driver for the entire period. An older driver is more likely to know the locations sought and is best recruited in advance. Remember to make it clear that the mosque at Chauburja is not the Per Gaib mosque; most taxi drivers think it is.

Netaji Subhash Marg the road facing the Red Fort, leads northward, passing beneath the railway bridge, where it becomes Lothian Road. On the right, entered beneath a low tower, is the **Lothian Cemetery**. Buried here is a British mercenary hero of the Mutiny, Thomas Dunn: the large sandstone memorial to him was paid for by Colonel James Skinner, commander of his brigade.

In the centre of Lothian Road, facing the Telegraph Office, is an archway remnant of the British Magazine. On 10 May 1857, mutineers rioted at Meerat, just 31 miles (50km) from Delhi; on the following day the British blew up their own ammunition stored in the magazine, in order to prevent its capture by the freedom fighters who were marching on Delhi. Lieutenant Willoughby and eight others died here in the ensuing fighting, and are commemorated.

An Anglo-Indian telegraph officer gave the British army the first warning of the mutiny from a point at the begining of the road island ahead, and a granite obelisk was erected to commemorate the event.

On the right hand side of Lothian Road, the house with a colonnade was occupied by Sir David Ochterlong in 1803, when it became the first British Residency in Delhi. It now accommodates the **State Department of Archaeology**. The façade of the building is early nineteenth century, but behind this is the former library of Prince Dara Shukoh, older brother of Aurangzeb.

Further ahead, on the same side of the road, **St James's Church**, Delhi's oldest, was dedicated in 1836. Colonel James Skinner commissioned the building (1778-1831), in redemption of his pledge to build a church if he survived injuries received on the battlefield: a lady from a nearby village nursed him back to health. Baroque in style, and boasting a large dome raised on an octagonal base, the church is painted ochre, with white pilasters and columns; porticos are set on three sides, their pediments supported by Doric columns.

In the lawned churchyard, which is always kept in splendid condition, several tombstones commemorate members of the Skinner family. Potted flowers contribute to the atmosphere of an English garden. The church is entered from the south side, after passing the SPCK bookshop. Monuments within include those to William Fraser, murdered in 1835, Sir Theophilus Metcalfe (1785-1846), who was the British resident in Delhi (1811-19), and officers of Skinner's regiment. The front pew was reserved for the Skinner family.

James Skinner (c1778-1841), was the son of a Scottish officer in the East India Company's army, and a Rajput girl, who produced six children before committing suicide. It is said that James was not permitted to follow his father's army career, due to mixed blood; instead, he accepted a commission to serve in the French-run Mahratta army as a mercenary. In 1803, Skinner, together with several companions, was persuaded by Lord Lake to switch sides and form his own cavalry: this would achieve fame as 'Skinner's Horse'. Their valour was an important factor in the British defeat of the Mahrattas at the battle of Delhi in 1803. Skinner was appointed lieutenant colonel, and made a Companion of the Bath in 1828; he never, however, received the expected knighthood. Skinner's grave is marked by a marble slab in front of the altar.

The house occupied by Skinner overlooked open land facing the church. Near this, by tradition, the last Mogul emperor, Bahadur Shah II, was imprisoned by the British in a basement room, before being exiled to Rangoon, Burma, in 1857.

As Kashmiri Gate is approached, note **Varma's** leather shop, on the west side; its patrons were primarily the aristocracy of Delhi, and included Queen Mary, consort of George V. Details of their purchases have been kept in a book, which will be shown to visitors on request.

The **Kashmiri Gate** formed the north entrance to Shahjahanabad, and was apparently the city's most important, as double arches catered for two-way traffic, the only example in Delhi to do so. Built of brick with stone arches, some restoration has taken place in cement. Fragments of the adjoining wall have also survived. During the Mogul period, it was customary for the emperor to spend the summer months in Kashmir to escape Delhi's unpleasant climate, and his entourage passed in grand procession through the gate, which is why it is so-named.

On the inner face are commemorated British officers killed in the decisive battle to recapture Delhi, which took place at this point in September 1857. The fighting, between 5,000 British troops and their Indian allies pitted against 20,000 sepoy mutineers, lasted 6 days. At this time, the city wall was complete and had to be stormed.

Ahead, on the right, is the **Inter State Bus Terminal** (ISBT), the departure and arrival point for all important bus routes. Interestingly, it stands close to the stage where boat passengers were deposited on the west bank of the River Yamuna. On the opposite side of Lothian Road is **Tilak Park**, formerly Nicholson Garden; its statue of Brigadier-General John Nicholson has been removed.

To the north, on the far side of Boulevard Road, lies the **Nicholson Cemetery**. Directly ahead from the entrance is the grave of the commander of the British assault on Delhi, which began 14 September 1857. Nicholson, a tall, military man, insisted on leading his assault party from the front and was a sitting target for the sepoy sniper who shot him through the chest from the window of a house near the Kabul Gate (since demolished). Nicholson was taken to a hospital tent in agony, but survived until 23 September. It is said that some of his Hindu troops were so impressed by Nicholson's fortitude that they regarded him as a reincarnation of Lord Brahma.

Directly to the east, on the far side of Ring Road (Shamnath Marg), the shelling of the Kashmiri Gate began from **Qudsia Garden**. The garden was laid out in 1748 by Qudsia Begum, a dancing slave of the Mogul emperor Muhammad Shah; she later became his favourite mistress and the mother of his successor as emperor. The gardens once incorporated several buildings of interest but, apart from the west gate and small mosque, these were demolished long ago.

Further north, on Shamnath Marg, is the **Oberoi Maidens Hotel**, built in 1900. This, the city's most delightful colonial style hotel, has a four star rating and is very convenient for those wishing to spend some time in and around Old Delhi. The exterior is neo-Classical, with a profusion of balustrades and pilasters. Particularly attractive are the large fanlights on the ground floor. Lutyens resided here for a period when planning New Delhi. Refreshments are served on the lawn in the cooler months, much in the style of the Hotel Imperial.

A return southward followed by a left turn leads to Mahatma Gandhi Marg. Turn left again, continuing northward. On the east side of the road is **Ladakh Buddh Vihara**, Delhi's most important Buddhist temple. Although of no great antiquity, the façade is strikingly picturesque, and the prayer hall has a tranquil atmosphere. Many Tibetan pilgrims visit the complex, which incorporates a library of manuscripts from their country. Around the temple, small restaurants and stalls serve Tibetan food at very low prices.

Continuing northward, Mahatma Gandhi Marg, after a short distance, skirts the River Yamuna, providing a rare chance of viewing the famous river from a Delhi thoroughfare. On the west side of the road is **Metcalfe House**, built for the British resident of that name in the 1830s. Apparently, the interior of this colonial-style house has

The Oberoi Maidens Hotel, North Delhi

Oxen cutting the grass is a tradition that can be seen; this is outside the Government buildings

Throughout Delhi you will see different modes of transport

been well preserved, and many of Metcalfe's possessions, including his Napoleonic memorabilia, remain. Unfortunately, at the time of writing, India's Ministry of Defence occupies the building, and visitors are not, therefore, permitted.

Return southward and turn right at the first junction, which leads to the Ring Road (Alipur Road). On the right is the **Old Secretariat**, now partly comprising members of parliament's offices. This is another neo-Classical building, completed in 1912 for the Government of India's Secretariat, which remained here until Baker's Secretariat was completed in New Delhi. The building is a two-storey structure, with a central pavilion and flanking towers. An interesting feature is the crescent shape of the middle section. Visits are not permitted.

Much of this part of North Delhi, known as Civil Lines, was popular with British residents before the construction of New Delhi, and many of their houses remain. By returning southward and turning right, the road ascends to the heights of Green Ridge, where, from its north end, British troops stormed the city in 1857. The Ridge provides an important 'lung' for Delhi's citizens, but is gradually being eroded. However, protection societies have been formed and are pressing parliament to act before this oasis of greenery is lost. On the summit, British women and children were assembled at the outbreak of the mutiny, to await transport to take them away from Delhi to safety. In the centre of the road, a circular Flagstaff Tower was left to mark the spot.

The site of the Coronation Durbar of 1911 has been preserved as **Coronation Park**, and Britons who are still nostalgic for their empire may wish to make a sentimental visit. Bear in mind, however, that the park is some miles distant and there is not a great deal to see. All northbound roads lead to The Mall, which forms part of Ring Road. Follow this westward to Kingsway Camp (now officially Guru Teg Bahadur Nagar). From here, Bhai Parmanand Marg leads northward to the park. A granite column marks the position of the thrones of King George V and Queen Mary at the Coronation Durbar 12 December 1911. It was here that the King astonished the country by announcing the transference of India's capital from Calcutta to Delhi and, together with his consort, laid the foundation stones of the new city. However, as surveys were made in 1913, it became apparent that the area was too swampy and malarial; New Delhi, therefore, was built well to the south, and both foundation stones were eventually transferred to New Delhi's Secretariat.

The marble statue of George V, carved by Charles Jagger in 1936, originally stood beneath the canopy at India Gate, and has been re-erected here. Queen Victoria's bronze statue was also brought to the park from its site outside the Town Hall in Chandni Chowk, but it was vandalized and transferred to the College of Art. Various statues of viceroys include Lord Irwin (much deteriorated) and Lord Willoughby, both by Reid-Dick. The statue of Lord Chelmsford is of interest, as it was carved by an Indian, M.S. Nagappu (c1935). Part of the arena's foundations survive and the grounds are well kept.

A return to the Green Ridge via The Mall and, at its end, right, Vishvavidyala Marg, leads to Chauburja Marg. Off this, to the left, after ½ mile (1km), lies **Chauburja Masjid**, the 'Four Towers' mosque built by Firoz Shah Tughlaq in 1356, possibly in connection with his hunting lodge. Some believe that the building is part of a tomb; its qibla, unusually, is at upper level.

Rani Jhansi Road branches south-westward downhill to the **Hindu Rao Hospital**. Facing the hospital's entrance is Delhi's second **Ashoka Pillar** which, like the example at Kotla Firoz Shah, was transported to the city by Firoz Shah Tughlaq. This specimen originally stood in Meerut, and was erected on its present site in what were then the grounds of the Sultan's hunting lodge. Early in the eighteenth century, an explosion broke the column, which fell to the ground in five sections, and lay here for 150 years before being taken to Calcutta. In 1867, the pieces were joined together and brought back to Delhi by the British. The third-century BC pillar is 33ft (10m) high and inscribed with faded Brahmi script.

Forming the core of the Hindu Rao Hospital, which may be entered, is the white-painted stucco **Hindu Rao's House**, built around 1825 for a Hindu nobleman. This became the country house of the British Resident in Delhi, William Fraser, who was shot while riding on horseback near the Lahore Gate of the Red Fort in 1835. The assassin was captured and executed, but it was found that he had acted on the orders of Shams-ud-din, Nawab of Firozpur, on whom Fraser had issued a decree. The prince was also tried and executed. During the Mutiny, Gurkhas occupied the building, which later became a military hospital.

Near the water tower in the hospital grounds rises the **Pir Ghaib** 'Observatory'. Its name Pir (Saint) Ghaib (Vanished) refers to the tradition that a saint who worshipped here mysteriously disappeared without trace. Steps ascend to the west wall, which is designed as a mosque's qibla, and where Muslims still pray. Steep steps lead to the flat roof, which may have been used by Firoz Shah as an observatory, but was certainly part of his hunting lodge.

From the hospital, follow Rani Jhansi Road southward. On the left is the **Mutiny Memorial**, erected in 1863 to commemorate the regiments of the Delhi Field Force that had stormed Delhi 7 years earlier. Panels naming the forty-six officers who died have recently

The Indian Mutiny

At the beginning of the nineteenth century, India was predominantly a collection of individually run states, autocratically ruled by Hindu or Muslim rulers, none of them pre-eminent, but many involved in internecine warfare. The British East India Company, long-established traders on the sub-continent, saw the vacuum as an opportunity to extend its activities to embrace political control, and amassed a powerful 'private' army. Protection treaties were signed with most Indian states in 1818, but British suzerainty was the price that had to be paid for stability. The Rajput princes co-operated with the British in the same way as they had with the Moguls, and were permitted to maintain direct rule over their own states with little interference. No British troops were stationed in Delhi, and the last of the Moguls, the venerable Bahadur Shah II, although no longer emperor, was permitted to bear the title King of Delhi. However, as was inevitable, Western culture, education, religion and morality were unsympathetically introduced by the country's new masters, and many orthodox opinions of both Hindus and Muslims were disregarded.

An explosion was inevitable, and the spark to ignite it proved to be the new Enfield gun, which sepoys (from the Urdu word for foot-soldiers) employed in the company's army were required to load by biting off the ends of cartridges. It was believed, although officially denied, that the cartridges were lubricated with fat from the bodies of pigs and cows, the consumption of which was taboo on religious grounds for Hindus and Muslims alike. When sepoys at Meerat refused to load the guns, they were incarcerated in chains.

On the morning of 10 May 1857, the prisoners were released by their fellow sepoys, who had shot the British commanders. That same afternoon, the rebels marched the 50 miles (80km) south to Delhi, capturing the city virtually unopposed. British civilian officials, who had taken refuge in the Red Fort, were massacred, and Bahadur Shah II and his sons were persuaded to take command. In the euphoria, a total of forty-seven sepoy batallions mutinied, no more than seven supporting the British. Lucknow and Cawnpore also fell to the 'freedom fighters' but, unfortunately for them, only the deposed leader of the Mahrattas gave his support, the other states honouring their treaties with the company and staying neutral. Gradually, British reinforce-ments were acquired from Bombay, Madras, and even China, augmented by troops from England. The British took the Ridge overlooking Delhi on 8 June, but had to wait for the monsoon to end in mid-September before they could launch their attack on Delhi. After one week of fierce fighting, Delhi fell, Bahadur Shah was arrested, and his sons executed: retribution was exacted in the grim fashion of the time. In view of his age, Bahadur Shah was not put to death, but exiled to Rangoon in Burma, where he died. Other areas of resistance were overcome the following winter, and peace was formally established 8 July 1858.

The British government decided that it was now time to establish direct rule, and the East India Company, which had been founded by Elizabeth I, was abolished. India would be-come the 'Jewel in the Crown' of the British Empire, although Victoria was not proclaimed Emperess of India until 1876. Measures which had particularly offended India's religions were immediately dropped, and a Legislative Council established with an element of local representation.

It was at this time that India's greatest inheritance from the British, a modern communications system, was instigated, al-though the prime impetus for it was not the altruistic modernisa-tion of the country, but to speed British troop movements in possible times of insurrection. India's road, railway and tele-graphic systems were soon far and away the most highly developed of any colonial country. Some traditions, however, the British refused to countenance, among them sati, the ritual suicide by immolation of Rajput widows. As was inevitable, Western class structures gradually infiltrated, and the Indian caste system began to lose its inflexible hold: a middle-class gradually emerged. If the Indian Mutiny had succeeded, it seems likely that the country would have taken a great deal longer to reach the degree of mature stability and modernity that it has achieved. Most British visitors, however, will feel a certain pang of guilt for the rapaciousness of their forebears. 'Amendments' have certainly been made to British monuments, particularly in Delhi, but an understanding forgiveness of the former colonizers prevails, and today's British visitors are given the most affection-ate of welcomes.

been defaced by nationalists' graffiti. The tapering red stone monument is octagonal, its format being reminiscent of the medieval Eleanor crosses erected in England by Edward I. In 1972, to mark the twenty-fifth anniversary of India's independence, the memorial was re-named Ajit Garh (Tower of Victory), and now also commemorates the Indian freedom fighters who lost their lives during the struggle. The memorial stands on what were the British Lines, where 3,000 troops in the service of the East India Company, half of them sepoys (Indian born), were assembled from the Punjab. They encamped here throughout the monsoon, from June to mid-September, many of them dying of malaria and cholera before a shot was fired. By the time of the assault on the Kashmiri Gate, however, their number had been increased to 10,000. The Delhi Ridge was then treeless and offered clear views of the city below.

Grand Trunk road sweeps north-westward at the intersection of Rani Hansi Road and Boulevard Road, skirting Sabzi Mandi district. The **Sabzi Mandi Market** is the largest fruit and vegetable market in Asia. Unusual seasonal fruits include: chickoos, similar to Kiwi fruit, pethas, green pumpkins and kinos (lime-flavoured oranges).

To the west lies **Roshanara Bagh** garden, planted by and named after a daughter of Shah Jahan. She died in 1671 and is buried in the grounds.

Grand Trunk Road leads south-eastward to New Delhi Railway Station. Just before this is reached, follow Qutb Road, right, in the direction of Connaught Place. In the Aram Nagar district, on the west side, is the **Qadam Sharif**. Firoz Shah Tughlaq built this mausoleum, intending it for himself, but his eldest son Fateh Khan predeceased him and was buried here instead, in 1373. A footprint of Muhammad in stone was obtained from Medina and set beside the grave. Now it is displayed only during July, usually covered by water from the monsoon rains. At other times, the prophet's footprint, which gave the mausoleum its name, is kept in an adjacent house but may usually be seen on request. The tomb is enclosed by a fortified wall, and a mosque and college were added to the complex by Firoz Shah.

Additional Information

Places to Visit

OLD DELHI
Lal Qila (Red Fort)
Open: daily 6am-5.30pm.

Indian War Memorial Museum
Red Fort
Open: Sat to Thurs 10am-5pm.

Son et Lumière
At the Red Fort: in English daily
November to January 7.30pm, rest
of the year 8.30pm.

Museum of Archaeology
Mumtaz Mahal
Red Fort
Open: Sat to Thurs 10am-5pm.

Digambar Jain Temple
Chandni Chowk
Closes: 2.30-5pm.

Karim's Restaurant
Gulli Kabab-i-yan
Open: daily 7am-7pm.

EAST DELHI
Gandhi Memorial Museum
Jawaharlal Nehru Marg
Open: Tues to Sun 9.30am-5.30pm.

International Doll's Museum
Nehru House
Bahadurshah Zafar Marg
Open: Tuesday to Sunday 10am-6pm.

Pragati Maidan
Mathura Road
Open: daily 10am-5.30pm.

Crafts Museum
Bhairon Marg
Open: Monday to Saturday
10am-5.30pm.

Purana Qila (Old Fort)
Mathura Road
Open: daily 10am-5pm.
Museum Open: Saturday to
Thursday 10am-5pm.

Zoological Gardens
Mathura Road
Open: daily 8am-6.30pm in
summer, 9am-5pm in winter.

Karim's Nemat Kada Restaurant
168/2 Jha House
Hazrat Nizamudden West
☎ 698300
Open: 12noon-12midnight.

NEW DELHI
Gandhi Balidan Stal
5 Tees January Road
Open: Sun to Sat 9.30am-5pm.
Film shows 10am-12.30pm and
2-5pm.

Indira Gandhi Memorial Museum
1 Safdargang Road
Open: Sun to Sat 9.30am-5pm.

Jawaharlal Nehru Museum
Teen Murti Bhavan
Teen Murti Marg
Open: Sun to Sat 9.30am-5pm.

Parliament House (Sansad Bhavan)
Pandit Pant Road
Visitors Gallery Open: when
Parliament is in session. Passes
from the Notice Officer or in
advance, from the Government of
India Tourist Office.

Secretariat
Raj Path
Open: by advance application to
the Government of India Tourist
Office.

Rashtrapati Bhavan
Raj Path
Passes for the state rooms must be
applied for, in advance, to The
Military Secretary to the President.

Mogul Gardens
Rashtrapati Bhavan
Raj Path
Open: at varying times from
November to April, Friday to
Wednesday.

National Museum
Jan Path
Open: Thurs to Sun 10am-5pm.
Guided tours: 10.30am, 11.30am,
12noon, 2pm, 3.30pm.
Film shows at weekends 2.30pm
onwards.

National Gallery of Modern Art
Jaipur House
Fifteenth August Maidan
Open: Tues to Sun 10am-5pm.

Philatelic Museum
Dak Tar Bhavan
Patel Chowk
Open: Monday to Saturday
10.30am-12.30 & 2.30-4.30pm.

SOUTH DELHI
Rail Transport Museum
Shantipath Chanakyapuri
Open: Tuesday to Sunday
9.30am-5.30pm.

Tourist Information Offices

NEW DELHI
**Government of India Tourist
  Office**
88 Jan Path
☎ 332005
Open: Monday to Friday 9am-6pm.
Saturday 9am-1pm.

Delhi Tourism Corporation
N Block, Connaught Place
☎ 3313637

Chemist

NEW DELHI
Super Bazar (24 hour chemist)
Connaught Place
☎ 3310163

Accommodation

NEW DELHI
Imperial Jan Path
☎ 3324540

Janpath Jan Path
☎ 3320070

Park Parliament Street
☎ 352477

Samrat
Kamal Araturk Road
☎ 1603030

Taj Mahal
1 Man Singh Road
☎ 3016162

Maurya Sheraton
Sardar Patel Marg
☎ 3010101

The Oberoi
Dr Zakiv Hussain Marg
☎ 363030

Le Meridien
Windsor Place
☎ 383960

Holiday Inn
Barakhamba Avenue
☎ 3320101

NORTH DELHI
Oberoi Maidens Hotel
7 Sham Nath Marg
☎ 2525464

Agra

✳ AGRA

2

For more than 150 years, Agra was the Lodi and Mogul capital, until Aurangzeb transferred it officially to Delhi on usurping his father's throne in 1658. In the seventeenth century, the city was compared favourably with London, and its architectural master-pieces from the Great Mogul period are world famous. In view of all this, most visitors expect to find an attractive, well-planned city, with at least vestiges of its former glory. Alas, they will not. The streets of the old city are narrow, its buildings, apart from the Jama Masjid, lack interest, and a general air of dilapidation and squalor prevails.

With the rapidly diminishing power of the Moguls in the second half of the eighteenth century, Agra became a battleground for the Mahrattas and the Jats, who took it in turn to control the city; much destruction occurred during their disputations, particularly in 1764, following a Jat raid. The British made Agra the regional capital once again, early in the nineteenth century, and built a large cantonment to the south, which even today represents half the entire city.

preceding page; Agra Fort's Diwan-i-Khas. Shah Jahan virtually repeated its external design for his Red Fort at Delhi

Although no detailed record exists of the layout and appearance of Agra in its heyday, there would undoubtedly have been exotic bazaars, grand mansions, gardens, trees and, probably, water coursing through the main street. As at Shahjahanabad (Old Delhi), virtually all has gone.

Fortunately, the Jats and Mahrattas, although they were Hindus, spared Agra's Muslim tombs and mosques, all of which, apart from the Jama Masjid, stood in open country, well outside the city: the Taj Mahal to the south-east, the Tomb of Itimad-ud-Daulah to the east and the Tomb of Akbar to the north-west, in the suburb of Sikandra. Agra Fort was untouched, presumably because it was needed to house the respective conquerors.

Primarily, therefore, it is the peripheral monuments of Agra, in particular the Taj Mahal, that people come to see, rather than the city itself; the overall impression that Agra gives is of a crown of base metal studded with exquisite jewels. A better impression of the splendours of Mogul cities is gained from a visit to Akbar's 'dead city' of Fatehpur Sikri, 23 miles (37km) distant. Its great Jama Masjid and royal palace have been almost untouched by time, although little else remains.

For the sake of convenience, due to proximity, a brief excursion is made into Rajasthan, via Mathura and Vrindaban, to explore Deeg and Bharatpur, with its Keoladeo National Park, an ornithologist's paradise. Before leaving Agra, many will wish to make an excursion southward to Gwalior, which possesses the finest of all Indian forts, and a series of enormous Jain rock carvings.

The Taj Mahal

The Taj Mahal, of course, symbolizes not only Agra but the entire country, and for many holidaymakers it is the chief reason for coming to India. Like Venice and the pyramids of Egypt, the Taj Mahal more than lives up to expectations, and effortlessly avoids becoming a cliché of itself. Even the most cynical will be overwhelmed. This incomparable mausoleum was built by Shah Jahan for his favourite wife, Arjumand Banu Begam. When her husband ascended the throne in 1628, she became known as Mumtaz-i-Mahal (Greatest Ornament of the Palace): Taj is an abbreviated version of Mumtaz, hence the name Taj Mahal. Although without doubt the world's most famous physical demonstration of love, the Taj Mahal was not an expression of grief by a king for the loss of a young and beautiful wife, as most believe. Mumtaz (1592-1631), died in her fortieth year, while in labour for the fourteenth time, and is unlikely to have been what most would now consider a conventional beauty. Nevertheless, although Shah Jahan had much younger wives, she remained his firm favourite, and he was devastated with grief at her sudden passing. Not a great deal is known about Mumtaz, but she appears to have been an ardent Muslim, personally campaigning against Christian missionaries in India, which was hardly surprising in view of the intolerance of Hinduism shown by the Portuguese in Goa at the time.

Work on the walled complex began shortly after the death of Mumtaz, suggesting that Shah Jahan already had a plan for such a tomb in mind. Within 6 months, the body of Mumtaz had been brought from Burhanpur, where she had died during one of Shah Jahan's campaigns in the Deccan, to a temporary grave in the garden of the Taj Mahal, and it remained there until the mausoleum was ready. In the early stages, 20,000 are reported to have been working on the project, but this number had been reduced to 1,000 craftsmen within 9 years. Scaffolding of brick rather than timber was erected, indicative of the importance of the scheme. All was completed by 1653. It seems only right that such a magical building should have its share of mysteries and unproven allegations, and this is indeed the case. There are three chief unsolved questions: Who was the architect? Did Shah Jahan plan a separate 'mirror image' tomb for himself on the opposite side of the river? Why are the two cenotaphs not positioned side by side within the mausoleum's main chamber? Self-confident guides who give unequivocal answers to these questions should not be believed.

The Mogul emperors wished to take personal credit for their most important building projects, and only rarely was the name of the chief architect officially recorded. It is primarily for this reason that some have credited the Emperor himself with the design of the Taj Mahal. There is, however, no evidence whatsoever that Shah Jahan possessed architectural abilities, only that he served as an enthusiastic patron. Nevertheless, due to the great cost of the material, it seems likely that he was responsible for specifying the exclusive use of marble for the structure: Shah Jahan would certainly have seen the nearby tomb of Mumtaz-i-Mahal's grandfather, Itimad-ud-Daulah, similarly clad entirely in marble, and one of only two such examples to predate the Taj Mahal.

Another contender is the Venetian jewellery designer, Geronimo Veroneo, who died at Lahore in 1640, and now lies in Agra's Roman

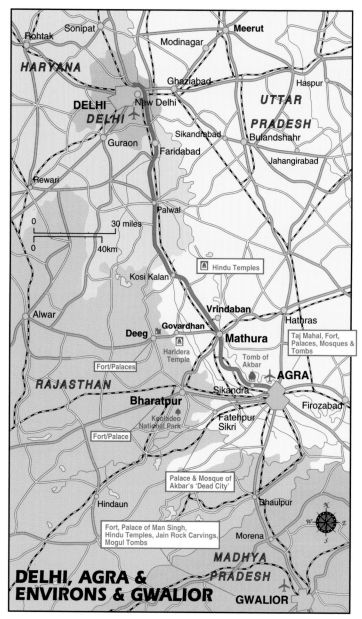

Rohtak
Sonipat
Meerut
Modinagar
HARYANA
Ghaziabad
Haspur
DELHI
New Delhi
UTTAR
DELHI
PRADESH
Sikandrabad
Bulandshahr
Guraon
Faridabad
Jahangirabad
Rewari
Palwal

0
30 miles
0
40km

Kosi Kalan
Hindu Temples

Vrindaban
Alwar
Hathras
Deeg
Govardhan
Mathura
Taj Mahal, Fort, Palaces, Mosques & Tombs
Haridera Temple
Tomb of Akbar
Fort/Palaces
AGRA
RAJASTHAN
Sikandra
Bharatpur
Firozabad
Keoladeo National Park
Fatehpur Sikri
Fort/Palace

Palace & Mosque of Akbar's 'Dead City'

Hindaun
Dhaulpur

Fort, Palace of Man Singh, Hindu Temples, Jain Rock Carvings, Mogul Tombs
Morena

MADHYA
DELHI, AGRA &
PRADESH
ENVIRONS & GWALIOR
GWALIOR

As the sun rises, the semi-precious stones of the Taj Mahal begin to sparkle

Catholic cemetery. His executor, Josef da Castro, stated that Veroneo was the architect of the Taj Mahal, and this claim was reiterated by a Spanish friar, Sebastian Manrique, but he was probably only repeating what da Castro had told him. There is no additional evidence, all other contemporary European visitors believing that a Muslim architect was responsible. It seems highly unlikely that a supremo would have been commissioned from Europe and, if he had been, that the news would not have spread. Persian records name Ustad Isa Afandi as the architect, but there are no other references to him; it is even uncertain whether he came from Persia or Turkey. Ustad Ahmad Lahori (from Lahore in what is now Pakistan) was certainly Shah Jahan's favoured architect at the time, and the names of the individuals responsible for the dome, caligraphy and petra dura work, etc, are recorded. Possibly, the Taj Mahal was the work of a spectacularly talented committee, presided over by Shah Jahan. The chief argument against this is the notorious failure of committees to produce outstanding designs: a sardonic tale might be recalled about the committee which set out to design a horse and ended up with a camel. Could any committee really produce such a sublime masterpiece? This mystery, and some others which are dealt with later, will surely never be solved to everyone's satisfaction.

On arrival at Agra, most visitors understandably rush straight to the Taj Mahal, and they are quite right to do so. The building's appearance changes as the sun rises and falls, and while the consensus of opinion seems to favour early evening, the time chosen for a first visit is not of overwhelming importance. What is important, however, is that return visits should be made (in spite of the recently-liked entrance changes for foreigners): dawn, sunset and midday present the Taj Mahal in completely different aspects. Unfortunately, terrorist threats have led to the closure of the compound at 7pm, and it is therefore no longer possible to observe the full effect of moonlight on the building. Some wicked tourists, however, have been observed on winter nights hiding in dark corners, thus prolonging their stay until 7.30pm, much to the aggravation of some of the generally good-natured guardians: offers of backsheesh will not get an extension! It should be borne in mind that only at sunrise and moonrise can the sparkling of the semi-precious stones, which are set in the marble, be observed. The tricks played by this three-and-a-half centuries old magician seem inexhaustible — there are more to come.

Although some fortunate residents of the Taj View Hotel may now be able to spy on the Taj Mahal, it was originally intended that the building should be completely hidden from the city by its high wall (it has always been possible to admire the mausoleum from the north side of the River Yamuna). This concealment adds to the visitor's astonishment on entering the complex and being confronted suddenly and dramatically by the wondrous apparition. Sadly, an ill-advised decision was made quite recently by the authorities in connection with security precautions. The finest view of the mausoleum is the initial one, gained from the arch of the **Great Gateway** (1648), and the scale of the entire scheme was obviously engineered that this should be so. Until recently, all visitors entered through the south gateway, and were thus immediately confronted by the knock-out vista, as intended. Now, security checks have been set up on the right hand side of the gateway, so that visitors have to sneak into the compound at an angle, and are thereby deprived of that first, astounding, symmetrical view, framed by the archway. Some brazen it out with the guardians, and insist on first looking through the arch (which is now the exit only); others, who are prepared, avert their eyes from the mausoleum and make directly for the inner side of the gateway before drinking in the view. It must be hoped that the system is soon reversed.

No more reading of this book should now take place until the wonder of the Taj Mahal has had its effect — an effect that may well, surprisingly, lead to tears, tears of pride that mankind has been able to create such beauty. A fairly lengthy stay at the gateway is recommended (at no other point will the view improve), followed by a slow, silent walk along the central canal, as if traversing the nave of a great cathedral. To accompany this magical experience by reading facts about the building would be as profane as to study the score of Beethoven's *Ninth Symphony* throughout a first hearing. Only after returning to the gateway should reading recommence, as a prelude to retracing one's footsteps...

...Many visitors to the Taj Mahal will already have seen some of its predecessors, the majority of which are in Delhi. These are generally buildings of high quality, and most comprise elements in their composition which are repeated in the Taj Mahal. Why then is Agra's mausoleum so unquestionably pre-eminent? Fairly obvious differences are: sheer size, its overall height of 240ft (73m) is almost identical to that of Dellhi's Qutb Minar tower (possibly not a coincidence); the entire structure is faced with marble; delicate, tapering minarets frame the mausoleum at the four corners of its podium; *chattris* cluster around the dome as if seeking maternal protection, thus making their contribution to the compactness of the design; the three bays between each *iwan*, one of which is angled, are identical, and lead the eye around the octagonal building, thereby augmenting its three-dimensional quality; absolutely nothing but sky impinges on the purity of the building's contours, and as this, at least in the tourist season, is invariably pale blue, the Taj Mahal evokes a floating desert mirage.

The dome plays a more prominent part in the design of the Taj Mahal than in any other Mogul building. It towers over the four *iwans*, even at close quarters, evoking a white balloon swelling with air, which is about to float gently skyward taking the remainder of the structure with it. The similarity of form between the minarets and space rockets increases this illusion; at any moment, it seems, they might ignite to assist take-off! Each of the marble slabs that make up the minarets is firmly delineated by black pointing, possibly to prevent the eye being directed from the composition by slender white towers melting into the hazy sky. It is said that the minarets are slightly tilted, so that they would not strike the mausoleum if they fell.

But perhaps the most important feature of the building is its dimensions. Uniquely among India's Mogul buildings, the height above podium level of the Taj Mahal almost precisely equals its diameter: the building would thus fit neatly within a cube. Renaissance architects discovered that, for some unkown reason, cubic dimensions are particularly appealing, a discovery that was put into practise by the great English architect Inigo Jones, who invariably designed his rooms in multiples of cubes.

Shah Jahan was particularly fond of Hindu-style cusped arches, even the Jama Masjid in Delhi demonstrates this, but here, the clean lines of the Persian arch appear throughout, with no examples of foliation. In fact, appart from the four *chattris* clustered around the dome, and the metal finials, this is a very 'Persian' building.

The four-part *charbagh* garden is the only Mogul example in either Agra or Delhi where water still courses regularly through it. However, this is cut off at intervals so that the channel may be cleaned; work usually takes 3 days, and then visitors will unfortunately miss the reflection of the Taj Mahal in the water. Peach trees originally flanked the channel, but they have been replaced by cypresses. The garden was completely restored for Lord Curzon (1899-1905), and its English appearance is a result of this work, rather than one of Lady Willingdon's enthusiasms, which might have been suspected.

As the steps to the podium are reached, it will be noted that they form the only asymmetrical feature of the building. It seems strange that a double flight was not constructed, thus preserving complete symmetry. Footwear must be discarded at this point.

It is said that the entire Koran is incised on the marble of the Taj Mahal's arches

On the pavement of the podium, the marble shimmers, but is clearly not dead white in the manner of Italian Carrara marble, as it often appears to be in photographs. Almost every slab incorporates veins of grey and cream; some even have a green or pinkish hue. The stone comes from the Makrana quarry, near Jaipur, and was the marble used almost exclusively for Mogul buildings; its smokey quality is chiefly responsible for the material's pearl-like appearance and changing response to variations in light. Makrana marble is still quarried and utilised for better-quality artefacts.

It soon becomes apparent that the decorative themes of the Taj Mahal are restricted to calligraphy or stylized floral patterns. Allegedly, the entire Koran is incised on the stonework of the complex. On the archways, the calligraphy is executed so that the actual size of the characters increases with height, thus giving an impression of uniformity. Most floral patterns are in multi-coloured petra dura work, but some below dado level are monochrome reliefs, an effective combination.

A promenade around the mausoleum will confirm that each side is identical. On the north side, the River Yamuna flows directly beneath the Taj Mahal. It was formerly possible to take a ferry to and from the opposite bank, but this service has been terminated as a security measure. Tavernier, a contemporary French traveller, reported that Shah Jahan intended to build his own private mausoleum in the form of a black marble facsimile of the Taj Mahal, on the north bank of the river; both mausoleums were to be linked by bridges. Apparently, Aurangzeb, on seizing the throne in 1658, ordered the scheme to be abandoned. However, there is no corroboration of this story, which was probably based on a fanciful rumour.

What may be seen on the far bank of the river is a small mosque, a rare building from Humayan's interrupted reign.

The mausoleum's interior is entered from the south side. Originally, silver doors closed the entrance, but they were taken by the Jat raiders in 1764 and never replaced. Visitors were not admitted to the tomb chambers during the Mogul period. The octagonal central chamber is situated directly beneath the great dome; smaller corner chambers lie, symetrically, below the four *chattris*.

In the main chamber, the cenotaphs of Mumtaz and Shah Jahan are enclosed by an exquisitely carved marble screen, designed to filter the light. That of Mumtaz is centrally positioned, while her husband's, inscribed as usual with a pen box to indicate the male sex, lies to one side, set on a slightly higher base. This asymmetrical configuration is taken by some to indicate that Shah Jahan intended to lie elsewhere; hence, possibly, the derivation of the black marble mausoleum story. However, the tomb of Itimad-ad-Daulah and his wife exhibits a similar configuration, and was certainly planned that way.

Originally, the chamber was somewhat lighter, but birds became a nuisance, and it proved necessary to erect glass panels to keep them out. The walls of the chamber are decorated with Koranic calligraphy and petra dura work, but the finest example of the latter is on the cenotaph of Mumtaz, where the gradation of the colours of the flower petals is exquisite. Viceroy Lord Curzon presented the lamp suspended above the cenotaph in 1905.

As is usual, the graves of the mausoleum's occupants lie in a chamber below. This is unlit, however there is usually someone who will loan a torch for a few rupees. Originally, the chamber was lined with gold sheets, but Aurangzeb removed them after his father's death.

The two buildings erected on either side of the mausoleum are identical. On the west side is the **mosque**, built of red sandstone and surmounted by three domes. A strange optical trick occurs here: walking from the back of the mosque towards an arch in its screen, the Taj Mahal appears to retreat; in the reverse direction it appears to advance. Only from this mosque, shortly after dawn, does the sun appear adjacent to the Taj Mahal, thus providing a popular composition for photographers.

The mirror-image building on the east side is known, understandably, as the **Jawal** (Echo). It appears to have been constructed primarily for reasons of symmetry. Claims that visitors were accommodated within, or that it served as an assembly hall, are pure guesswork. It is undoubtedly the best place from where to watch the semi-precious stones set in the marble of the mausoleum sparkle, as either the sun or the moon rises. From November to January it is possible to gain some impression of the moonlight effect, even at 7pm (but better at 7.30pm). Few visitors appear to know that this sparkling occurs: it is rather as if a myriad gloworms were colonizing the mausoleum. Set in the pavement in front of the Jawal is a representation of the finial of the Taj Mahal's dome.

One last question remains. Is the Taj Mahal the most beautiful building in the world? There is, of course, no answer to this, because, as is well-known, beauty lies in the eye of the beholder. But perhaps it can be said with some confidence that no other building moves so many people entirely through the abstract purity of its architecture.

⚏ Agra Fort

A lively street of shops and restaurants leads from the Great Gate of the Taj Mahal to the area where all vehicles must park.

Although a fair amount of propositioning of tourists will have been noted in the environs of the Taj Mahal, mostly by postcard

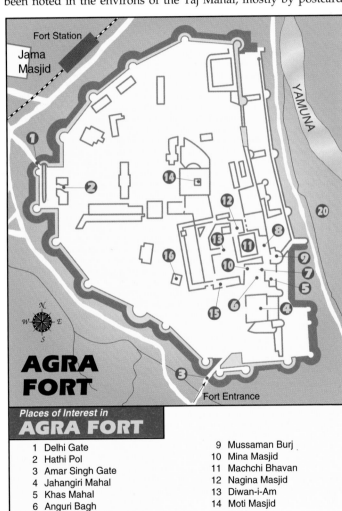

Fort Station

Jama Masjid

YAMUNA

AGRA FORT

Fort Entrance

Places of Interest in
AGRA FORT

1 Delhi Gate	9 Mussaman Burj
2 Hathi Pol	10 Mina Masjid
3 Amar Singh Gate	11 Machchi Bhavan
4 Jahangiri Mahal	12 Nagina Masjid
5 Khas Mahal	13 Diwan-i-Am
6 Anguri Bagh	14 Moti Masjid
7 Sheesh Mahal	15 Café
8 Diwan-i-Khas	16 Salimgarh Kiosk

vendors, it is nothing compared with the hassle which visitors to the Agra Fort must endure; by far the worst in India. Remember, you have already sent postcards and are returning home tomorrow, you have bought all your presents, your guide is ahead. And good luck!

Akbar's impressive Amar Singh Gate, the main entrance to Agra Fort. Its design was greatly influenced by the Hindu gateway to Gwalior Fort, and the designs of the ceramic tiles are the only Islamic features

Having said this, the layout of the buildings is much more confusing than at Delhi's Red Fort, and there are no identifying plaques. Some may, therefore, wish to engage the services of a guide, merely for identification.

After the Taj Mahal, the Agra Fort is the most important of the city's sights. Most readers will have seen the Red Fort at Delhi a few days before, and it must be admitted that, superficially at least, the two great complexes have much in common, even though Delhi's fort is twice the size. Both are orientated north/south and occupy the west bank of the River Yamuna, they are surrounded by similar castellated walls of dressed red sandstone, and the most important pavilions are built of marble in the distinctive style of the Shah Jahan period. Historically, however, there are great differences. No earlier defensive structure occupied the site of Shah Jahan's Red Fort, whereas Agra Fort owes its present appearance to two emperors, Akbar and Shah Jahan, and was built over an earlier fort, constructed of brick by Sikandar Lodi.

It was to Agra Fort that Humayun was despatched by his victorious father, Babur, immediately following the defeat of Ibrahim Lodi at Panipat, 50 miles (80km) north of Delhi, in 1526. Babur understood that the Lodi jewels were kept in the fort, and Humayun was instructed to secure them. An unexpected bonus was that members of the Maharajah of Gwalior's family were discovered sheltering in the fort, guarding their own jewels. In order to gain Humayun's favour, they presented him with an enormous diamond, believed by some to have been the Koh-i-Noor, which is now (in cut down form) one of the Crown Jewels of England.

Two years later, Babur defeated the Rajputs, and celebrated his newly-won status as Emperor of Hindustan at Agra Fort. Babur had little interest in building, preferring to lay out Persian-style gardens but, in any case, he spent so much time fighting to establish his dynasty during his short reign that little opportunity occured. Within 4 years, Humayun had succeeded his father as emperor, and appears to have carried out some construction work at the fort, none of which has survived; on Humayun's death in 1556, his son Akbar, then aged 14, inherited the throne, which he immediately and successfully defended against Shah Adil, the nephew of his father's conqueror Shah Sher Sur. From 1565, Akbar began to rebuild Sikandar Lodi's Agra Fort in an enlarged form, a task which took 16 years to complete. The walls, gates and one important pavilion are all that survive with certainty, from Akbar's period; almost all the remainder is the work of Shah Jahan.

The walls were built as a double structure, innner and outer defences being separated by a moat; Quaim Khan, Akbar's surveyor, was in charge of the project. As at Delhi, three gateways punctuate the wall, on the west, south and east sides. The most important was the west gate; at Agra this is called the Delhi Gate and it leads directly to a second, inner gateway, the **Hathi Pol** (Elephant Gate). Unfortunately, neither may be inspected closely, as the entire west section of the fort is now occupied by the military. Within the inner arch of the **Delhi Gate** is inscribed the date 1600, indicating that it was rebuilt soon after Akbar's return to Agra in 1599.

Between the Delhi Gate and the Jama Masjid stood the Tripulia Court, in which stood the Naubat Khana, from where musicians played to announce the arrival of important guests. Both the courtyard and the Naubat Khana were demolished by the British when they constructed the railway line.

The only public entry to the fort is now from the south, via the **Amar Singh Gate**. The name of this gate commemorates Rao Amar Singh, originally destined to become Maharajah of Jodhpur, but disinherited by his father in favour of his younger brother Jaswant Singh. Apparently, Rao suffered from an uncontrollable temper, which led to unacceptably rash deeds. His rashest, and last, took place in the Diwan-i-Am of Agra Fort, when he took exception to statements made by the court treasurer and killed him; all this in the presence of Emperor Shah Jahan, who was not impressed. Allegedly, Rao, sensing that this time he might have gone too far, mounted his horse and attempted to leap the wall of the ramp and escape from the fort. The horse fell and threw Rao to the ground, where he was set upon by guards and put to death. The Amar Singh Gate was stormed by General Lake in 1803, instilling such fear into the occupying Mahratta force that an immediate surrender to the British ensued.

Tickets are purchased to the left of the public entrance, the first of three structures that make up the gate. The path curves right to the second archway, but further on, located at right angles to the path, is the most impressive part of the Amar Singh Gate. Great domed towers, connected by an open gallery, flank a relatively small archway. Apart from the stylized, floral patterns of the blue tiles, the appearance of the structure is entirely Hindu, and typical of the early period of Akbar's reign, when his architects departed from the Muslim architectural tradition which had been long-established in India. Similarities between the Amar Singh Gate and the main entrance to the Rajput fort at Gwalior have been noted. It was near this point that Amar Singh was slain, hence the gateway's name.

To the right, at the end of the ramp linking the southern gateways with the royal pavilion, stands the red sandstone **Jahangiri Mahal**,

Jahangir completely remodelled and extended the exterior of his father's palace at Agra Fort, renaming it the Jahangiri Mahal

Built by Akbar, the Jahangiri Mahal makes more use of Hindu than Muslim architectural features. Note the typically Hindu brackets in the courtyard

believed to have been built by Akbar in 1570. Salim, Akbar's son and successor, adopted the name Jahangir (Seizer of the World), on ascending the throne in 1605; the change of name was evidently made to avoid confusion with Sultan Selim of Turkey. In view of this, the building could not have been called the Jahangiri Mahal in Akbar's time. Its name appears to reflect that Jahangir, shortly after becoming emperor, added a new façade to his father's palace, also probably extending it, which explains why the exterior and interior of the building are completely different in style. Due to its location and single access point from the west side, the palace is believed to have formed part of the female quarters. A tradition that Jahangir remodelled the building specifically for his adored wife, Nur Jahan, might well be true. Fronting the building is the Hauz-i-Jangiri, an enormous tank of red porphyry rock, believed to have been built in 1611. Its inscription refers to Jahangir.

The façade of the Jahangiri Mahal is Islamic in form, although Hindu *jarokhas*, *chattris* and *chajjas* are incorporated, as was normal in Mogul buildings. Here, they are unmodified in any way, and a combination rather than a fusion of styles results. White marble architraves delineate the blind arcades flanking the central *iwan*. A fringe of lotus buds decorates the arches, echoing the fourteenth-century work of the Khalji sultans.

Within, the vestibule is basically Hindu in style, although its exquisite carving is Saracenic. A gloomy, domed hall follows, and then Akbar's extraordinary courtyard is reached. Apart from the pointed arches of its gallery, this is entirely Hindu in style. Sumptu-ously carved columns and brackets, square-headed apertures, and the general design appear to be inspired by Gwalior Fort. At Agra Fort, for the first time since the Muslims had ruled in India, they commissioned buildings in the Hindu architectural style, with very limited Islamic detail, rather than the other way round. Akbar, of course, may have built other similar structures at Agra Fort which preceded this example, but his later work, at Fatehpur Sikri, still survives to demonstrate effectively the strong influence that Hindu architectural traditions held on him in the middle of his reign.

Akbar was the least religiously bigoted of the Great Moguls, and permitted his subjects complete freedom of worship. He studied the religions of Hindus, Buddhists, Sikhs, and even Christians, eventu-ally evolving his own philosophy, known as Din-Ilani (God's Reli-gion), a merging of basic precepts common to all. It appears that Akbar's views were genuinely held, and only incidentally provided a way of uniting the subjects of his newly-formed empire; however, Akbar may have had this unifying aspect in mind when he gave precedence to Hindu architectural styles over Islamic. Alternatively, it may have been simply a question of local craftsmen better understanding the former. There is no conclusive evidence to support either view, and experts disagree.

To the left lies the north hall, its roof supported by stone crossbeams, which are sinuously carved with dragons. Opposite, the south hall, similar in style, is much narrower. The east hall, which retains some original stucco work (restored by the British), leads to an open quadrangle, from where its pillared façade may be admired. From here also is the first of the fort's viewpoints of the River Yamuna and the distant Taj Mahal sited on its bend. The slender columns of the rooftop *chattri*, approached right, frame the scene even more attractively (beware the dangerously low balcony rail).

The northward route continues, leading, via an archway, to a small, walled courtyard, which announces Shah Jahan's marble rebuilding of his grandfather's work. It is generally considered that Shah Jahan's buildings at Agra are even finer than those at Delhi, particularly with regard to their decorative inlay. On the east side of the courtyard, right, is the 'Gold Pavilion', named from its gilded copper roof; it is one of a pair which flank the larger pavilion ahead: all make up the **Khas Mahal** (House Palace), built by Shah Jahan for his private relaxation in 1636. It is representative of the mature Mogul period of architecture, in which both Islamic and Hindu forms are simplified and merged into a synthesized but distinct style, with Makrana marble the dominant building material.

The roof of this side pavilion is in three parts; the central, curved section being known as bangaldar, as it imitates the roofs of Bengali huts. There is a fanciful tale that Shah Jahan intended the side pavilions to serve as quarters, respectively, for his two favourite daughters, however, it was uncommon for areas to be set aside for an exclusive use in this way.

The central pavilion ahead is approached from the courtyard, and it will probably be apparent immediately to those who have visited Delhi that this was the inspiration for the Red Fort's Diwan-i-Khas. The interiors of the Khas Mahal were partly restored in 1895. Dampened screens of grass were fixed between the columns in summer to reduce the heat; in winter, thick curtains protected occupants from the chill evening air.

As has been seen, Agra Fort combines work by Akbar, Jahangir and Shah Jahan, built at different periods, and therefore lacks the homogeneity of planning and design of Delhi's Red Fort. However, the British demolished far less here than at Delhi, and it therefore remains more pristine.

From the east side of the pavilions, as at Delhi, animal fights and other spectacles could be observed below on the then narrow piece of land between the fort and the river. At Agra, the Yamuna is only a trickle compared to the wide, fast-flowing river that it formerly was: Delhi now takes so much more of the water upstream for its vastly increased population.

A pool is set in the raised platform on which the Khas Mahal is set; from this, water was channelled to form a cascade falling into the **Anguri Bagh** (Grape Garden) below. This may have been a vineyard, but a contemporary traveller recorded that the garden's name came from red and green jewels set in its marble screens, now lost. The garden is laid out in the usual *charbagh* style, its four sections divided by curbs into a jigsaw-puzzle pattern. Originally, this pattern was emphasized by planting flowers of different colours in each subdivision; now, most of the planting is of herbs with floral borders. It is said that fertile soil was brought from Kashmir to establish the garden. Immediately north of the Khas Mahal's central pavilion, the side pavilion precisely matches its twin.

To the north of this, three chambers comprise the gloomy **Sheesh Mahal** (Glass Palace), so-named from the mirror work decoration of its rooms. Originally, illuminated fountains and cascades were fitted within.

From the small courtyard, steps lead up to the **Diwan-i-Khas** (Hall of Private Audience). Built in 1637, this is a more open structure than its later equivalent at Delhi and, instead of wide piers delicate, twelve-sided columns set in pairs, support the roof. The carving and petra dura work is also superior to that at Delhi. It is said that the royal treasury was housed beneath the building.

Set on the same terrace, to the north, is a black marble throne, from which, in private audience, the emperor would receive important visitors, who would be seated on the white marble chair facing him. The inscription on the throne refers to Salim's change of name to Jahangir. A fissure in the throne is said to be damage received during the eighteenth-century Jat occupation of the fort. A hall and the royal baths once stood to the north of the terrace.

A staircase from the Diwan-i-Khas leads to the octagonal **Mussaman Burj** tower; its name refers to the muezzin's call to prayer, which could be heard from it; there are, however, alternative appellations: Jessamine (Jasmin) Burj, and its abbreviation, Saman Burj.

Shah Jahan began rebuilding the palaces of Agra Fort in 1628, and it is believed that he intended that the Mussaman Burj would be the private apartment of his adored Mumtaz, but she died shortly before it was ready for occupation. Shah Jahan left Agra for his new fort at Shahjahanabad (Old Delhi) in 1648 and probably spent little further time at Agra until his enforced return 10 years later, when, by tradition, he was imprisoned in this tower by Aurangzeb until his death in 1666. Jahanara, who had become 'first lady' on the death of Mumtaz Mahal, cared for her father here throughout his exile, but Roshanara, his other daughter, abandoned him, and supported her unscrupulous brother. Aurangzeb never met his father again after

Agra Fort's Diwan-i-Khas

imprisoning him at Agra. Shah Jahan was permitted a harem but few clothes or writing materials.

If the Mussaman Burj were indeed Shah Jahan's place of exile, it must have been the most splendid prison of all time; the carving of the marble, the petra dura work, and the pierced screens are unmatched elsewhere in either Agra Fort or the Red Fort at Delhi. The rows of niches probably supported lamps and scent bottles, and a pool is carved in the pavement of an outer room. Views from the octagonal gazebo are superb; it is said that Shah Jahan would gaze sorrowfully for hours at the distant Taj Mahal, where his beloved Mumtaz lay. Beside the tower, the tiny mosque, known as the **Mina Masjid**, was allegedly built by Aurangzeb for the exclusive use of his imprisoned father, in order to restrict his movements within the fort. Marble slabs on the floor of the terrace that faces the tower are laid out to resemble the board of a game known as *pachisi*. The surrounding screens show signs of damage from cannon fire, probably dating from the Mutiny.

Below the Diwan-i-Khas is the **Machchi Bhavan** (Fish House), a garden courtyard enclosed on three sides by a two-storey cloister, possibly built by Akbar, who certainly brought the bronze gates, on the north side, from Chittaurgarh Fort. Formerly, pools stood in the centre, and these, assuming that fish swam in them, would probably account for the name. The Jats removed the marble pools and their fountains in 1761. By tradition, bazaars had been held in the court-yard before its pools were excavated, and the courtesans flirted between the stalls; it has even been surmised that Jahangir met Nur Jahan, and Shah Jahan met Mumtaz for the first time at one of them. The severe Aurangzeb is reputed to have commissioned the pools in order to put a stop to such immodest behaviour.

Reached from the north-west corner of Machchi Bhavan's upper arcade is the mosque built of marble by Shah Jahan for the ladies of the court. In spite of its small size, the **Nagina Masjid** (Gem Mosque) is triple-domed.

Return to the west side of Machchi Bhavan's courtyard and descend the steps to the **Diwan-i-Am** (Hall of Public Audience), a great hipostyle, built of plastered red sandstone. It is more than twice as long as the similar hall at Delhi, but only slightly wider. Shah Jahan was responsible for the present building which, it is alleged, replaced an ancient structure of wood erected by Humayun. Women were permitted to watch the proceedings through screens set in the rear wall. In the centre of this wall is an arched recess decorated with petra dura work. From here, throughout most mornings, Shah Jahan presided over administrative matters, adjudicating and sentencing criminals, and hearing the pleas of his subjects. On becoming emperor in 1627, Shah Jahan commissioned the Peacock Throne, in which would be incorporated his finest jewels; the throne took 7 years to complete and first stood in this recess, which was made to accommodate it.

Immediately north of the north range of the Diwan-i-Am's court-yard is the most important of the fort's mosques, the **Moti Masjid** (Pearl Mosque). This has been closed many years for restoration and, at the time of writing, there were still no signs of it being re-opened.

Shah Jahan built the mosque, but it was not completed until 1653, 5 years after he had transferred the court to Delhi. Considering that it was only planned to serve the palace, the dimensions are surprisingly large. Red sandstone forms the courtyard's external wall and its east gate, which is reached from a double stairway; within, however, all is faced with marble, carefully selected for its whiteness. On three sides of the courtyard, the cloister is supported by fifty-eight marble columns. An ancient sundial on an octagonal pillar stands south-east of the central ablutions tank.

Chattris decorate the roof line, but, architecturally, the design of the mosque is less successful than most of Shah Jahan's work, the three identical domes failing to provide a focal point above the seven-arched screen. A black marble inscription likens the mosque to an exquisite pearl.

On returning to the fort's exit, passing the exterior of the south-west corner of the Diwan-i-Am's courtyard, the small Salimgarh Kiosk, in early-Mogul style, is passed. This may have been built by Islam Shah Sur during his brief reign. Nearby, in the south range of the courtyard, is a cafeteria.

Jama Masjid

As has been seen, three mosques were built within the fort, but Agra's largest, the Jama Masjid, stands in the centre of the old city and, since it was constructed, has been the most important centre of worship for local Muslims. Strangely, even though all four of Agra's mosques were designed during the finest period of Mogul architecture, none are particularly successful compositions. It must be admitted, however, that before the British ran the railway track between the mosque and the fort, the Jama Masjid would have been much more impressive.

Not only did the iconoclastic British demolish the square and the Naubat Khana, they also destroyed the original main gateway of the mosque, which was replaced with the present unexceptional structure. It is recorded on this that Shah Jahan built the Jama Masjid for his daughter, Jahanara, in 1648.

The mosque and its courtyard follow the normal practise of being raised on a plinth. An unusual zig-zag pattern of white marble bands give zest to three red sandstone domes. For some reason, the five arches of the prayer hall's screen were separated by unduly wide pillars, and the ponderous appearance that has resulted is the chief reason for the mosque's lack of appeal.

Agra City ☀

The labyrinthine streets of the old city wind sinuously behind the mosque. There is nothing of great architectural interest to see, as Agra's fame rests on its fort and its mausoleums, which were built in what was then the surrounding countryside. However, it is possible to watch craftsmen at work, and shopping for bargains can be most rewarding. Agra's thoroughfares are narrow and, except on Mondays, when most bazars close, claustrophobically jammed with people, most of whom seem to be riding bicycles or carts drawn by buffalo and loaded with goods. They weave nonchalantly between assorted animals, which never fail to amaze and amuse western visitors. Pigs snuffle, goats munch cigarette cartons, oxen masticate plastic bags, gibbering monkeys perform tight-rope acts on overhead wires (sometimes chosing a live one and ending up grilled monkey), green parakeets survey the scene from vantage points. It is as if the *Tour de France* had collided with a travelling circus. The liveliest time is late afternoon/early evening, but if any form of festival is being held it will be impossible to move at more than a snail's pace. Most streets of greatest interest intercommunicate, and shopkeepers will explain how to reach them; however, those who prefer to be guided will find many cheerful young men willing to assist for a few rupees.

Behind the mosque is the cloth market; to the right of this, the main shopping thoroughfare of Old Agra snakes northward, beginning as Johri Bazar. On the left-hand side, a well-known shop, **Damodar Das Mammo Mal**, sells *dhurries* (flat woven rugs), which can be made to specific designs and colours. Traditionally, the patterns are geometric and the yarn used is cotton, but slightly cheaper wool versions are also available. The store's post-home service is completely reliable.

Walking sticks with carved handles in a variety of designs are sold in a fascinating shop further up on the right. The street now becomes Kinari Bazar, where many jewellers are to be found. Panni Gali, an alleyway to the right, leads to the workshops of Shams Uddin, a world-famous master of gold-thread embroidery.

Returning towards the Jama Masjid, a left turn leads to the Malka Bazar, renowned for its kite makers — and ladies waving from upper windows, who seem to think they know you.

An interesting crafts area, north-west of the city, **Nai Ki Mandi**, is where the art of petra dura inlay is continued by many descendants of those who worked on the Taj Mahal. Trays, table tops and small boxes, all of Makrana marble, are the most popular items produced, and it is fascinating to watch the painstaking and highly-skilled

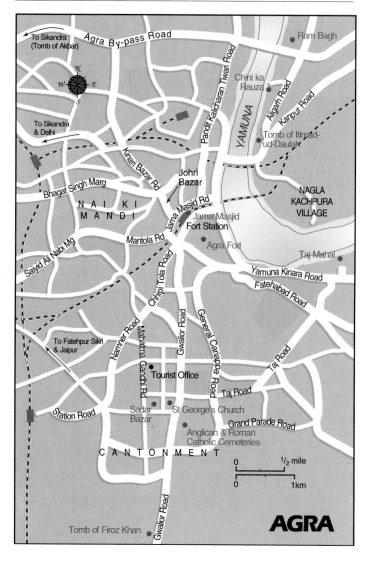

insetting of the semi-precious stones. Beware if buying, however, as the majority of the smaller pieces are in 'Italian marble' (alabaster) or even a composite made from marble dust. These will be dead white in appearance, without the grey and cream veining of the genuine marble; as the base is softer, these materials are much easier to work and articles made from them are, therefore, cheaper to buy. However, they stain and chip easily, and the real thing should be sought. As this is a Muslim trade, no work takes place on Fridays, which is always a religious holiday. Another traditional Agra trade in Nai Ki Mandi is shoemaking, the craftsmen working within tiny kiosks.

The British built their **cantonment** to the south of Agra. Similar residential areas were planned on the outskirts of many Indian cities of importance from the early nineteenth century onwards. Like New Delhi, Agra's cantonment is laid out with spacious, leafy avenues, which are too spread-out to tour comfortably on foot. Anglican and Roman Catholic **cemeteries** are located beside each other in Grand Parade Road, to the south; a colourful Victorian Gothic gatehouse forms the entrance. It is a surprise to discover that an envoy of Elizabeth I, John Mildenhall, who died in 1614, is buried here.

Gwalior Road crosses Grand Parade Road and, beside the Madhanagar market, 1 mile (2km) to the south, a turning right is signposted to the **Tomb of Firoz Khan**, a minor Mogul. His mausoleum, raised on a plinth, is prettily reflected in water, in the manner of the Taj Mahal.

Returning northward, look out for **Subhash Emporium** in Gwalior Road, a reliable place from which to buy petra dura work in Makrana marble at reasonable prices. Munro Road is an interesting shopping street; **Oswal Emporium** (30) also sells petra dura articles, **Ganesha** (18) metal goods and **Cottage Industry** (also 18) *dhurries*. Jewellery is probably best purchased in Jaipur, but **Jewel Palace** in Pratabpural, and Chirali, near the Hotel Amar, in Fatehabad Road (east of the Taj Mahal), will both design to order and are reliable on delivery.

St George's Church, built in 1826 by Colonel J.J. Boileau, is Agra's Anglican church. It stands at the Gwalior Road / Taj Road junction.

One of Agra's most popular, medium price restaurants, almost entirely the preserve of tourists, is Sonam at 51 Taj Road. Murg sammandar (for 2) is the house speciality. Nearby, at 25 The Mall, Sonar's menu includes a range of chicken dishes.

East Bank of the River Yamuna

An early start is recommended to avoid rush-hour traffic jams on the approach to the narrow bridge, that crosses the river. The most impressive views of Agra Fort's ramparts are gained from its north side: keep a lookout for them to the right, once Fort Station has been passed. Most drivers will want to turn left onto Aligarh Road immediately the east bank of the river has been reached; insist, however, that they turn right to the village of Nagla Kachpura. From here, a short walk to the river provides another aspect of the Taj Mahal, sited on the opposite bank. Since the ferry service was stopped, there are few tourists, and the atmosphere is predominantly rural. Unfortunately, neither the sun nor the moon directly strike this north face of the mausoleum, and dawn or night-time visits are not really worth the effort. Hurnayun's mosque facing the Taj Mahal is of historic interest.

 ## Tomb of Itimad-ud-Daulah

A northward return, continuing just past the bridge, leads to the Tomb of Itimad-ud-Daulah. The complete facing with marble, and the extensive petra dura work of this mausoleum's exterior presaged the Taj Mahal. In form, however, it is very dissimilar, corner minarets being mere stumps, compared with the high, slender examples of the Taj Mahal (or the gateway to Akbar's Tomb), and they rise from the tomb itself, not its plinth, thus competing with the flat dome for visual priority. For these reasons, it hardly seems necessary to make an effort to visit this tomb before the Taj Mahal is seen, as some purists recommend. It will be noted that, unusually, the entrance is from the east rather than the south side, presumably to give the building a river backdrop. Unlike the Taj Mahal, this tomb stands in the centre of, not at one end of, its *charbagh* garden. The tomb was built between 1622 and 1628 for her parents by Nur Jahan, the most favoured and influential wife of Emperor Jahangir.

Mirza Ghiyas Beg, a Persian nobleman, fled with his family from Teheran, and proceeded to India, via Randahar, where he had been robbed of all his possessions apart from two mules. Employed at Akbar's court, he eventually became Jahangir's chief minister, gaining the title Itimad-ud-Daulah (Pillar of the State). His second daughter, initially called Mihr-an-Nisah, wedded an Afghan noble, who died campaigning for Jahangir. A disputed tradition is that the Emperor had already fallen in love with the young girl, and arranged that her husband should be put in a dangerous position on the battlefield where he was almost certain to be killed. Initially, so it is said, the recently-widowed Mihr-an-Nisah rejected Jahangir's advances, but eventually married him, in 1611. As Jahangir became increasingly dependent on opium and alcohol, his wife assumed great power. She was renamed Nur Mahal (Light of the Palace) and, later, Nur Jahan (Light of the World). Eventually, together with her father, Itimad-ud-Daulah, and her brother, Asaf Khan (father of

Mumtaz Mahal), she effectively administered her husband's empire, and became the most powerful woman in Mogul history. Itimad-ud-Daulah's death at Agra in 1622, closely followed that of his wife, and Jahangir recorded that he believed grief to be the cause.

Whatever view is held on the quality of the architectural assembly, this is undoubtedly one of the finest and most extensive examples of inlay work in India. It was not, however, the first, as the gateway to Akbar's tomb at Sikandra preceded it by 14 years. The inlay techniques employed show a great advance on previous work but, although the geometric and floral patterns are exuberant, the colours are muted; nowhere here are to be found the vibrant hues of the Taj Mahal's petra dura.

Internally, above dado level, the walls and ceilings were plastered and gilded, but deterioration has been extensive; a section of the vestibule was restored by Lord Curzon around 1905. The tombs of Itimad-ud-Daulah and his wife are of yellow marble, probably from quarries near Jaisalmer. They are matched by cenotaphs in the pavilion with the Bengali-type roof, which is set on the terrace directly above. It will be noted that only the upper sections of the domes escape the filigree decoration of the rest of the building's surface.

The Tomb of Itimad-ud-Daulah was the first example of a building entirely clad with marble to be commissioned in India (1622), but the Chaunsath Khamba necropolis at Nizamuddin (south Delhi), although not begun until 1623, was also finished that year, 5 years before Itimad-ud-Daulah's tomb. Jahangir soon tired of Agra, and spent most of his remaining years in Kashmir. He died at Lahore in 1627, and Nur Jahan commissioned a similar tomb to that of her parents for him at Shahdara; it is the only other example of this type to have been built.

The long Aligarh Road continues northward, passing through market gardens of great charm. After ½ mile (1km), a rustic lane, left, leads to the **Chini ka Rauza** (China Tomb). This is believed to be the tomb, which was built for himself, by Alami Afzal Khan Shirazi, a cultured Persian, who became Shah Jahan's chief minister, dying at Lahore in 1639. Now rather dilapidated, the severe, Persian-style mausoleum is still worth visiting, as it was the only building in India to be completely covered in tiles, fragments of which survive. The glazed, Chinese-style tiles (*chini-mitti*) have given the domed building its name. They are predominantly blue and white, with turquoise, orange and yellow variations, and were set in plaster on a brick base in the manner of a large-scale mosaic; designs illustrate flowers in a stylized form. It is on the north side that the most extensive sections remain. An enormous *iwan* gives entry to the interior, where there is little to see; it is thought that both tombs were originally faced with marble, but only brickwork survives.

Half a mile (1km) further along Aligarh Road (shortly after the Agra bypass crossroad), again on the left hand side, is a rare survival of a formal garden laid out by Babur, founder of the Mogul dynasty. Its original name, Aram Bagh (Garden of Repose), was gradually abbreviated to **Ram Bagh**. Established as a Persian *charbagh* by Babur in 1526, this may have been the first garden of its type in India. Much in need of restoration, the original layout of the four-part garden is still in evidence. Their narrowness here demonstrates that a

Remains of the ceramic tiling, which originally covered the unique Chini ka Rauza tomb at Agra

charbagh's water channels were originally intended for irrigation only; they were not regarded as the decorative features that they eventually became, for example, at the Taj Mahal. By tradition, Babur was buried here for a short time, immediately following his death in 1630; the first of the Great Moguls now lies in a simple grave in Kabul, Afghanistan.

Nearby is a similar garden, the **Zahara Bagh**, which some believe was laid out even earlier. The Agra By-Pass Road crosses the River Yamuna; it links with the Mathura Road, which lies to the north-west, and leads to Akbar's Tomb at Sikandra, 5 miles (8km) distant. It is no longer necessary to return first to the centre of Agra.

SIKANDRA

Marking the city limits of Agra, the Delhi Gate was built by Shah Jahan. Almost 4 miles (6km) further north, in the direction of Sikandra, the terracotta **figure of a horse** allegedly commemorates a favourite steed of Akbar's that died nearby. Half a mile further on, standing back on the right hand side of the road, is the **Gura ka Tal**, a water tank built of red sandstone; it retains octagonal towers and a channel.

Tomb of Akbar

Work probably began on the tomb before Akbar's death in 1605, however, it was not finished until 1612, and his son, Jahangir, certainly altered the design as work progressed. Some allege that, in 1607, he demolished a third of what had been built.

Tribes of monkeys haunt the area of Akbar's tomb

Views of the complex from the gateway's roof, and Akbar's cenotaph set on the upper terrace of the mausoleum, are of prime interest to visitors but, at the time of writing, both were closed 'for security reasons'. Unusually in India, peanuts are sold at the entrance for feeding the monkeys, but beware — like all monkeys, these are amoral thieves, and personal belongings should be guarded constantly.

The **gateway** to the tomb complex is a superb composition in red sandstone, which is inlaid with white marble and colourful mosaics. Four corner minarets, entirely faced with white marble for the first time in India, give added delicacy to the work. If the gateway's roof is out of bounds, visitors should proceed directly ahead to the tomb, following the paved causeway through the large *charbagh* garden where, as usual, water no longer flows through the irrigation channels.

The podium has four identical façades, a central *iwan* on each side being flanked by five arched bays of a cloister. Above the podium, four storeys rise to form a flattened pyramid structure, best viewed from some distance. The lower three storeys, built of red sandstone, are open halls supported on spindly columns, evoking bird cages. Surmounting the ensemble is a verandah of marble screens, within which is a courtyard and the cenotaph of Akbar (not visible externally). *Chattris* decorate the roof at all levels.

The lack of a dominant focal point is an undoubted architectural weakness of the building, and some have suggested that a central dome may have been intended. How much of the original design was altered by Jahangir is not known, but the solidity of the gateway and the podium is in strong contrast with the airiness of the upper storeys.

The entrance through the south *iwan* leads to a vaulted **vestibule**, the colourful decoration of which is now in poor condition. Ahead, the passage descends gently to the **crypt**, where the marble sarcophagus of Akbar stands, covered by a cloth; the lamp above it was donated by Lord Curzon. In 1691, the Jats rebelled against Aurangzeb's religious bigotry and raided the tomb of his great-grandfather, looting much of its ornamentation, including the bronze gates. It is said that Akbar's remains were taken from his tomb and burnt; a particularly inappropriate act considering the tolerance that the Emperor had shown towards Hindus.

Every attempt should now be made to ascend to the terraces above. On closer inspection, the top floor is revealed to comprise a courtyard surrounded by a cloistered verandah. *Jalis* screen the outer sides of the verandah, none of their geometric panels being identical in design. A triple-domed **pavilion** shelters Akbar's symbolic cenotaph. Inscribed on its sides are the ninety-nine names of Allah; the words Allahu Akbar (God is Great) on the north side, and Jalla Jalalahu (May His Glory Shine) on the south side. It has been alleged that the short marble pillar behind the cenotaph once supported the Koh-i-noor diamond. However, as has been said, the history of the diamond is controversial.

After leaving the tomb, some may wish to continue ½ mile (1km) northward to see what may be the remains of the late fifteenth-century Bavadari Palace, now better known as 'y **Mariam's Tomb**'. The town of Sikandra, in which both this building and Akbar's Tomb stand, was established in 1492, and named after its founder Sikandar Lodi, Sultan of Delhi from 1488 to 1517. He left Delhi in 1502 to take up residence here in his Bavadari Palace, built 7 years earlier.

The façade of this two-storey, red sandstone building is now somewhat dilapidated, partly due to its various uses before being purchased by the government in 1912. Within is the tomb of Mariam uz Zamani (Mary of the Age), a Hindu wife of Akbar, who was the mother of Jahangir. By tradition, she became a convert to Christianity hence presumably, her name.

Having seen Akbar's tomb, it is appropriate from an historical viewpoint to continue to the dead city of Fatehpur Sikri, approximately 30 miles (48km) distant, where the finest display of buildings from Akbar's period is to be found. Fatehpur Sikri lies due west of Agra and may be reached by bus or train, the former being preferable, due to greater frequency. An alternative route for those with time available, and involving at least one overnight stay, is to continue northward to Mathura and Vrindaban, with their strong Krishna connections. From Mathura, an excursion across the Rajasthan state border can then be made to Deeg and Bharatpur, returning to Agra via Fatehpur Sikri. This route is now followed, but those proceeding directly to Fatehpur Sikri will find its description on page 169.

MATHURA

Mathura, like Fatehpur Sikri, is 30 miles (48km) away from Sikandra, but due north. Traditionally, Mathura is the birthplace of Krishna, and therefore an important centre of worship for Hindus. Unfortunately, Aurangzeb destroyed all its ancient temples, including the famous Kesava Deo Temple. On its foundations was built an elevated Idgah mosque of red sandstone, from which there are good views of the city.

Mathura Museum contains an impressive collection of objects found locally, which date from the Buddhist Mauryan period. Outstanding sculptures include a fifth-century standing Buddha, a colossal second century figure, and a depiction of Naga the serpent god.

Perhaps the most attractive part of Mathura lies along the west bank of the River Yamuna, north of the bridge, where two splendid Hindu residences overlook the water, respectively the **House of Guru Parshotamdas** and the **House of Ballamdas**. Ahead rises the **Sati Burj**, a red sandstone tower, built around 1675 to honour a widow of the Maharajah of Amber, who committed sati on her husband's funeral pyre. The steps of **Viskant Ghat** descend to the river, where many still bathe. Here, each evening, at dusk, the ceremony of blessing the river takes place, and the abundant cows, monkeys and large turtles are fed; a temple stands nearby.

✻ VRINDABAN

Six miles (10km) north of Mathura, Vrindaban lies just off the main road, and is known as 'the town of a thousand shrines'. The site of the legend in which Krishna steals the clothes of the bathing Gopi (cowherds) is reputed to have been Vrindaban's riverside. As the River Yamunhas since changed its course, the most important sights for visitors are the collection of late-sixteenth-century Hindu temples. The best, the **Gobind Deo** (Divine Cowherd) **Temple**, lies just outside the town. Unusually, its porch is vaulted in European Gothic style, one of only two examples to be observed in a north Indian temple. Although its tower (sikhara) has gone, the linear forms result in an exceptional exterior. Other temples of particular interest are **Madan Mohan** and **Jugal Kishor**, near the Kesi Ghat. Amateur 'guides' will also point out the (symbolic) tree that Krishna climbed carying the Gopi's clothes.

✻ GOVARDHAN

A return to Mathura must be made before proceeding westward to Deeg, on the Alwar Road. After 16 miles (26km), Govardhan is reached. Krishna is alleged to have held up the range of hills behind the town on one finger for a week, in order to protect his fellow cowherds from monsoon floods. In consequence, the town is a centre of pilgrimage, its houses encircling the huge **Manasi Ganga** tank. Built during Akbar's reign is the **Haridera Temple**, a work commissioned by the Maharajah of Amber. Its design is reminiscent of Romanesque churches in southern France, and may have been influenced by Christians, who were welcomed at Akbar's court. Two Maharajahs of Bharatpur are commemorated by early nineteenth-century **cenotaphs** in the form of *chattris*.

DEEG ❋

Deeg (or Dig), 19 miles (30km) westward on the Alwar Road, lies just within the Rajasthan state border. Entered from its north gate is the **fort**, with its massive walls and bastions. A large cannon stands on Lakla Burj, the highest of the fort's towers. In 1804, an important battle took place here between Jaswant Rao Holkar's supporters and the British; General Lake's army forced withdrawal after a 3-day siege.

Of greatest interest to visitors, however, is the superb mid-eighteenth-century **palace** of the maharajahs of Bharatpur, which comprises a series of pavilions. The most important of them is the **Gopal Bhavan**, built in 1763, and retaining original furnishings. A unique architectural feature of the palace is its double cornices; opportunities for decoration have been gleefully accepted. Flanking pavilions are named after the periods of Rajasthan's unreliable monsoon: Sawan (July and August), and **Bhadon** (August and September). On the terrace opposite, a marble arch formerly served as the frame for a swing on which young girls celebrated the Choti Tij festival, swinging gently backward and forward and singing religious songs. To the north-east is the **Nand Bhavan**, a ceremonial hall.

The Suraj Bhavan, of marble, with mosaic decoration, lies to the south, adjacent to the Harder Bhavan, part of the female quarters, and which, like the other halls, is built of gold sandstone.

Water in the tanks and Rup Sagar Lake cooled the summer heat at Deeg, and this was the reason for its popularity. Bangaldar curved roofs are a feature of many buildings in the town, a well-known example being the **Suraj Mal Laveli**.

BHARATPUR ❋

Bharatpur can be reached directly by bus from Deeg, the journey taking just over an hour. Although it is possible to continue westward from Deeg to Alwar direct as an alternative, most will prefer to visit that town from Jaipur, and it is therefore described in Chapter 3. Bharatpur has a magnificent fort, but chiefly attracts tourists due to Keoladeo National Park, a mecca of international importance for bird-watchers.

Bharatpur's **Lohargarh** (Iron) **Fort**, begun in 1732, took many years to complete. In 1805, Ranjit Singh repulsed four British attacks, and a peace treaty was ratified. However, the fort fell to the British eventually, in 1805, after withstanding a siege for 3 weeks. It was then deliberately weakened, the outer defensive walls being demolished.

A causeway crosses the moat to the main gateway, which is flanked by rounded towers. The inner fort stands in the north-east section of the complex and incorporates three palaces, which are named, from left to right; the **Kamra Palace**, **Palace of Badan Singh** and the **Mahal Khas**. The Kamra Palace accommodated the fort's armoury, and formerly the treasury of the maharajahs until it was looted by the British. Preserved within the Mahal Khas are the apartments of Balwant Singh, created in the mid-nineteenth century.

The State Archaeological Museum (closed Fridays), founded in 1944, incorporates the **Palace of Badan Singh**, which forms the core of the palace, being constructed in 1733. Most exhibits come from the eastern half of Rajasthan. An important figure of the elephant-headed god Ganesh dates from the tenth century. In the north-west corner, the **Jowahar Burj** may be ascended for the best views from the fort. Another tower, the **Fateh Burj**, is named to commemorate the resistance against the British in 1805.

The maharajahs of Bharatpur are descended from Churaman, a Jat warrior, who rebelled against Aurangzeb in 1681. An iron pillar, however, is far more genealogically ambitious; it is inscribed with the family tree, commencing with Lord Krishna!

🐦 Keoladeo National Park

An overnight stay at Bharatpur is recommended so that an early morning start (dawn if possible) can be made to see the birds at their best in Keoladeo National Park. Within the sanctuary itself, accommodation is available at Bharatpur Forest Lodge (prior reservation essential) or Shanti Kutir Rest House, but other hotels exist in and around Bharatpur town. It is ironic that a location in which so many birds were slaughtered for 'sport' has now become a sanctuary for them.

The park encompasses a fresh-water swamp, which was excavated to form a lake by the Maharajah of Bharatpur in 1902. As recently as 1938, it is said that no fewer than 4,273 birds were massacred in one day's shoot, a participant being King George VI's viceroy Lord Linlithgow. Since the park was created in 1956 the birdlife has completely recovered, 350 species now being recorded annually. It should be remembered, however, that many of the birds are in transit, and only sojourn here for short periods. December to March are the most spectacular months, when the star attraction, the rare Siberian crane, makes an appearance.

Local ornithologists will act as guides and add much to the experience; they may be hired from the information centre. Boats silently cruise the lake at dawn as the birds begin to wake, and this is the most memorable time to observe them. In addition, bicycle rickshaws and four-wheel drive vehicles follow paths which have been laid out in the sanctuary. As may be expected, binoculars and a camera with a powerful telephoto lens are rewarding accessories for this trip.

FATEHPUR SIKRI

Fatehpur Sikri can be reached directly by bus from Agra's Idgah bus station (23 miles/37km) or Bharatpur (15 miles/24km). There is also a train service from Agra, but this is less convenient. Due to its international fame, visitors expect to discover a complete 'dead' city but, in reality, little apart from the Jama Masjid has survived outside Akbar's palace. The great sixteenth-century complex, nevertheless, has the appearance of a city, and its pristine condition is remarkable.

In spite of having 300 wives, Emperor Akbar, at the age of 26, had been unsuccessful in producing a son to survive infancy. Akbar was a great admirer of the ascetic Chishti sect of Muslims, and made annual pilgrimages to the shrine of Khwaja Muin-ud-din, a Chishti saint, at Ajmer. Near Agra, on a ridge beside the village of Sikri, lived in seclusion another Chisti saint, Shaik Salim. He first met Akbar in 1568, when 89 years old, and predicted that the Emperor would father three sons. Akbar's first Hindu wife, Jodhai Bai, became pregnant almost immediately, and spent her pregnancy at Sikri in order to be near Shaik Salim and thereby give encouragement to his prophecy. The future Emperor Jahangir was born to much jubilation and, in gratitude, Akbar named him Salim after the saint; further sons were born in 1570 and 1572, also at Sikri.

Soon after Salim's birth, Akbar began to build a great mosque on the ridge at Sikri, and then decided to construct a royal palace behind it, which would replace Agra as the emperor's seat of government. Residential accommodation for courtiers followed, and the city was protected on three sides by a wall, 7 miles (11km) in circumference; the north-west side was not walled, but fronted by a huge artificial lake, now dried up. A local abundance of malleable but durable red sandstone aided construction, and the city was virtually complete within 7 years. It was given the name Fatehpur (Victory) Sikri, possibly in celebration of Akbar's conquest of Gujarat in 1572, although some claim that it refers to Babur's victory over Sangram Singh at Bayana in 1527. All appeared set for a glorious future for

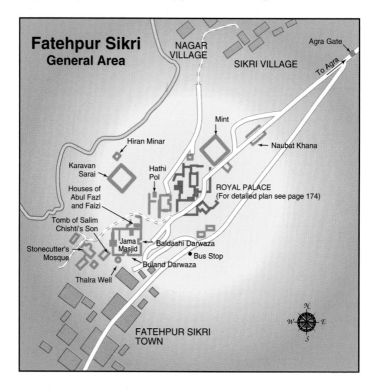

Fatehpur Sikri under the still young, popular and successful emperor but, in 1585, Akbar left the city with his army to put down a rebellion in the Punjab. His new base was Lahore (now in Pakistan) but, following his victory in 1586, the Emperor's return to Fatehpur Sikri was expected. Instead, Akbar remained in Lahore, which became the new capital. In 1599, the Emperor eventually returned to Agra, where he died 6 years later.

Parts of Fatehpur Sikri had become ruinous by 1610, but Jahangir stayed in the palace for some months with his son, the future Shah

Jahan, as late as 1619, in order to escape the plague raging in Agra. It has been mooted that the city was vacated by Akbar because its water supply had dried up, but if that were so, why did some still live there, Jahangir's mother, for example? The more likely reason seems to be that both Akbar and Jahangir found the damper and cooler climates of Lahore and Kashmir more appealing than the aridity and heat of either Fatehpur Sikri or Agra. It was not uncommon, in any case, for the Moguls to abandon grand projects: their great wealth did little to deter such profligacy.

Many visitors to Fatehpur Sikri arrive by private transport or excursion buses, and are deposited at the north-east entrance to the palace, which they will then visit before the mosque. Local buses, however, terminate in the modern town, from where can be seen, on the ridge above, the mosque's great gateway. This is reached by climbing a narrow pathway, which runs directly off the main road and is by far the most impressive approach to the deserted city. The ascent is not arduous. Before entering the mosque, boys may be seen diving into the Thaira well outside the west end of its wall: they expect a few rupees.

Jama Masjid

A short flight of steps makes the final ascent to the base of the **Buland Darwaza** (Lofty Gate), the monumental entrance to the Jama Masjid. This was added in 1576, 4 years after the completion of the remainder, in order to celebrate Akbar's victory in Gujarat. The gateway is also known as the Fatehpur Darwaza (Victory Gate), presumably a reference to the same Gujarat campaign. Architecturally, this is the most Islamic feature of Fatehpur Sikri; deeply recessed pointed arches are fringed, harking back to the fourteenth-century style of Delhi's Khalji sultans. Detailing emphasises the vertical nature of the structure, which is amplified by the steep approach.

A Persian inscription within the arch, left, refers to a return visit to the mosque made by Akbar in 1601, following his conquests in the south of India. Apparently, on that occasion, Akbar continued directly to Agra and did not spend a night in the city he had founded. On the opposite side, within the arch, words of Jesus (Isa) are quoted, a reminder of Akbar's interest in faiths other than Islam. It is common practise for sick people to fix horseshoes to the gates and pray to Shaikh Salim for a cure.

When built, Fatehpur Sikri's Jama Masjid was one of the largest mosques in India, its courtyard measuring 360ft x 139ft (109m x 142m). The arcade of the three-sided cloister consists of pointed arches, behind which mullahs occupied cells. All roofs, except that of the marble shrine ahead, are lined with *chattris*, evoking rows of soldiers on parade. Each range is interrupted by a central *iwan*. The form of the **prayer hall**, to the left, was apparently based on that at Mecca, but its flanking domes are partly obscured by the *chattris*, and an unusually high *iwan* almost conceals the central dome.

Although the prayer hall is typically Mogul externally, within the flanking chambers Hindu brackets support both domes, and the ceilings rest on columns which are also Hindu in style, although elongated. This latter feature is seen elsewhere only in Gujarat mosques, leading to the supposition that stonemasons from that state were employed here.

In front of the prayer hall is the white marble **shrine of Shaikh Salim** (1479-1572), the Chishti saint who inspired the city's foundation. His cenotaph is inscribed with the dates 1571-80, which refer to the construction of the shrine. It is believed that Jahangir refaced this with most of the present marble, and provided the screens, although its original dome of red sandstone remained until 1868. Unusual serpentine brackets support the *chajja* eaves and the porch, those of the latter again extending from 'double height' Hindu columns. Each panel of the exquisite *jali* screens is perforated with a different pattern.

Within, an ambulatory with painted walls surrounds the cenotaph, the canopy of which is embellished with mother-of-pearl decoration. As usual, the actual tomb of the saint lies below. The shrine is still venerated, in particular by barren women, who tie a piece of string to the screen and pray for a child. Musicians perform in front of the shrine every Friday.

To the right is the red sandstone tomb of Islam Khan, the saint's grandson, who was appointed Governor of Bengal by Jahangir. Other male members of the family also lie within: female members are buried in the cloister to the rear. On the east side of the courtyard, the **Baldashi Darwaza** (Royal Gate) gave direct entrance to the palace.

⌂ The Royal Palace

A pathway leads from the Baldashi Darwaza to the south-west section of the palace complex, at Jodh Bai's Palace, but this involves a 'back-to- front' tour, and it is better to continue north-eastward to the last building on the left, the Diwan-i-Am. On the way towards this, the **Daftar Khana** (Record Office) is passed on the right. A rear staircase leads to its roof. Those approaching the palace directly from

Agra will have reached this point via the Agra Gate in the city wall, passing through the **Naubat Khana**, with its musicians gallery, the ruined **Treasury**, left, and what is referred to, optimistically, as the **Mint**, right. The palace complex is laid out around courtyards on a fairly narrow ridge, which runs diagonally north-east/south-west. First seen is the public area, followed by the male and then the female sectors. Most buildings are given name plaques, and visitors should have little difficulty in following a logical route.

A sunken, cloistered courtyard faces the **Diwan-i-Am** (Hall of Public Audience). The hall itself is insignificant compared with those at Delhi and Agra. Here, the design is Hindu, rather than Muslim, with the exception of the *jali* screens on either side of the central bay reserved for Akbar. The purposes to which the other buildings in the palace were put cannot be identified with certainty, and the names by which they are now known were conceived comparatively recently, without much historic basis.

Reached from a rear doorway is the enormous courtyard of the *mardana* (men's sector), the most important area of the palace. At the north end, right, rises the best known of Fatehpur Sikri's buildings, the apparently two-storey pavilion, now generally called the **Diwan-i-Khas** (Hall of Private Audience). With its corbelled *chajjas* and four *chattris*, no Muslim elements are incorporated in its design.

On entering the building, it is immediately obvious that this is not a two-storey, but a single-storey hall, designed for a specific purpose, but what that purpose was is disputed. Uniquely in a Mogul building, a central octagonal pillar, with the aid of a huge, richly-sculptured corbel capital, supports a seat, which is linked by mid-air walkways of stone to the four corners of the hall. Some believe that this was the Ibadat Khana (House of Worship), completed in 1575, where Akbar discussed religion and philosophy. However, that building is described by a contemporary as comprising four separate halls. Others claim that the hall was a jewel house, but it would surely be asking for trouble to provide a jewel house with four entrances. Perhaps the best clue that we possess comes from the writing of Akbar's close friend and chronicler Abu'l Fazl, who describes the Emperor dispensing justice from his 'throne of sovereignty in the lofty hall' (ie the Diwan-i-Khas), a description which does fit this building. However, from his 'perch' here it would not have been possible for Akbar either to see or be seen by his audience, apart from those of high rank in the galleries, although he obviously could be heard from all parts of the hall. Perhaps the Emperor preferred that his four ministers, seated one in each corner, should conduct the accused and supplicants along the walkways to his presence high

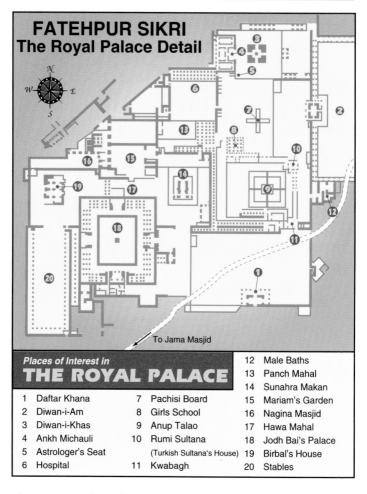

FATEHPUR SIKRI
The Royal Palace Detail

To Jama Masjid

Places of Interest in
THE ROYAL PALACE

1	Daftar Khana	7	Pachisi Board	
2	Diwan-i-Am	8	Girls School	
3	Diwan-i-Khas	9	Anup Talao	
4	Ankh Michauli	10	Rumi Sultana	
5	Astrologer's Seat		(Turkish Sultana's House)	
6	Hospital	11	Kwabagh	

12	Male Baths
13	Panch Mahal
14	Sunahra Makan
15	Mariam's Garden
16	Nagina Masjid
17	Hawa Mahal
18	Jodh Bai's Palace
19	Birbal's House
20	Stables

above most of the audience in order to attain greater intimacy. Each walkway is reached by flights of steps built into the walls, and these continue to the roof. The screens to the windows are modern.

Immediately west of the hall is the strangely-named **Ankh Michauli** (Closed Eyes). It is said that this three-roomed building served as a treasury, gold and silver being lodged in deep recesses protected by stone doors: hence 'closed eyes'. Once again, however, it seems strange that a treasury should have so many entrances.

The room with the flat ceiling has supporting struts carved in the form of traditional monsters, their purpose perhaps being to put fear into any would-be burglar. One of the least likely stories about the palace testifies that this building's 'closed eyes' name refers to the game of Blind Man's Buff played here by Akbar with his concubines.

To the south lies a small *chattri*; its cupola, resting on Hindu serpentine brackets, was originally painted inside. Akbar, like most eastern leaders at the time, was absorbed by astrology and its portents. It is said that an astrological adviser of the Emperor meditated here, and the structure is known as **The Astrologer's Seat**.

Immediately behind, to the west, the **palace Hospital** retains some of the stone partitions which created the wards. Roofs are carved to appear as tiles, but they are, in reality, stone slabs.

In the centre of the *mardana's* courtyard, lines appear to represent a large **Pachisi board**, used to play a game similar to ludo. It is said that Akbar sat in the centre, using slave girls as pieces. The simple, stone building south-west of the 'board' is known as the **Girls School**.

Further south, a square pool, **Anup Talao** (Peerless Pool), is laid out with four walkways leading to its central island. Facing the pool's north-east corner is the **Rumi Sultana** (Turkish Sultana's House). Akbar had a Turkish wife but she would certainly not have

Fatehpur Sikri's Royal Palace, the centrepiece of Akbar's 'Dead City'

resided in the male section of the palace. Although small, this is one of the most beautiful of Fatehpur Sikri's pavilions. Again, its stone roof imitates tiles; the walls and columns are carved with geometric and floral patterns.

Within, the walls of the single chamber are entirely covered with intricate designs, which give the appearance of a lattice screen. The glorious dado comprises eight panels depicting forest scenes; the animals' heads are now lost, as they have been chiselled out by an iconoclastic vandal, presumably a Muslim bigot who objected to the depiction of life.

In the south-east corner is the **Kwabagh** (House of Dreams), where a Hindu priest is supposed to have lived. Persian calligraphy appears above the doors, but the finest work in the building is the carved set of pillars supporting its platform. The **male baths** are approached immediately right, by returning northward.

To the west of the great courtyard lies the **zenana** (female sector), which occupies two-thirds of the total area of the palace. Linked by a covered walkway to the Girl's School is the pagoda-like **Panch Mahal** (Five Palace), so-named from its five superimposed halls. The lower four stages are flat-roofed, each providing a terrace for the floor above. Columns are reminiscent of a Hindu temple, although they are higher on the first floor, where the variety of corbel capitals is finest. Particularly outstanding is the group of four capitals in the north-west corner. There are indications that *jali* screens were originally fitted, emphasising that this was a palace for women. It is possible to ascend to the upper *chattri* for excellent views. Apparently, the walkway approach was an afterthought, as the join is unsatisfactory from an architectural viewpoint. A delightful flower garden lies to the north.

The **Sunahra Makan** (Golden House), or Mariam's House, lies in a separate courtyard directly to the south. The first name refers to the gilded murals, which were originally painted both internally and externally; the second to Mariam-uz-Zamani, mother of Jahangir, who is believed to have lived here. Mariam, born a Hindu, is said to have converted to Christianity, and it has been suggested that the existing fragment of a mural depicting angel's wings formed part of an Annunciation scene. To add to the theological mystery, brackets include depictions of Hindu deities, including Rama and Hamuyan the monkey god. It seems unlikely that Mariam would have remained here during Akbar's lengthy sojourn in Lahore, but she may have returned after her husband's death.

The remains of **Mariam's Garden**, to the north-west, incorporate a bath with a central column in its south-east corner. A passageway, with Fatehpur Sikri's only surviving stone screen, leads westward to the **Nagina Masjid** (Ladies Mosque), which retains traces of a Turkish bath.

Immediately south of the garden, projecting from the north wall of Jodh Bai's Palace, the **Hawa Mahal** (Wind Palace), is so-named because its isolated situation seems designed for the ladies to catch any breezes. According to Abu'l Fazl, Akbar often slept here at night with his chosen partner. A covered walkway, stretching northward from the Hawa Mahal to the Hathi Pol (Elephant Gate), provided the women with partly-concealed access to their quarters.

Walls 34ft (10m) high, immediately to the south, enclose the largest courtyard in the women's sector, known as **Jodh Bai's Palace**. Jodh Bai, a Rajput, was Jahangir's first wife, whom he married when he was just 16 years old, in 1585, the year that Akbar vacated Fatehpur Sikri. She may have resided in this palace for a short time, but there is little doubt that many of Akbar's favourite wives lived here, sharing common areas but occupying private chambers. The pre-eminent of them, Rakiya, was also Akbar's first cousin.

The walls are basically plain; their squat-domed viewing towers at the corners, in Rajput style, were designed so that the women could look out without being observed. Projecting lattice work on the north side creates a small room from which they could also view Mariam's Garden. Left of the entrance gateway, which is located on the east side, is the guardroom. Older females acted as guardians within the gate, but outside, eunuchs and troops, in addition to the porters, formed an impregnable barrier to any would-be paramour.

Within the courtyard, the layout is reminiscent of a Rajput palace, in contrast with the Muslim-style planning seen elsewhere at Fatehpur Sikri. Each range incorporates, in its centre, a two-storey block. Turquoise enamelled tiles to the gabled roofs were inspired by those of the Man Mandir Palace at Gwalior. A corridor links ground floor reception rooms on three sides; the finest carving is found in the west room, where there is a fireplace.

Outside the north-west corner of Jodh Bai's Palace stands the two-storey **Birbal's House**, completed in 1571, and therefore one of the earliest pavilions to be built in the complex. Raja Birbal was Akbar's favourite courtier, and the only important Hindu to follow the Emperor's composite religion of Din-Ilahi. By tradition, this house was built for his daughter; however, as the girl was not one of Akbar's wives, there seems no reason why she would have been accommodated within the Royal Palace. The building has two upper terraces, now open, but which originally would have been screened; they are arranged diagonally, so that each receives shade in turn from one of the first floor rooms. Crisp carving throughout is outstanding and remains in fine condition; Muslim geometric decoration and painted arches are combined with Hindu features, such as elaborate corbels, *chajja* eaves and *jarokha* balconies.

Internally, the geometric carving is even more profuse, the frieze of the cornices in the ground floor rooms and the corner brackets supporting the cupolas of the upper rooms being particularly outstanding. Although the craftsmanship throughout is of a very high standard, some find that the combination of so many disparate elements results in a jerky, unresolved overall appearance.

South of Birbal's House is a puzzling courtyard, still known generally as the **Stables**. Each 'manger' is fitted with a stone ring, to which horses, and possibly camels, may have been tethered. The problem is that stables were never located adjacent to the women's quarters; riding was a completely male preserve, and the fragrance of the animals' excretia appealed little to the fair sex. A current theory is that the 'mangers' were in fact cells for female servants' occupancy or, alternatively, that they accommodated market stalls.

North-west of the courtyard is the **Hathi Pol** (Elephant Gate), the north entrance to the city. Two damaged life-size figures of elephants stand on the west face. Ahead lies the **Karavan Sarai** courtyard, where merchants travelling in groups would repose; its south-east range was originally three storeys high. Outside the north corner rises the circular **Hiran Minar** (Deer Minaret), so-named from the tradition that Akbar shot deer from it. The tower is supposed to be constructed above the grave of Akbar's favourite elephant, hence the stone elephant tusks protruding from the structure. Occasionally, after a heavy monsoon, part of the site of Akbar's artificial lake to the north again fills with water.

Visitors who have arrived at the palace directly from Agra will now wish to proceed westward to the mosque. Three points of interest are sited north and west of its walls. Buildings north-east of the mosque are known as the **Houses of Abul Fazl and Faizi**, brothers and favourites of Akbar, both of whom followed his religion. Faizi, the poet-laureate, died in 1595, and Fazl, Akbar's chronicler, was murdered in 1602, at the instigation of Jahangir, who was jealous of his father's affection for him. It is now believed, however, that the houses were in fact part of the royal nursery.

Outside the mosque's west wall a small **tomb** set within an enclosure, is said to be that of Shaikh Salim's 6-month-old son, who was sacrificed so that the future Emperor Jahangir might live. As Shaikh Salim was 90 years old at the time, quite an age for fathering a child, the story is hard to beieve.

A short distance to the west stands the **Stonecutter's Mosque**, built for the Saint by masons before the city was begun; he apparently lived in a cave within (no admission to non-Muslims). The serpentine brackets served as models for those on the saint's shrine.

On returning to Agra, it is thought-provoking to reflect on the diary of Elizabeth I's messenger, Ralph Fitch, written during a visit in 1584: 'Agra and Fatepore are two very great cities, either of them much greater than London. Between, all the way is a market.'

GWALIOR　　　　　　　　　　　　　　　　　　　 ❋

Before proceeding to Jaipur, and thereby completing the 'Golden Triangle', some will wish to continue from Agra to the Rajput city of Gwalior, 85 miles (137km) to the south. Buses and trains link the cities; the Delhi-Agra-Gwalior 'Taj Express' is the quickest way to make the journey, if its timing is convenient — check in advance. Even though practically every major town in Rajasthan state has a Hindu fortress/palace of note, that of Gwalior, in Madhya Pradesh State, is considered by many to be the finest in all India. An added bonus is that, adjacent to Gwalior Fort, there are a unique series of gigantic rock carvings honouring Jain prophets.

Gwalior was ruled by the Pal kings from the tenth to the twelfth centuries, followed by the Parihara Princes for another hundred years. Tomar took the fort in 1398 and founded Gwalior's greatest dynasty. Its most famous member, Man Singh (1486-1516), repelled both Sikandar and Ibrahim Lodhi. From 1526, the Moguls, Mahrattas, Jats and British succeeded as rulers of Gwalior. During the Mutiny, the Maharajah personally remained loyal to the British, but most of his troops did not, and much carnage resulted when the fort was stormed in 1858.

The major sights of Gwalior can easily be seen in one day. It is preferable to visit the fort via its main, north-east entrance. On the way, ask the driver to stop at two tombs, which are close to each other. The **Tomb of Muhammad Gaus**, a Muslim saint venerated by both Babur and Akbar, is a fine example of Mogul architecture. Originally, its dome was clad with blue-glazed tiles.

To the south-west, the **Tomb of Miya Tansen** is the site of a pilgrimage by musicians in December, when a music festival takes place in the town. Miya Tansen was a singer greatly admired by Akbar. By tradition, a voice will be improved by chewing leaves from the adjacent tamarind tree.

Gwalior's **Jama Masjid**, a white sandstone mosque, stands outside the fort's entrance. Its gilded domes combine effectively with the high minarets, resulting in an harmonious design. Much of the building dates from 1661.

♖ Gwalior Fort

Many visitors will note architectural affinities between Gwalior Fort and Akbar's Palace at Fatehpur Sikri. As at Amber, it is possible to ascend to the fort on the back of an elephant. Six gates in succession are passed. The first two are named, respectively, **Alamgiri** and **Badalgarh** (or Hindola). To the right, the **Archaeological Museum** is housed in the **Gujari Palace**, built for his favourite Gujari wife, Mriganaya, by Man Singh around 1500. Exhibits include sculptures, miniature paintings and copies of the Buddhist frescoes in the Bagh Caves near the Gujarat border. Like the other museums in Gwalior, it is open Tuesday to Sunday. A third gate, Bansur (Archer's), has been demolished.

The fifteenth-century **Ganesh Gate** incorporates a pigeon house (Kabutar Khana) and a small, square temple commemorating Gwalipa, from whose name the city of Gwalior is known. By tradition, Gwalipa, a hermit living on the Gopagiri Hill, the site of the fort, gave a drink of water to Suraj Sen, a Kachchwaha chieftain who was on a hunting expedition. Suraj Senof his leprosy, was cured by the water, and renamed Suhan Pal by Gwalipa, who promised him that his dynasty would rule the area as long as the name Pal was kept. Eighty-three descendants did so, but the eighty-fourth changed his name to Tej Karan and, surprise, surprise, was defeated. A tiny **mosque** is dated 1664.

Ahead, the **Chatarbhujmandir shrine** to Vishnu is built into the rock face. An inscription within is dated 876.

Steps lead to a group of small **Jain figures** carved in the cliff, but larger examples lie to the south; these include a 15ft (4½m) high Shiva killing Gaja, one of the earliest carvings at Gwalior. Gwalior's finest sculptures, however, are carved on the south side of the fort and seen later.

The final gate, **Hathiya Paur** (Elephant Gate), was built by Man Singh in the late fifteenth century.

Undoubtedly the most important building within the fort is the **Palace of Man Singh**, also known as the Man Mandir, or Chit Mandir (Painted Palace). The east and south façades are punctuated by towers surmounted by *chattris*, which are linked by lattice-work parapets of exceptional delicacy. There are two storeys above ground level, but two more below. In one of the subterranean appartments, Aurangzeb imprisoned his younger brother Murad Baksh in 1659, ordering his execution 2 years later. In this instance, Aurangzeb had little option; Murad had murdered his finance minister, whose family would not accept financial compensation. Under Islamic law, therefore, they were able to demand the death penalty. However, Aurangzeb did murder his nephew, Suleiman Shukoh, the son of his elder brother Dara, at Gwalior — by weakening him with opium. Dara's younger son Sipihr was also imprisoned at Gwalior by Aurangzeb, who eventually permitted him to marry one of his own daughters. They then lived together under house arrest at Salimgarh Fort in Delhi. Aurangzeb even imprisoned his own eldest son, Muhammad Sultan, at Gwalior, perhaps fearful that his treatment of his own father might be repeated.

Built around two small courtyards, the rooms above ground level are decorated with a profusion of brightly-coloured wall tiles, which have given the building its alternative name 'Painted Palace'. The long south wall is windowless, but clad with the most exquisite tiles in the palace, primarily depicting birds and elephants. This work is the finest of its type in India and should not be missed.

None of the other buildings in the fort compare in beauty with the Palace of Man Singh, which is linked to the west with the Karan Palace (or Kirti Mandir), built in 1516. To the north are the Jahangiri and Shah Jahan Palaces with, north-west of them, the Johar Kund, a tank named to commemorate the ritual suicide of the Rajput women as the forces of Iltutmish approached in 1232.

Half way down, on the east side of the fort, are the two **Sasbahu Temples** (Mother-in-Law and Daughter-in-Law). The larger was built in 1039, probably as a Jain temple, and it originally possessed a sikhara tower. Figures of Vishnu are now carved above the entrances. The smaller temple, decorated in similar style, is probably contemporary with it.

Further south, but on the west side, rises Gwalior's highest building, a temple dedicated to Shiva, the **Tele-ka-Mandir**, believed to date from the ninth century. Restoration in 1881 included the facing gateway, which was built from fragments discovered at the time. A Garuda surmounts the entrance and indicates that the building was originally a Vishnu temple. The roof is south Indian in form.

It is necessary to leave the fort by the south-west gate in order to see the other glory of Gwalior, the Jain carvings executed between 1425 and 1455. There are five recognised groups, the best of which are the Arwahi group and, the finest of all, the south-east group. Most of the sculptures depict Jain tirthankaras (prophets). The **Arwahi group** is located at the bottom of the Arwahi ravine, from which it is named. The **south-east sculptures**, 1 mile (2km) distant, cover a ½km mile (1km) of cliff, and were all carved within 5 years (1468-73); they are the last of their type in India.

Lashkar (camp) is the name given to the 'New City', founded by Daulat Rao Scindia to the south of the fort, after taking Gwalior in

1809. Its lively Sarafa (Merchant's Area) is typical of north Indian bazaars. **Jai Vilas Palace**, although still occupied by the former Maharajah of Gwalior, a descendant of Rao Scindia, is partly open as a museum. The collection displayed is esoteric to a degree, highlights being (rather surprisingly) erotica, stuffed tigers, and a model railway designed to serve the maharajah's guests with brandy and cigars. Slightly to the north-east, similarly located in Phul Bagh, part of the **Moti Mahal** (Pearl Palace) is also open as a museum.

It is possible to proceed to Jaipur, Rajasthan state's capital, from Gwalior without returning to Agra, but public transport is arduous. However, the journey can be broken at Sawai Madhopur by those wishing to tour the famous Ranthanbore tiger sanctuary, and from Sawai Madhopur there is a direct link by rail with Jaipur. Most, however begin their tour of Rajasthan from Agra.

Additional Information

Places to Visit in Agra

Agra
Taj Majal and Agra Fort
Open: daily 7am-7pm.

Old Agra's Bazars
Close: Mondays, but Muslim craftsmen take their religious holidays on Fridays.

Accommodation in Agra

Hotel Mughal Sheratoh
Fatehabad Road
☎ 64701

Hotel Taj View
Fatehabad Road
☎ 64171

Hotel Clarks Shiraz
54 Taj Road
☎ 72421

Eating Out in Agra

The best food is served in the restaurants of the aforementioned hotels

Agra Tourist Office

Government of India Tourist Office
191 The Mall (Sadar Bazar area)
☎ 72377

Other Places to Visit

Bharatpur
Fort State Archaeological Museum
Open: Saturday to Thursday 10am-5pm.

Deeg
Palace
Open: daily 8am-12noon & 1-7pm.

Gwalior
Museums
All museums in Gwalior are open Tuesday to Sunday 10am-5pm.

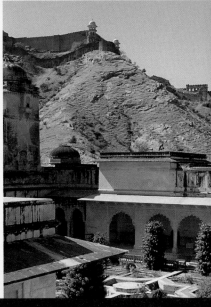

Jaipur & East Rajasthan

3

✳ JAIPUR

A brief incursion into Rajasthan from Agra, due to reasons of proximity, has already been described. Most visitors, however, begin their tour of the state from Jaipur, one of the three points of the 'Golden Triangle'. A circular tour, either clockwise or anti-clockwise, will then take in the state's locations of greatest interest. Jaipur serves as the centre for east Rajasthan, from which, with overnight stays, excursions can be made: southward to Ranthambore Wildlife Sanctuary, Kota and Bundi, westward to Ajmer and Pushkar, eastward to Alwar and Sariska Wildlife Sanctuary, and northward to the Shekhavati region (on route to Bikaner).

Bikaner is the centre for north Rajasthan, Jaisalmer for west, Jodhpur for central, and Udaipur for south. Delhi, Agra, Jaipur, Jodhpur and Udaipur are all linked by air, train or bus, but there are no civil flights to Bikaner or Jaisalmer. Buses ply throughout the state, as do trains, but there is no direct train link between Bikaner and Jaisalmer.

preceding page; (left) the richly carved Sikhara Tower of this Pushkar temple is more typical of South Indian architecture. (right) Amber's sixteenth-century fort is overlooked protectively by the much smaller Jaigarh Fort, built by Jai Singh II in 1726, just one year before he began the construction of Jaipur

Some fortunate visitors have plenty of time at their disposal, and will be able to see everything described in Rajasthan; however, at least three weeks will be needed, and those with shorter schedules will perforce have to be selective. Night travel by train between Jodhpur and Bikaner, and Jaisalmer and Jodhpur, and flights between Jodhpur and Udaipur, and Udaipur and Delhi, are recommended, in order to increase the sightseeing time available. It is difficult to advise what should be omitted from tight schedules, but the following suggestions might be considered. Visit either Ranthambore or Sariska Wildlife Sanctuaries, not both, and omit Alwar, Kota and, regretfully, Bundi and the Shekhavati region, thus saving almost one week. Additional time could also be saved by cutting out Bikaner, thereby reserving all of north Rajasthan for another trip. In the Udaipur region, there are superb Jain temples at both Ranakpur and Mount Abu, and some may decide to omit the latter, which involves a long and tiring journey from Udaipur, even by private car. Due to its remoteness, many are tempted to give Jaislamer a miss; try not to, as it is unique, and can be reached easily by the overnight train from Jodhpur. As can be seen, the permutations available are numerous: the decision is yours.

If some time has been spent at Delhi and Agra, which are rather flat topographically, it will be pleasant to discover that, in contrast, Jaipur is surrounded by hills. Another difference, and a refreshing one, is that although Jaipur is one of India's larger cities, most of interest to visitors lies within the walled, eighteenth-century precinct, and may consequently be seen on foot without great exertion. Auto-rickshaws or taxis, of course, will be needed for the outlying forts, and some may also prefer to be driven to the Albert Hall, which houses the Central Museum.

Although Jaipur bustles like any other Indian city, its streets are wide and laid out in a simple-to-follow grid pattern. Immediately noticeable are the men's brilliantly-coloured turbans and exuberant moustaches: usually turned upward for Hindus, downward for Muslims. Unless the wearer is a Sikh, which is rare, the turban is not designed to protect uncut hair, and it never seems to have had any religious significance for Rajputs. It is also in Jaipur that many will see working camels and elephants for the first time, although most of the latter's tasks take place in nearby Amber, and consist of transporting tourists from the town up to the fort.

A helpful aide-memoire to travellers in recalling their visit to Rajasthan is that the five major towns are basically different in colour: Bikaner red, Jaisalmer gold, Jodhpur blue and Udaipur white. Jaipur is pink and, as at Jodhpur and Udaipur, the colour is achieved by paintwork, not by a natural building material, most of which is rubble. To mark the visit to Jaipur of the Prince of Wales, later King Edward VII, in 1876, Ram Singh II decreed that Jaipur's buildings within the walled area should be plastered and painted pink, to imitate the ubiquitous red sandstone of north India's Mogul monuments. Upkeep by the owners became, and still is, mandatory.

The completely new city was devised by Jai Singh II, a descendant of the Kachchwaha Rajput warriors that had ruled the region from nearby Amber Fort for over 600 years. It was intended from the outset that it would eventually be the capital of a united Rajput territory, but this did not come about until the state of Rajasthan was created after Indian independence. Construction began with the laying of the foundation stone in 1727 by Jai Singh, who named the city after himself. An unusually harmonious relationship appears to have developed between the patron and his architect, a young man named Vidyadhar Bhattacharaya, who had been appointed by Jai Singh initially to serve as a priest in his temple at Amber Palace. Apparently disenchanted with the priesthood, Vidyadhar took up secular duties, including engineering, and proved himself so indispensable that he eventually became Jai Singh's chief executive (Desh Diwan).

Jaipur was the first completely planned city of importance to be built in northern India (Fatehpur Sikri developed piecemeal around the palace), and its architect rigidly controlled all aspects of construction, personally inspecting building materials as they were delivered. He divided the city into six blocks, each of which was allocated to a specific trade. These blocks were separated from each other by wide avenues, and narrower streets criss-crossed each block in straight lines. In the centre of the city was sited a separately walled palace for Jai Singh, who moved to it from Amber Fort. Jaipur's important buildings were completed by 1733, and a water supply was connected to the new city by a canal from the River Darbhawati 2 years later. However, piped water and street lighting was not introduced until the late nineteenth century.

A castellated wall surrounds the eighteenth-century city, which may be entered from ten gates, five of which punctuate the south wall. Even in the earlier years of the twentieth century, every gate was locked nightly, to the inconvenience of surprised travellers.

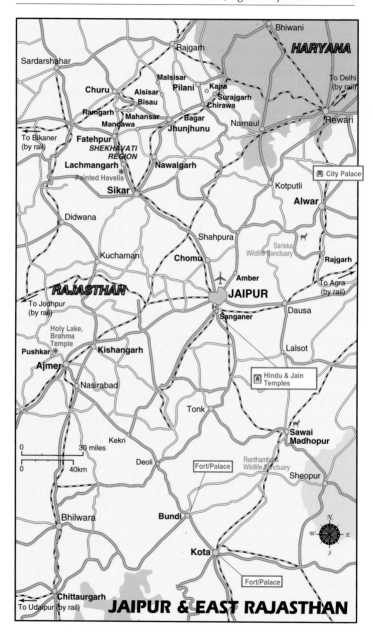

JAIPUR & EAST RAJASTHAN

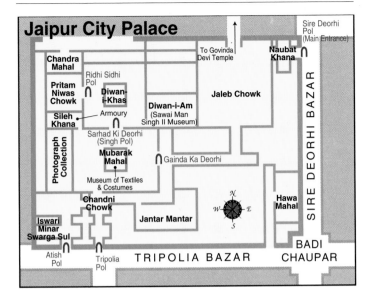

If an early start is made, Jaipur's chief sights may be seen in a single day, but an additional half day at least should be allocated to Amber. As is usual in Indian cities, most of the large tourist hotels are situated some way from the centre, primarily, in the case of Jaipur, to the west. Many will wish to head intitially to the City Palace, where transport is likely to deposit them in **Jaleb Chowk**, a small square within the palace precinct, having passed though the outer gateway, **Sire Deorhi Pol**, originally the main entrance to the palace, and the **Naubat Khana**, from where, as is usual, musicians played to announce important guests.

Jaipur City Palace

The palace was completed in just 7 years, although there have been many additions since. It will soon be apparent that the palace did not follow the pink colour scheme stipulated for the rest of the city, most of it being built of cream or white stone. A path through the archway ahead leads to the **Gainda Ka Deorhi** (Rhinoceros Gate), formerly the servants entrance, where tickets are purchased (a further ticket office and admission point is sited at the Tripolia Gate to the south-west of the complex).

In the centre of the courtyard ahead stands the **Mubarak Mahal** (Palace of Welcome) added by Madho Singh II in 1900 to accommodate guests; it later housed the royal secretariat. In 1959 the **Museum**

of Textiles and Costumes was opened on the upper floor of the building. Madho Singh I (ruled 1750-68) apparently stood 7ft (2m) high and weighed 495lb (225kg); his enormous *atamsukh* (soul's pleasure) garment of pure silk and gold thread is the most impressive item on display. Also look out for the wedding robes of Pratap Singh. Exquisitely made musical instruments, blue Jaipur pottery and royal toys are incorporated in the collection.

In the north-west corner of the square, the **Sileh Khana** (Armoury) houses the Armour and Weapons collection, again on the first floor. Curved swords, Mogul daggers, and a helmet designed as a turban for Jai Singh I are suitably exotic, although there is no example of elephant armour, which might be expected by those visitors who have already seen a specimen in the Royal Armoury's Oriental display in England.

Immediately south of the building is exhibited the **collection of early photographs** taken and developed by Ram Singh II (ruled 1835-80). He was encouraged and aided in his work by T. Murray, a pioneer British photographer.

The splendid **Sarhad Ki Deorhi** (or Singh Pol) gateway, on the north side of the square, is flanked by marble elephants, which were added in 1931 to mark the birth of Bhawani Singh, the first son to be born to a maharaja of Jaipur for two generations. His delighted father, Man Singh II, supplied so much champagne to celebrate the event that the infant's nanny gave him the nickname Bubbles, which has stuck. Although all hereditary titles have been abolished in India, Bhawani Singh is still regarded by many as the de facto Maharaja of Jaipur; he resides in the Chandra Mahal section of the palace, seen later.

In the smaller courtyard ahead stands the **Diwan-i-Khas** (Private Audience Hall). While the courtyard itself is typically Rajput in design, this hall is more reminiscent of Mogul work. It was rare in Hindu palaces for areas to be isolated and set aside for special functions, but the maharajas of Jaipur had a long tradition of close contact with the Mogul emperors, and were obviously influenced by their taste. The unusually large dimensions of the Diwan-i-Khas indicate that it had formerly served as the Diwan-i-Am (Public Audience Hall) before the present building was erected specifically for that purpose. Although partly built of marble, economies appear to have been made on this building, as architectural features are trompe l'oeil rather than carved.

Exhibited are the largest articles in the world ever to have been produced in silver: two great urns, each with a capacity of 1,800 gallons (8,181 litres). They were made in 1901 for Madho Singh II to transport Ganga water from India to London, so that his health would not be at risk from drinking 'dangerous' English water during his attendance at the coronation of King Edward VII. British visitors who have been warned of the perils of drinking fresh water anywhere in India may doubt the veracity of the tale, but it is undoubtedly true.

The present **Diwan-i-Am** is approached from the south-east corner of the square; formerly, its main entrance was from Jaleb Chowk. This was added by Sawai Pratap Singh in the late eighteenth century to accommodate durbars and great banquets, hence its enormous size. Unlike a Mogul Diwan-i-Am, this example is enclosed. Since 1959, the building has accommodated the **Sawai Man Singh II Museum**. Exhibits within the columned hall include four enormous seventeenth-century carpets, miniature paintings, manuscripts and, at the far end, on a central dais, a set of exotic furniture. *Jali* screens at upper level permitted the royal ladies to watch proceedings unobserved.

The spectacular **Pritam Niwas Chowk** (Peacock Courtyard) of Pratap Singh, lies west of the Diwan-i-Khas. Each of its doorways depict Kartikkaya, the son of Shiva, riding on the back of a peacock.

On the north side rises the highest building in the city palace, the seven-storey **Chandra Mahal** (Moon Palace), which is still the residence of the former maharaja and his family. For this reason, it is only possible to view the ground-level hall. Part of its floor is painted, as an alternative to carpeting, a feature which is apparently repeated elsewhere in the palace. This was not a measure forced on this very wealthy family by economic factors, but to keep down temperatures in the hot summer months.

By returning to the exit at Gainda Ka Deorhi and turning right, visitors will reach the **Jantar Mantar Observatory**. Jai Singh II built five observatories, the first, at Delhi, being completed as a prototype in 1727. Jaipur's example, the largest, was begun the following year. Great scientific instruments are built of stone and, even today, the Raj Yantra is used to establish the following year's Hindu calendar. An enormous sundial, the Samrat Yantar (Supreme Device), is consulted to predict the date of the arrival of the forthcoming monsoon.

Beside the three-arched royal entrance to the palace, **Tripolia Pol**, in the south-west corner, rises a minaret. This is the **Iswari Minar Swarga Sul** (Minar that Pierces Heaven) erected by Iswari Singh, the son of Jaipur's builder, who succeeded him in 1743. Iswari Singh showed none of his father's fortitude and, at the approach of the invading Mahrattas in 1751, took poison. In case that failed to do the trick, he also arranged to be bitten by a cobra — the combination worked.

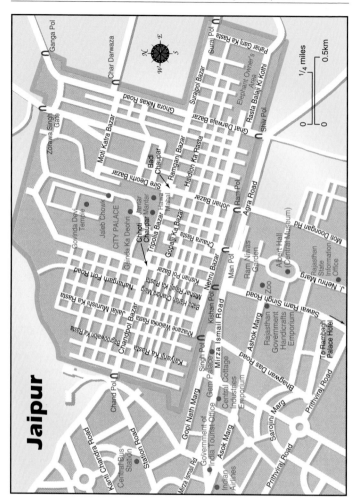

To visit the **Govinda Devi Temple** it is necessary to return to the ticket office at Gainda Ka Deohri, continuing to Jaleb Chowk. An archway immediately ahead leads to the temple. In 1735, Jai Singh rescued an image of Krishna from a temple in Mathura before it

opposite; Jaipur's Palace of the Winds, one of India's best known structures, is just one room deep. It was built so that the royal ladies in purdah might view processions without being seen. There are 900 apertures

could be demolished by Aurangzeb, and brought it to Jaipur to be worshipped as the patron deity of his dynasty. Govinda is the most revered of Krishna's six forms, in which he became a cowherd. As Govinda, he is always shown with a blue-painted face and plays a flute. The idol, hidden from view by a curtain, is revealed at each puja, seven times daily; the 5pm puja is always the best-attended. Jai Singh aligned the temple so that he would have good direct views of the idol from the Chandra Mahal.

Return to Jaleb Chowk and turn left to the Sire Deorhi Gate, which opens onto Sire Deorhi Bazar; cross the road and proceed southward. On the opposite side of the road, just before the Badi Chaupar junction, stands Jaipur's most famous building, the **Hawa Mahal** (Palace of the Winds). Pratap Singh commissioned the five-storey building in 1799 specifically for the royal ladies in purdah to watch state processions from behind delicately screened windows. It has been estimated that there are at least 900 apertures in the façade. In addition to hiding the women from view, the building was designed so that cooling breezes would be admitted (hence the palace's name) while, at the same time, the sunlight was filtered.

Although the appearance of the façade is exotic, it is, in fact, extremely functional. It is also symmetrical, vertical rows of domed *jarokhas* alternating with curved-roofed bays. So delighted was Pratap Singh with the building that its architect Lalchand Usta and his descendants were given tax exemption in perpetuity.

To enter the building (from the rear only) it is necessary to continue to Badi Chaupar, turn right into Tripolia Bazar and first right again through a narrow street. The Palace of the Winds, built around two courtyards, is not nearly as impressive from the rear, but it is amusing to ascend the ramp, floor by floor to the top, in the footsteps of the royal ladies. Surprisingly, the famous elevation is just one room deep throughout, and the street-facing wall only 10 inches (25cm) thick; quite a structural achievement. There are good views from the upper floor of the hills around Jaipur.

From Badi Chaupar, many will opt to hire an auto-rickshaw if proceeding to the **Central Museum**, located at the south end of Ram Niwas Garden. The foundation stone of the Albert Hall was laid in 1876 by the Prince of Wales, who named the building after his deceased father, Prince Albert. Since 1887, it has housed the museum and, in a separate wing, the Durbar Hall. Sir Swinton Jacob designed the building, apparently inspired by the function, although not the appearance, of London's Victoria and Albert Museum. Jacob spent 10 years designing buildings in India, all of which were eclectic in style.

Externally, the decorative features of the Albert Hall are primarily Indo-Saracenic but, internally, the European Gothic Revival dominates. As in so many Indian museums, the displays have become rather old-fashioned and grimy. There is, as would be expected, a splendid collection of Jaipur glazed pottery. This was introduced in the eighteenth century, died out, and is now manufactured once again. A *phad* (folding screen), 30ft (9m) long and 5ft (2m) high, has been described as a portable novel: it relates the tale of Pabuji Ramadeo and his 'magic man' Kesa Kali. While in Rajasthan, most visitors staying at the larger hotels will see stylized marionette (*kathputli*) performances, based on ancient legends. There is a splendid collection of puppets in Rajput costumes displayed in this museum: each specimen has a face of wood, while the body, always legless, may be made either of wood or cloth. A carving and a terracotta depicting, respectively, a lady and a gentleman wearing turbans, date from the second century BC, indicative of the long period during which this headwear has been worn by Rajputs.

On the upper floor, miniature paintings from Jaipur, Bikaner, Jodhpur and Kota are displayed. More surprising is a model of an ancient Egyptian camp, and an Egyptian mummy. Another tableau depicts the execution of a Rajput by the British.

The **Durbar Hall** is reached by leaving the Central Museum, accompanied by an attendant, who will unlock it. Ask to see the **Carpet Museum**, which the hall now accommodates. Outstanding is an enormous carpet, one of India's most spectacular, but made in Kirman, Persia, in 1632. Entirely woven from silk, scenes from a Persian garden are depicted; fish can be seen in the irrigation canals, which are flanked, as was usual, by fruit trees, not the cypresses which have gradually replaced them in India's surviving Mogul gardens.

Ram Singh II laid out the **Ram Niwas Garden**, in which the Central Museum stands, employing a Dr de Fabeek to landscape their 36 acres (14 hectares). For those with a desire to see yet more animals, there is a small zoo on the west side of the garden.

Just 4 miles (6½km) north-west of Jaipur, at **Gaitor**, *chattri* cenotaphs of Jaipur's royal family are grouped romantically together within an enclosure. Most impressive is the white marble cenotaph of Jaipur's founder, Jai Singh II (1699-1744), supported on twenty columns and decorated with scenes from Hindu mythology. Nearby, that of his second son, Madho Singh I (died 1779), is carved with peacocks. Other maharajas commemorated are Ram Singh, Pratap Singh and Man Singh II.

Above Gaitor, at the south-west spur of the Kali Khoh Ridge, is **Nahargarh** (Tiger) **Fort**, one of the fifty constructed by the Kachchwaha chieftains. From here are gained the finest overall views of Jaipur. Jai Singh II added this fort to the series in 1734, specifically to protect his new city. An upper floor was constructed a century later, and extensions were made in 1903. Nahargarh Fort housed the royal treasury until 1942.

Nahar, after who the fort was named, is reputed to have been a hermit who lived on the hilltop and took umbrage at not being consulted about the new fort proposed by Jai Singh. He cursed the project, causing work during the day to be 'miraculously' demolished at night until a due apology was made — it was.

Within the Ajmeri Gate of the city wall, which immediately faces Ram Niwas Garden, runs Nehru Bazar. Here, the **Hotel Sweet Dream** has a west-facing roof terrace (Ashiana Restaurant), ideal from which to view Jaipur's sunset while sipping a drink (non-alcoholic). As can be imagined, the 'pink city' is at its pinkest at this time, and an ethereal glow pervades all.

Late afternoon and early evening on weekdays is the best time to amble through the shopping streets of Jaipur, which are at their liveliest around Johari Bazar. **Nehru Bazar** (closed Tuesday) specializes in hand-painted cottons in vibrant colours, also in perfumes, but these, like Indian confectionery, are generally too cloyingly sweet for Western tastes.

Facing the outer side of the Ajmeri Gate is the **Rajasthan Government Handicrafts Emporium** where, as in similar shops in other large tourist cities, prices are fixed and the quality reliable. Mirza Ismail Road, an extremely long thoroughfare, runs eastward in front of the city wall, passing New Gate. **Johari Bazar** (part closes Sunday and part Tuesday) runs northward from the next entrance, Sanganeri Gate. Half way along on the left, **LMB** is a Jaipur institution, with first-rate ice creams and vegetarian snacks: *dahi bara* and *rasmalai* are recommended.

Jaipur is regarded as the jewellery centre of India, and prices are at their keenest here. The reason for this is the abundance of local craftsmen (around 30,000 stone cutters are permanently employed) and the low wages which they receive. Gold itself is not a particular bargain in India, most of it being purchased from Dhubai in the Persian Gulf. Bargaining is expected in most shops, but purchasers should ensure that the supplier is reliable. **Haldion Ka Rasta**, fourth right, is a famous street of jewellers, and, just off it, in Lal Katra, can be found the showrooms of the renowned **Bhuramal Rajmal Surana** which has, supplied the present Prince of Wales. Prices are fixed and the establishment is renowned for its diamonds and enamel-backed pieces in Mogul style, for which nothing less than twenty-two carat gold is used. However, more modest examples of Surana's work, including necklaces incorporating semi-precious stones, for only twenty rupees, are available. The company guarantees to repurchase any item for the price paid.

Gopalji Ka Bazar runs westward from Johari Bazar, facing the entrance to Haldion Ka Rasta, and many of its shops sell sweetmeats of the usual very sweet type; there are also more jewellers. Ahead lies the Badi Chaupar intersection from which, to the right, runs **Ramganj Bazar**. On the north side are concentrated shoe shops, many of which specialize in black, embroidered Jaipur slippers. **Tripolia Bazar**, which runs westward from Badi Chaupar, is the centre for costume jewellery and also a strange combination, cooking utensils. On the north-west corner of **Badi Chaupar**, salesmen of enamelled bangles entice young ladies with their wares. North of Badi Chaupar, the main street is called **Sire Deorhi Bazar** where, just past the Palace of the Winds, fireworks are sold. On the opposite side are puppet-makers and more shoe shops.

The long **Mirza Ismail Road** has several shops of interest in addition to the Rajasthan Government Emporium already mentioned; these include **Central Cottage Industries Emporium**, for crafts, and **Gem Palace**, for cheap and reliable precious stones. Also in this road is **Niro's**, Jaipur's most popular restaurant outside the tourist hotels. Its chicken tikka butter marsala is outstanding; as elsewhere in Jaipur restaurants, no alcoholic drinks are served.

Jaipur is particularly well-endowed with hotels that have been converted from former palaces; pre-eminent is the **Rambagh Palace Hotel**, which is worth a visit if only to take tea on the lawns or sip a drink in the bar. Ram Singh II converted exisiting pavilions into a hunting lodge in the mid-nineteenth century and, soon after succeeding as maharaja, the athletic Madho Singh II commissioned Sir Swinton Jacob to adapt the lodge into a sports complex. This later became the principal residence of Madho Singh's adopted son, Man Singh II, who ruled Jaipur State from it. When the rank of maharaja was abolished in India in 1949, Man Singh, known to his intimates as Jai, and his wife Gayatra Devi (Ayesha) moved to the smaller Raj Mahal Palace, where they resided until Man Singh was appointed India's ambassador to Spain. He was an enthusiastic polo player, regularly practising on his father's ground, which still survives adjacent to the Rambagh Palace Hotel, and where matches take place every March. In a match at Cirencester, England, in 1970, Jai, aged 54, fell from his horse and was killed; the hotel's Polo Bar commemorates his great passion for the sport. From the polo ground can be seen, to the south, the **Moti Doongri**, a mock-medieval castle, to which the royal treasury was transferred from Nahargarh Fort. If possible, try to have a peek at the Rambagh Palace Hotel's Princess Suite, one of the loveliest hotel rooms in India.

Other 'heritage' hotels in Jaipur include the **Raj Mahal Palace** (the last home of Jai and Ayesha), which was built in 1729 by Jai Singh for his favourite consort, and later became the British Residency in Jaipur; the **Narain Niwas Palace**, built in the nineteenth century for Thakur Kanota; and the **Hotel Samod Haveli**, a former residence of Rawal Sheo Singhji, a chief minister of Jaipur; this is the only one in the group to be conveniently sited within the old city — near the north wall's Zorawa Singh Gate.

AMBER

🏰 Amber Fort

Amber Fort, 7 miles (11km) north of Jaipur, and generally regarded as the finest in Rajasthan, may be reached by regular bus services, which depart from outside the Palace of the Winds, and follow a route between arid hills which is surprisingly lush. It is not certain how Amber acquired its name; suggested sources are Ambarisha, a famous king of Ayodha, one of India's seven sacred cities, or Amba, goddess of fertility. Equally uncertain is the early history of the region before 1037, when the Kachchwahas defeated the Minas, who then occupied the fort. For some reason, the Minas were permitted to stay on in a subsidiary role, evidently serving their conquerors with great fidelity. However, it was their ability to form amicable relationships with India's non-Hindu masters that was mainly responsible for the Kachchwahas' undisturbed rule of 600 years. A particularly stong liaison with the Moguls began in 1562, when the youthful Akbar, on returning from his first Ajmer pilgrimage, met and married a daughter of Amber's Raja Bhar Mal, Mariam-uz-Zamani, who would give birth to the future Emperor Jahangir.

Man Singh I acquired so much booty in the service of both Akbar and Jahangir that he could afford to replace his old fort with a new complex, which followed Mogul layouts; work began around 1600 and was continued by Jai Singh I.

The bravery of Jai Singh II in combat on behalf of the Moguls even met with the enthusiastic approval of Aurangzeb, who awarded his dynasty with the title sawah maharaja (one and a quarter maharaja). Jai Singh immediately increased the size of his banner by a quarter, to assert Jaipur's superiority over the other maharajas. Following the death of Aurangzeb in 1707, Jai Singh II refused to support his successor, Bahadur Shah I, and eventually forced the now divided and weakened Moguls to end their suzerainty of Amber. In 1729, the fort was abandoned for Jaipur.

Elephants depart from the town for the slow climb up to the fort; the price is fixed per elephant, not per person, and four people can be seated on each howdah. If walking up, steps to the right provide a shorter route. The main entrance to the palace is called **Jai Pol** (Victory Gate) or **Surya Pol** (Sun Gate), the latter probably referring to the fact that it faces east and hence the rising sun. Elephants deposit their passengers in Jaleb Chowk, the first and largest of the palace's courtyards, and then make a limited perambulation from the west side for those who have walked up and just want a short ride (some find that the swaying movement can induce slight nausea). From a balcony, reached via the café, there are good views down to the earlier Kadmi Palace. Lowering down from a crag above is Jaigarh Fort.

Steps, right of the main entrance to the palaces, on the south side, ascend to the **Shila Devi Temple**, which is best visited immediately, as it shuts between 12noon and 4pm. This was built in 1604 by Man Singh I for private use by the royal family to honour Kali, the fiercest manifestation of Shiva's consort, Parvathi, who is known at Amber as Sila Mata, goddess of war. Although this is a Hindu, not a Jain temple, socks as well as shoes must be removed, and no leatherware is permitted within. In 1939, Man Singh II survived an aircrash, and his wife, in thanks, presented the silver entrance doors as a votive offering to the goddess. It had long been traditional for every new maharaja on inheriting the title, to worship at the temple and sacrifice a live goat, and Man Singh II, in spite of being cultured, charming and worldly-wise, similarly propitiated Kali in this way. Within, the columns are apparently of expensive Carrara marble, imported from Italy and renowned for their whiteness. However, it was decided to cut them in imitation of palm trees and paint them green, which seems rather a waste. The idol, of black marble, was brought from East Bengal in 1604.

Return to Jaleb Chowk and enter the palace proper by **Singh Pol** (Lion Gate), the double archway adjacent. To the left, in the court-yard ahead, stands the **Diwan-i-Am** (Public Audience Hall), added by Jai Singh. It will become apparent that the buildings are approached north to south in reverse order to their construction. This hall is Amber's most successful Rajput imitation of middle-period Mogul architecture. Apparently, Emperor Jahangir was not entirely pleased when told of its high quality, and Jai Singh, not wishing to make him unduly jealous, plastered over the structure to reduce its

Amber Fort

Jai Pol (Surya Pol)

Jaleb Chowk

Path
to
Amber
Village

Singh Pol

Diwan-i-Am

Ganesh
Pol

Shila Devi
(or Sila Mata)
Temple

Jai Mandir
Diwan-i-Khas
Sheesh Mahal
Jas Mandir

Sukh
Niwas

Zenana

Man Singh's
Building's

LAKE
MAOTA

N
W   E
S

*opposite; one thousand convex
mirrors cover the interior of
Amber Fort's Moti Mahal*

Amber Fort may be approached by elephant

splendour. Students of English history might recall a similar situation, when Henry VIII became jealous of Wolsey's Hampton Court Palace. The terrified Wolsey presented it to the King, but was never again in favour. It is possible to ascend to the upper terrace on the south side of the courtyard.

The vibrant **Ganesh Pol**, built by Jai Singh in 1639, was probably remodelled in the eighteenth century. This gateway depicts the elephant-headed god Ganesh above the arch, hence its name; decoration combines paintwork with glass mosaics. The structure marks the division between the public and private areas of the palace.

Ahead, the central courtyard of the palace takes the form of a sunken formal garden with, on its west side, Sukh Niwas and, facing it, the Jai Mandir. **Sukh Niwas** (Pleasure Hall) is renowned for its ingenious air conditioning systems, open walls being placed at different heights and angles to create drafts; the air then passes over water which cascades from an upper cistern through marble screens. Pastel-colour decoration throughout is influenced by Mogul work, and flower vases are a recurring theme. Doors of sandalwood and ivory inlay are noteworthy. A water channel runs through the centre of the hall as an additional cooling device.

The **Jai Mandir** (Hall of Victory), reached by a ramp, was built to accommodate his private apartments by Jai Singh, and is the loveliest section of the palace; no finer interiors will be seen in Rajasthan. Floral, hunting and battle scene murals, painted throughout, are still in remarkable condition, due to the quality of the top coat of plaster, in which was incorporated ground particles of eggshells, marble, and even, it is said, pearls. Once again, the colours are delicate, and there is no hint of the gaudiness which can sometimes mar Hindu work in western eyes.

On the ground floor is the arcaded **Diwan-i-Khas** (Private Audience Hall). Much of the interior is lined with examples of the mirror work for which Jaipur is famous. An attendant will unlock the **Sheesh Mahal** (Mirror Hall), shut the door so that all light is excluded, and light a candle; the effect is magical, each section of mirror mosaic twinkling in turn. The Sheesh Mahal is believed to have been the royal bedroom. Off this, in a small dressing room, a face will be reflected 1,000 times in small pieces of mirror glass — quite an unnerving experience.

Occupying the upper floor is the **Jas Mandir** (Hall of Glory), its opening screened by full-length *jalis* of alabaster, and more examples of mirror-glass decoration within. Its huge roof terrace possesses superb views.

The oldest part of Amber Fort, at its south end, was built by Man Singh; this eventually formed the female quarters (zenana), but is now dilapidated.

Jalgarh Fort

Looking down on Amber Fort is the much smaller and much longer-established Jalgarh Fort, rebuilt and expanded by Jai Singh II in 1726. Four-wheel drive vehicles will conduct visitors to it, but the fare demanded is outrageous — bargain heroically! It may also be visited on foot, but although only 1 mile (2km) distant, the uphill path should not be attempted by the elderly or infirm. The fort, opened to visitors in 1983, is the only part of Amber still in the private ownership of the former royal family. Obviously, the views are the chief attraction, but at the south end many will be enthralled by what is claimed to be the world's largest cannon, Jaivan, constructed in 1720, with a 20ft (6m) long barrel. It was only fired once, on test, and the cannon ball was propelled a distance of 24 miles (39km). The armoury collection includes the great five-key lock to the royal treasury, originally located at Jaigarh. At the end of Jalgarh's **Jaleb Chowk** courtyard, a miniature cannon will be fired on payment of a fee. The fort's gun foundry of 1584 still exists; when it was built, the Moguls believed that only they knew how to make gunpowder in India, and were not particularly pleased to discover that Man Singh I had obtained the secret direct from Kabul. The **palace** section of the fort is sited at the north end of the spur.

Before finally leaving Amber, it is pleasant to stroll around, or even boat on, **Lake Maota**, directly below the fort, which it reflects so romantically. Near the formal **Dilaram Gardens** is a small **Archaeological Museum**.

SANGANER ❋

Less than 10 miles (16km) south of Jaipur is the crafts town of Sanganer. Over 7,000 are involved in the block-printing industry, many of whom welcome visitors to watch them at work. Block-printing is a hand process by which materials are dyed with brilliant colours in traditional designs. If material is purchased, ensure that it has been blocked rather than silk-screened, and that natural, not chemical dyes have been used. Paper-making by hand is another Sanganer industry, based on silk and cotton waste rather than timber.

While in Sanganer, visit the **Krishna Temple**, with its superbly carved wooden door, and a **Jain temple**, which exhibits the usual sumptuous carving. Of greatest interest, however, is the **Sitaram Temple**, due to its marble pillar, 6ft (2m) high, on which are carved Brahma, Vishnu and Shiva accompanied by Parvati and Ganesh.

ALWAR ❋

Alwar is fractionally nearer to Jaipur than to Agra, and some accompanied tours pass through the town on route to the Sariska Wildlife Sanctuary, a short distance away. However, although Alwar is a pleasant city, it is not a 'must' by Rajasthan standards, and only worth a special detour if time is unrestricted. The quickest approach from Jaipur is by rail on the Pink City Express, which continues to Delhi.

Pratap Singh, a member of Jaipur's royal family, broke away to become independent in 1771, and took Alwar Fort from the Jats. He created his own state with the acquiesence of the emperor of the by now weak Moguls, Shah Alam, who also did not oppose the title Sawai (Maharaja and a quarter), which Pratap Singh awarded himself in emulation of Jaipur's maharajas.

The present City Palace was built by Vinai Singh in 1840, and named after him as the **Vinai Vilas Mahal**. This is located at the far end of the town, separated from the hills by a water tank. Designed in a variety of styles, the complex is of historical interest as it was the last example of Rajput palace architecture to be built. Unfortunately, the municipal authorities have taken over most of it, including the famous library. A **museum**, on the upper floor, however, is of importance, and displays a splendid collection of manuscripts, miniature paintings and armour; some of the swords, inset with jewels, are alleged to have belonged to the son-in-law of the Prophet Muhammad. Overlooking the tank is a **Shish Mahal**, lined with mirror-glass mosaic in the style of Amber. The **Durbar Hall** may be open to visitors, but it is safer to obtain permission in advance from Alwar House in New Delhi.

An elephant carriage is displayed in a building immediately right of the palace entrance. In emulation of a London bus, it is a double-decker, which could accommodate fifty passengers; the carriage, when full, was pulled by four elephants.

On the west side of the tank (remove shoes), an enclosure incorporates temples and memorials. Of chief importance is the marble **cenotaph of Maharao Raja Bakhtawar Singh** (1781-1815).

Located near the railway station is the domed Mogul **tomb of Kateh Jang**, an important minister of Shah Jahan; it is dated 1547.

Those who wish to visit **Bal Qila Fort**, with its superb views (but little else of interest), must obtain special permission, as the fort now accommodates a radio station. In addition, a four-wheel drive vehicle must be hired or else slog up an extremely steep path, so steep that elephants had to turn back half way up. No refreshments are available.

🐃 Sariska Wildlife Sanctuary

Buses between Alwar and Jaipur skirt the Sariska Wildlife Sanctuary. This is much larger than the more famous Ranthambore Sanctuary, but there is little chance of seeing a tiger. However, unlike Ranthambore, it is possible to visit water holes at night, by far the best time for viewing the fauna. The most popular is at the **Kaligati Ranger Post**, reached by a daily bus service, but only mattresses are supplied in its watch tower, and there is no food — very much a basic, but great fun, safari. From here, the fortunate may see panthers, and leopards, but tigers are now rare. Night safaris and boat trips on the **River Rupa** can also be booked from nearby hotels. **Tiger Den Tourist Bungalow**, at the sanctuary, is convenient, but the smart place to stay is **Hotel Sariska Palace**, the former hunting lodge of Jai Singh, built in 1900 and facing one of the sanctary's entrances. Much original Art Deco furniture has been retained.

A return to Alwar might be made via **Rajgarh**, where Pratap Singh rebuilt the ancient palace fort in 1771.

Ranthambore Wildlife Sanctuary

India's most frequented wildlife sanctuary is the Ranthambore Tiger Reserve near Sawai Madhopur, which is situated on the main Delhi/Bombay railway line.

Wart-hogs wallowing at Ranthambore

The reason for Ranthambore's popularity with tourists, prior to 1991, was the virtual certainty that they would see a tiger in the wild. India's Project Tiger, introduced to save the animal from extinction, was founded here in 1973, and the area decreed a national park in 1981: a measure which involved the relocation of sixteen villages. Ranthambore's tiger population was built up to around forty, and the big cats gradually became so used to humans that they would roam around during the day as well as nocturnally. Fuelled by greed, the corruptibility of guardians, and the mistaken belief of some Chinese and Koreans that various parts of the tiger's body have medicinal and potency qualities, tiger slaughter began in earnest at Ranthambore in 1991, and within 2 years poachers had reduced their number to less than twenty. By 1993, sightings were rare, only occasionally exceeding two per week and, although rigorous security has been introduced, it is an uphill job, and would-be visitors, whose only motive for coming to Ranthambore is to see a tiger, should check the current position. It should, perhaps, be borne in mind that the present 'slaughter', although reprehensible, pales into insignificance compared with the estimated total of 39,000 tigers, which the British and Indians shot in the name of 'sport' between 1900 and 1971, when it was banned.

For security reasons, night excursions have been terminated, and the Jogi Mahal Hotel, within the sanctuary, is now closed. All accommodation at Sawai Madhopur, however, is a fairly short drive away from the sanctuary. A pleasant 'time-warp' experience awaits guests at the **Sawai Madhopur Lodge**, the former hunting lodge of the last Maharaja of Jaipur, built in the 1930s. Few changes have been made by the Taj Group in converting the building to a hotel, all fixtures and most furnishings being original. In addition to fourteen standard rooms, two suites are available, that were occupied, respectively, by Elizabeth II and the Duke of Edinburgh, when they took part in a tiger shoot at Rathambore, 21-23 January 1961. Some guests, therefore, have a rare opportunity to sleep in a bed which was once occupied by the Queen of England, and wrestle with the same solid brass bathroom and toilet fittings; one hopes that Her Majesty's maid understood the workings of vintage plumbing devices. Tea on the lawns is a delightful experience, and the management and staff, even for India, are outstandingly helpful.

Early-morning and late-evening tours by bus or jeep (the latter cost more but can explore minor tracks) should be booked from hotels the night before they are required. It is recommended that both should be taken, as different routes are followed: preferably the morning trip by jeep and the afternoon tour by bus. In order to do this, two nights accommodation must be booked. Tigers are most likely to be seen early in the morning. It is engrossing to watch the ranger examining spore, nodding his head and saying, hopefully 'Tiger near'. If he is right, confirmation will soon be given by the deep-throated baying of terrified sambah deer, the tiger's favourite meal, which gets more frenetic as the beast approaches. Great silence must be observed, and one half expects the menacingly staccato *Jaws* theme to be played on a jungle tannoy. The central lake is generally visited in the afternoon, when crocodiles can always be seen basking in the sun. Even without the animals, Ranthambore would be worth visiting, as the hilly, partly-wooded scenery is idyllic, and the birdlife varied. Leopards, caracels (Indian lynx) and bears are more numerous than tigers, but rarely seen, as they are nocturnal.

Perched on a 65ft (215m) high ridge above the reserve's entrance is the ruinous **Ranthambore Fort**; there is no road approach, but the climb, up steps, is not as difficult as it looks. The Delhi Sultan, Ala-ud-din Khalji, stormed the fort in 1303 and it is said that 20,000 women committed mass suicide in a johar. Akbar took the fort in 1569, after a 12 month siege but, as has been seen, the Moguls developed a close liason with the Maharaja of Jaipur, and the fort was soon returned to him. The entrance gate pierces a wall, 4 miles (7km) in circumference; it is studded with nails to prevent aggressors using elephants to break it down, an oft-repeated feature in Rajasthan forts. Views over the reserve are magnificent, but little of architectural interest within the fort has survived.

Most will return from Sawai Madhopur station to Jaipur, however, it is possible to continue southward by train on a 3 hour journey to Kota (and later Bundi), returning to Jaipur via Ajmer and Pushkar or, alternatively, proceeding by road from Bundi to Udaipur via Chittaurgarh. The relatively isolated position of Kota and Bundi, which involves lengthy direct journeys from either Jaipur or Udaipur, has meant that these 'twin' towns, only 25 miles (40km) apart, are not included on most tourist's Rajasthan itineraries. Kota has become semi-industrialized, but Bundi, almost untouched by the modern world, seems little changed in appearance, or attitude, from Rajasthan's pre-tourist days. Its 'virginal' nature is quite unique in the state and a visit will be most rewarding.

KOTA   ✳

Historic Kota has grown tremendously since independence, and is now an industrial town with a population of around half a million. It lies on the east bank of a tributary of the River Yamuna and is primarily visited for its City Palace, begun by Rao Madhu Singh in the seventeenth century within an exisiting fort, and added to at various times up to the twentieth century. Locations of interest all lie well to the south of the railway station, and follow a virtually straight route.

Kota was taken from the Minas around 1346, by Chauhan Rajputs, who had also been victorious at Bundi a few years earlier, and it was immediately incorporated into Bundi State. However, Ratan Singh, ruler of Bundi, permitted his son to create an autonomous Kota State in 1624.

The modern palace, **Umed Bhavan**, which is not open to visitors, overlooks the River Chambal to the north of the bus stand.

Mid-sixteenth-century **tombs** of two brothers who ruled Kota, Kesar and Dokkar Khan, are close to the **Kishor Sagar** artificial lake, in the centre of which is the island palace of **Jag Mandir**, built for Maharani Brij Ranwar in the eighteenth century.

Kota Fort, within which the Old Palace was built, overlooks the **Kota Barrage**; not only does this barrage control floodwater and irrigate canals, it also serves as an alternative bridge in the monsoon season.

⛬ Kota Fort

The fort is entered at **Hathia Pol** (Elephant Gate), built by Maharao Madho Singh. Sculpted figures of rampant elephants are an eighteenth-century addition by Maharao Bhim Singh (1707-20). The elephant theme, an obvious inspiration from Bundi, is repeated on the columns of the **Arjuna Mahal**, the walls of which are decorated with nineteenth-century murals.

More early work by Bhim Singh follows in the two-storey **Lakshmi Bandar Tribari**, and the **Raj Mahal**, where stands the 'coronation' throne on which new maharaos were anointed. Bhim Singh also added the **Bhim Mahal**, to provide the Durbar Hall of the palace, and the **Bara Mahal**, with its superb murals and displays of early Kota miniatures; both buildings formed a new wing of the male section of the palace.

Wrestling appears to have been a favourite sport of the maharaos of Kota, the **Akhade-ka Mahal** having been built by Durgan Sal specifically for contests, in the eighteenth century; the present hall is a late nineteenth-century replacement by Umaid Singh (1888-1940), who was also responsible for the two unimpressive **pavilions** built for his wives.

Two museums are accommodated within the palace, the **Rao Madho Singh Museum** being by far the most important: weapons, banners, costumes, photographs and archaeological fragments are exhibited.

Laid out a short distance south of the palace are the attractive **Chambal Gardens**, which incorporate a pond shared by crocodiles and flamingoes; surprisingly, there is no jealous animosity or cases of murder.

Although Bundi is a much more attractive town than Kota, accommodation is severely restricted. The best hotel in the area is the former British Residency in Kota, now the **Brij Raj Bhawan Mahal;** its restaurant is also the best in town, but only for residents. The bus from Kota to Bundi takes less than an hour to make the journey; it leaves from the bus stand and immediately crosses the 'Irish' bridge.

BUNDI   ✳

Bundi is a walled town with a palace/fortress, which has retained its unique charm because its inhabitants do not realise how unique and how charming it is. Visitors are welcomed with surprised interest rather than as a source of income, hence restaurants and accommodation (what there is of it) are generally aimed at Indian, not Western, travellers. However, Bundi can be seen easily in a day before returning to Kota, or continuing to Chittaurgarh or Ajmer.

The relatively small size of Bundi makes the town easy to explore on foot, and its intimate, lively streets, and the colourful dress of its inhabitants are a constant delight. An unusual feature of Bundi is the succession of stepped *baoli* water tanks which are passed on route to the palace. Bundi lies in a narrow valley running between the Araval range; *bindo*, meaning a cleft in the hills, gives the town its name. The palace and fort are sited on high ground above a reservoir, Jait Sagar.

Taragarh Fort   ♜

In 1342, the Minas were expelled by Hara Chauhan Rajputs, who built the present Taragarh (Star) Fort 30 years later; the adjacent palace was begun around 1600. Bundi's fort and its palace are spread over the hillside in a protective rather than a menacing way, evoking a town within a town rather than a defensive bastion.

It will quickly become apparent to those who have seen it already, that Kota Fort owes much of its inspiration to Bundi. **Hazari Pol**, the first gateway passed, is followed by **Hathi Pol** (Elephant Gate) which, as at Kota, is embellished with carved elephants, their trunks entwined.

The **Ratan Daulat** courtyard, now entered, incorporates the former stables of the royal horses. Steps ascend to the **Diwan-i-Am** (Public Audience Hall), the small size of which indicates that the general public were kept well back in the courtyard, only a few being admitted to the maharao's presence at a time. It was built by Patan Singh (ruled 1607-31), whose marble throne is displayed.

Chitri Shali (ruled 1748-70) built the **Chattar Mahal**. From what remains, the decoration of its courtyard appears to have been influenced by Mogul work. In its west hall, known as the **Hathi Sala**, elephants are carved on the columns, again an obvious source of inspiration from Kota. Entered opposite are the private apartments, one of which, on the south side, displays seventeenth-century murals. The finest wall paintings at Bundi, however, are located in the **Chitra Shali** (Picture Gallery) of Umaid Singh (ruled 1739-70).

Scenes of hunting expeditions, elephant fights, historical events and, most important, Krishna playing with Gopis (female cowherds) cover the walls. Umaid Singh was a devout follower of Krishna, and retired from office to become a monk. Taragarh Fort is situated on Bundi's highest point, from where Kota can usually be seen.

North-east of the palace, in the centre of **Jair Sagar**, is the eighteenth-century royal summer palace, **Sukh Mahal** (Palace of Happiness).

The young Rudyard Kipling stayed at Bundi and recorded his visit in *From Sea to Sea*, published in 1889. Bundi seems to have changed very little since.

From Kota and Bundi it is possible to continue direct by bus to: Ajmer and Pushkar (5 hours), Chittaurgarh (6 hours), or return, by rail via Sawai Madhopur to Jaipur (a lengthly business). Most visitor's to Ajmer, however, take the bus or train direct from Jaipur (2½ hours). It must be said that Pushkar is a much more attractive place in which to stay overnight than Ajmer. Frequent buses from Ajmer to Pushkar leave from the bus stand, but also, and more frequently, from outside Ajmer railway station; the journey takes around half an hour.

✳ AJMER

Although the town of Ajmer has little general appeal, it does possess some important monuments: a Muslim shrine, a small fort built by Akbar, a Jain temple, romantic marble pavilions constructed by Shah Jahan beside Lake Ana Sagar, remains of the early mosque of Adhai-din-ka Jhopra, and the ancient Taragarh Fort. Historically, it is a unique Muslim enclave in Hindu Rajasthan.

Akbar's fort occupies a central position north-west of the railway station, just within the town's east wall, and now accommodates a museum. The fort was constructed with double-thickness walls in 1570 to provide impregnable shelter for Akbar during his annual pilgrimages to Ajmer. It is known that at least two of these pilgrimages were made on foot from Agra. The fort's plan is almost square, with octagonal towers located at the four corners of its red sandstone wall. On the west side, the gateway is built with stones of various colours, and displays fine *jali* screens within the entrance arch.

Accommodation consists solely of a rectangular, gold sandstone pavilion, divided internally to provide nine rooms. In 1616, Jahangir received James I's ambassador, Sir Thomas Roe 'with courtly conde-scension' in the pillared **audience chamber**, which rises two storeys high. Akbar had taken Ajmer from Maldeo of Malwar in 1556; in the first half of the eighteenth century, the late-Moguls lost and regained the town but, from 1750, the Mahrattas held Ajmer almost continuously until it was ceded to the British by their leader Daulat Rao Scindia in 1818. The other states which now make up Rajasthan were permitted by the British to remain under the direct control of their princes, albeit as vassals.

Within the fort, the **Government Museum** exhibits Hindu sculpture, coins and rather uninteresting armour; some ravishing miniature paintings are the pride of the collection. Jahangir resided at Ajmer (1613-16), not in his father's fort, however, but in the Daulat Bagh Palace, now in ruins.

Dargah of Khawaja Muin-ud-din Chishti

South-west of Akbar's fort is the shrine of the Muslim saint, Khawaja Muin-ud-din Chisti (1142-1236), who was born in the Chishti sector of Sanjar in Persia. By tradition, the Saint, during a pilgrimage to Mecca, was instructed in a vision to live at Ajmer, and eventually did so, probably arriving with Shahab-ud-din Ghori's army around 1193. The enclosed area of the shrine is entered (remove shoes) from the south side through a gate donated by the Nizam of Hyderabad. Passed on the right is the **mosque** built by Akbar.

Two iron cauldrons, the larger set on a stepped pyramid, the smaller beneath a domed kiosk, are nineteenth-century replacements of the originals presented, respectively, by Akbar and Jahangir. Wealthy Muslim pilgrims cast money for the needy into the cauldron, and when sufficient has been deposited, rice to fill both cauldrons is purchased and boiled in them. On cooking day all is pandemonium as the cauldrons are 'looted' of their contents. It is said, however, that little is now eaten by the poor, who prefer to sell their sanctified rice to the virtuous at a high price.

Shah Jahan's mosque, of white marble, stands in an inner court-yard ahead, its screen comprising eleven arches.

Iltutmish appears to have begun the shrine in the Saint's lifetime, but it was not completed until the sixteenth century, when Humayun commissioned further work. Not only must heads now be covered (a handkerchief will suffice) but it is forbidden to stand on the steps. The domed superstructure of marble has a silver archway, and a rail of silver surrounds the plain brick tomb of the Saint. Donations are requested, and the names of subscribers entered in important-looking books. However, payment is certainly not obligatory and should never exceed one rupee from non-Muslims. Nearby, masked by lattice *jalis*, is the **tomb** of the Saint's daughter, Bibi Hafiz Jamal

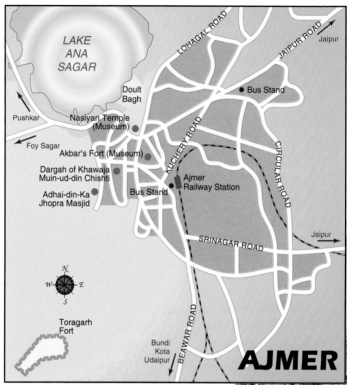

and, beside it, that of a daughter of Shah Jahan, Chimni Begam. Non-Muslims may not approach the former too closely. The mosque in the courtyard was built by Aurangzeb.

On rising ground, a short distance away to the south-west, is one of India's earliest mosques, the **Adhai-din-ka-Jhopra Masjid**. It is possible that Qutb-ud-din Aibak remodelled an exisiting Jain theological college around 1200 to form the prayer hall, but the seven-arched screen was not erected until 1266. When completed, the mosque was significantly larger than the same builder's Quwwat-ul-Islam mosque in Delhi, begun in 1193, and which it resembles. Although only one of its four sides has survived, and that is partly ruinous, the beauty of the structure still enthrals. The mosque's name translates as 'Hut of two and a half days', apparently referring to a religious festival which lasted for that length of time, not the number of days that the remodelling of the building took to complete (which would have been impossible without divine intervention).

An unusually high *iwan* (56ft/17m) has been given short minarets; the delicate seven-arched **screen**, of which it is the centrepiece, and its caligraphic decoration, are some of the finest work to be found in an Indian mosque, in spite of dilapidation. It will be noted that four of the arches are cusped in the Hindu manner; also Hindu is the primitive method of arch construction.

Built in 1192, the arched screen of the Adhai-din-ka Jhopra mosque at Ajmer is the second oldest in India

Within the **prayer hall**, 124 reused Hindu columns, each apparently comprising three superimposed shafts, support the roof, which incorporates ten domes, all resting on short stone joists. The spectacular carved ceilings are Jain work, either from the college or reused from demolished temples.

Two miles (3km) further to the south-west, on a low hill, is the **Taragarh** (Star) **Fort**. Ajaipal Chauhan, founder of Ajmer, built the first fort here, one of India's earliest, in the seventh century. It was referred to as Ajaimeru (Unconquerable Hill), probably the source of Ajmer's name, and remained in the hands of the Chauhans until Prithviraj III's defeat by Qutb-ud-din Aibak's Muslim army in 1193. Views over Ajmer from the fort are superb. Unexpectedly ancient survivors within are a mosque and the shrine of an early Muslim governor of the fort, Sayid Husain, who died in 1202.

To the north of the town, in the direction of Lake Ana Sagar, is a nineteenth-century Jain temple, known as the **Nasiyan** (Red) **Temple**, now a museum. In its two-storey hall are displayed gilded wooden figures.

Lake Ana Sagar, backed by hills, was created by the Chauhan King, Ana, who dammed the River Luni in 1150. Shah Jahan built four pavilions in its park on the south-east bank, which is known as **Doult Bagh**. The **marble pavilions** were apparently located to gain as much breeze as possible from the lake, which unfortunately dries up when successive monsoons fail. It has been suggested that as the arches are not cusped, the pavilions must have been built early in Shah Jahan's reign, however, as the niches in the walls are cusped, that feature may not be conclusive evidence. As the sun begins to set, the pavilions reflect its golden light and appear to be illuminated: a magical sight. It is possible to drive around the entire lake.

A walk through Ajmer's Bazars should not be contemplated in the late evening, as it is then that the streets of its butchers' quarter, sited on rising ground, are hosed down, and an evil-smelling slurry pours through the bazars, up to ankle level. Strange this, in the town where the secret of making attar of roses, still an important ingredient of expensive perfumes, was discovered.

Near the Ana Sagar is Ajmer's most prestigious hotel, the Mansingh; the **Khadim Tourist Bungalow** is acceptable for those on lower budgets, and located just a short walk from the bus stop; it also has a bar that is popular with the locals, a facility rarely found in Rajasthan outside high-grade hotels. Ajmer's most popular restaurants, the **Elite** and **Honeydew**, are opposite the railway station. A very hard toffee, filled with cashew nuts, appears to be Ajmer's culinary high spot: those with dentures should take care!

The westward route from Ajmer to Pushkar winds uphill through the intervening hills, following Nag Pahar (Snake Pass), so-named (one hopes) from its serpentine route, rather than infestation by cobras. As Pushkar is approached, cacti and patches of sand appear, indicative that this is indeed desert country.

PUSHKAR ✳

In its appearance and atmosphere, Pushkar is one of the most westernized towns in India. Nestling around the most sacred lake in the country, bars, restaurants with terraces, and boutiques, all gleaming white, offer a home-from-home to foreign tourists. A unique bonus in Rajasthan is that between 9am and 4pm no motorized vehicles are permitted in Pushkar's streets, due to its holy status. Probably nowhere else in India, apart from the beach resorts of Goa and Kerala, will such a high proportion of non-Indians be seen. Most are young, stay for lengthy periods, and might once have been members of the hippy movement. Long hair is now rarely seen on the men, but the occasional, astonishingly hatless skinhead makes an appearance, in spite of the burning sun. Quite a large number of the youngsters discard jeans in favour of Indian dress, apparently believing, *wrongly*, that they will thereby melt into the background; however, this gives much harmless amusement to the locals. The friendly, laid-back atmosphere of Pushkar is hard to resist, particularly by those who have become temporarily exhausted by the 'Indianness' of India.

Many Pushkar traditions are associated with Brahma, the four-headed Hindu god of creation. The most important, related in the *Padma Parana*, is that Brahma, on discovering a demon devouring children, killed him with the lotus flower, which is his emblem, and three petals fell to the ground, forming the lakes of Pushkar. A less exciting variant of this is that Brahma merely cast the lotus petals at a band of his worshippers in recognition. The main lake of Pushkar directly faces the town, while the other two are some miles distant.

A few villainous locals attempt to perform private blessing ceremonies on the lakeside with unwary foreigners. Politely decline, as a ridiculously large 'donation' will invariably be demanded. Steps at Pushkar's fifty-two bathing ghats lead down to the holy waters, and notice boards at their approach warn, in several languages, that footwear must be discarded within 30ft (9m) of the shore. Other regulatory notices will prove worthy of careful study: 'Men and women please dress respectively', on one, was surely not intended

preceding pages; (left) The white town of Pushkar, with its sacred lake, introduces visitors to the carved mansions (havelis) of Rajasthan.
(right) One of Pushkar's colourful Hindu temples; there are, reputedly, more than 1,000 in the town

to infer that coachloads of transvestites had been arriving at Pushkar to the consternation of local residents. Some commercial posters will also cause surprise; they include those of Cadbury's for their ice-cream, which has been given the evocative brand-name 'Dollops'.

Kindness to animals is particularly apparent at Pushkar's ghats, where the greedy monkeys waiting for titbits frequently outnumber people. It is said that there are a thousand temples at Pushkar but, although many are appealing, every one is relatively modern, the intolerant Aurangzeb having destroyed all Pushkar's original Hindu places of worship in the eighteenth century. **The Gau** (Cow) **Temple** — note the Sanskrit base for both words — was built specifically to give refuge to cows which, of course, are sacred to Hindus but were slaughtered by the Moguls during Aurangzeb's reign. It overlooks **Gau Ghat**, from where the ashes of Mahatma Gandhi and Jawaharlal Nehru were scattered following their cremations in Delhi. Pushkar's most famous temple, distinguished by a pink spire, overlooks the lake and is dedicated to Brahma. Most say that this is the only Brahma temple in India, but another certainly exists in the south. The god's goose vehicle is depicted above the entrance.

Some visitors staying in Pushkar climb up to enjoy the fine views from the hillside **temple** to Brahma's consort Savitri (or Saraswati), approximately an hours trek from the town.

Hotel Sarovar, run by the Rajasthan Tourism Development Corporation, but once owned by the maharajas of Jaipur, is recommended for accommodation in Pushkar, but reserve in advance from Jaipur.

Every November, on variable dates, a 4-day fair is held at Pushkar. Originally a cattle fair, it has now become popularized by the inclusion of camel rides, folk evenings, puppet shows and general Rajasthan cultural activities. Literally hundreds of thousands turn up, and around 1,500 foreigners can be accommodated in temporary huts, tents and dormitories specially erected for the occasion. A foreign exchange counter and medical facilities are provided.

Many Pushkar visitors will wish to eat overlooking the lake, and there are several restaurants from where this is possible. The **Sunset Cafe** Shiva Restaurant and GR Rooftop Restaurant are established favourites. Pushkar's vegetarian specialities include *cashew nut curry* and *Malapura pancake*, but there are plenty of 'non-veg' opportunities as well.

From either Pushkar or Ajmer it is possible to continue to Jodhpur or return to Jaipur by bus, depending on the preferred itinerary. However, if visiting the exquisite, painted havelis in the Shekhavati region, a return to Jaipur will be necessary for those without private vehicles.

Towards Jaipur, just 18 miles (30km) from Ajmer, by road or rail, lies **Kishangarh**, divided into a new town and an old town which was founded in 1611. A close relationship developed between the ruling Singh family and the late Moguls, and the city prospered. Raj Singh promoted the development of Mogul-style miniature painting, and a unique Kishangarh treatment developed, which is much acclaimed by experts. Several royal palaces were built, one in the centre of the lake, as at Udaipur. The **fort** overlooks the **lake**; both may be visited, and another former royal building, the **Manjhela Palace**, provides overnight accommodation.

SHEKHAVATI REGION

Although the Shekhavati region's towns and villages are linked by bus services, a car is a much more convenient and quicker way of exploring them; in addition, a local driver will be invaluable in locating the havelis of greatest interest. At least one complete day is needed to appreciate the extent of the 'open air art gallery', as Shekhavati has been dubbed by promoters of its tourist potential. It is best to travel by bus or train (take the daily Shekhavati Express) from Jaipur to Sikar, the region's most southerly point, and hire a car there. Locations of greatest interest are found to the west and the north of the region. A convenient circular tour of Shekavati might include, in the following order: Sikar, Lachmangarh, Nawalgarh, Mandawa (stopover at Castle Mandawa Hotel), Fatehpur, Ramgarh, Mahansar, Bisau and Chura. However, its extent will obviously be dependent on time available and particular interests.

One of Rajasthan's most popular palace hotels is the century old **Samor Palace**, 26 miles (42km) north of Jaipur on route to Sikar; it is reached by taking a right turn after Chomu (served by train or bus). Richly decorated interiors include an enamelled **Durbar Hall** and a **Sheesh Mahal** mirrored hall. Advance bookings are recommended, as the hotel is popular with international tour operators throughout the winter season.

Between 1750 and 1939, the art of mural painting became so widespread in Shekhavati that this region of India has probably more outstanding examples than anywhere else in the world of comparable size. Although the earliest frescoes are found in cenotaphs, temples, forts and palaces, it is the havelis of the wealthy merchants for which Shekhavati is renowned. Most examples are external, therefore the question of arranging admission to the houses rarely arises.

Shekhavati was created in 1471 by incorporating a group of small autonomous areas into one administrative region. Its name, meaning Garden of Shekha, commemorates the first ruler, Rao Shekhaji, a member of Amber's Kachchwaha dynasty. Almost 200 years were to pass, however, before the famous murals made their first appearance: outside Nawalgarh, within the cenotaph of Shardal Singh. By that time, however, Shekhavati had been under direct rule from Jaipur for 12 years. It may well have been this closer contact with Jaipur which set in motion the popularity of murals in the region.

Initially, the method employed was fresco, by which means natural dyes are applied to wet plaster, a technique probably learned by the Moguls from Persia and passed on to their Jaipur allies. Whether or not the Persians had discovered fresco from the Italians is uncertain. An alternative theory is that Christian missionaries from Europe introduced the technique directly to India. It has been suggested that mural work, once learned, achieved its great popularity in Shekhavati due to the region's lack of natural colours, the land being flat and arid with few trees or flowers. There is no doubt, however, that it was the great wealth of the local merchants, particularly in the early nineteenth century, which enabled them to build their enormous havelis and commission artists to decorate them so splendidly. Haveli is a Persian word used to define a town mansion built around a courtyard or courtyards frequently shared by several families. Etymologically, it is tempting to speculate that a dilapidated example of a haveli might have been the source of the English word hovel, but there is no evidence for this.

Around 1870, some Germans perfected a blue dye, which until then had been impossible to produce. This was, of course, synthetically manufactured from chemicals, but gained immediate popularity in Shekhavati due to its novelty. Other chemical dyes quickly followed, but it was found that they could only be applied to dry plaster. However, the cheapness of the new dyes sounded the death-knell of both fresco (wet plaster) work and natural dyes, and there are few twentieth-century examples of either in Shekhavati. Both the longevity and delicacy of colour of the late murals have suffered in consequence.

Somewhat earlier, a change in subject matter had also taken place, mythological, religious and vernacular themes being replaced by depictions of the fashionable British way of life, with its modern appurtenances: telephones, trains, bicycles and European clothing, all of which made an appearance, painted in naive style. Although the earlier work is undoubtedly finer both from a technical and an artistic viewpoint, the later examples have an undoubted charm, and evoke the childlike wonder expressed by Indians as the products of Europe's industrial revolution appeared in their country.

Available in Jaipur, but not apparently in Shekhavati itself, is *The Guide to the Painted Towns of Shekhavate*, which includes specific details, useful for those wanting to explore the region thoroughly.

Sikar ✸

This town, founded in the seventeenth century, quickly became wealthy. Three temples, **Gopinath**, **Raghunath** and **Madan Mohan**, have good frescoes, as do the **Biyani** havelis, one of which is entirely blue.

Lachmangarh ✸

Overlooked by its fort, Lachmangarh only dates from the early nineteenth century, its regular street plan obviously being inspired by that of Jaipur. The **Gareniwala haveli**, in Char Chowk, built around four courtyards, is rated Shekhavati's most impressive. Other havelis worth seeking out are the **Chokhani** and **Rathi**, the latter decorated with a mural illustrating an Indian lady operating a wind-up gramophone.

Nawalgarh ✸

Nawalgarh and the villages and towns immediately north of it posseses the finest examples of Shekhavati's murals. Its **fort**, built in 1737, may occasionally be entered to view the painting of Jaipur city on its dome. Temples of **Ramdeoji** and **Gopinath**, the **Poddar**, **Bhayat**, **Dangaich**, Chokhani and **Chchawachcharia** havelis (the latter illustrating British riding bicycles, and a three-trunked elephant) should be visited. However, do not miss the kiosk of the **Bala Kila**, which has some of the finest examples of fresco work in Shekhavati. The **telephone exchange** is covered with murals. In Nawalgarh, it is possible to stay overnight at the **Roop Nihas haveli**.

Six miles (10km) east of Nawalgarh, at Parasampura, is the cenotaph *chattri* of **Shardul Singh**, decorated with the earliest (1750) frescoes in Shekhavati. Hindu sagas and scenes of famous battles are painted. Adjacent, with contemporary frescoes, is the **Gopinath Temple**.

❋ Mandawa

Castle Mandawa, its stable block converted to hotel bedrooms in 1980, overlooks the mid-eighteenth-century town. Very popular in the season, bookings may be made in Jaipur (☎ 522214). The castle's former Diwan-i-Am (Public Audience Hall) is now a **museum**, boasting an outstanding collection of sumptuous royal costumes. However, the hotel is not the only reason for staying in Mandawa, as there are well over a hundred painted havelis of distinction in the town; it may be of benefit to engage the services of a knowledgeable resident in order to identify them. The full range of mural styles is covered by the following havelis: **Chokhani**, **Ladia**, **Saraf**, **Goenka**, **Madan Zal**, **Harmukh**, **Mormoria** and **Newatia**. The Newatia haveli, which possesses one of the last examples of murals, was painted in 1937; it illustrates the Wright brothers, pioneers of aviation.

❋ Fatehpur

Fatehpur is much older than the towns previously described, being founded in the mid-fifteenth century by Fateh Khas, after whom it was named. Only ruined sections of the town's sixteenth-century fort have survived. Located on the main Jaipur/Bikaner road, Fatehpur's situation had much to do with the wealth of its merchants. Superb examples of frescoes are to be seen at the **Devra**, **Singhania**, **Goenka**, **Bhotika** and **Saraogi** havelis. Slightly later, more naive but amusing work is to be found at the **Jalan**, **Bhartiya**, **Poddar** and **Devra** havelis.

Buses and trains link Fatehpur with Bikaner and Jaipur.

❋ Ramgarh

The cenotaph *chattris* **of the Poddar family**, who founded Ramgarh in the late eighteenth century, are the chief attractions of this small town; in particular their vibrant frescoes, illustrating scenes from the Ramayana. Havelis of the **Poddars** and **Ruias**, and the **Ganga Temple** should also be sought out.

❋ Mahansar

Located midway between Ramgarh and Bisau, Mahansar, although not large, posseses some of the most exquisite fresco work in Shekhavati. Similarities in style indicate that artists employed at Bikaner Fort may also have worked here, which would account for the high quality. The Poddar family, in their **Raghunath Temple** and **Sonee-Chandi-Ki haveli** are, as at Ramgarh, responsible for the best known examples.

Bisau

Established, like many Shekhavati towns, in the mid-eighteenth century, Bisau, in addition to its **Sigtia**, **Khemka**, **Tibriwala** and **Kedia** havelis, exhibits sumptuous frescoes in the cenotaph *chattris* **of the Thakurs**.

Churu

Now technically just outside Shekhavati, Churu is the most convenient exit point from the region for those continuing to Bikaner or returning to Jaipur by rail. Before leaving, however, make for the six-storey **Surana haveli** (claimed to possess more than 1,000 doors and windows), **Kanhaya Lal Bugla haveli** and the **Kothari haveli**. Buses and trains link Churu with Bikaner or Jaipur.

For those with more time, the towns of Jhunjhunu, Khetri, Surajgarh, Kajra, Pilani, Alsisar and Malsisar, all in the northern sector, possess additional frescoed havelis of quality.

Additional Information

Places to Visit

Amber
Fort
Open: 9-4.30pm.

Shila Devi (Kali) Temple
Open: 5-12noon and 4-8pm.

Jalgarh Fort
Open: 9-4.30pm.

Jaipur
City Palace
Open: 9.30-4.45pm.

Palace of the Winds (Hawa Mahal)
Open: Saturday to Thursday 9-4.30pm.

Nahargarh Fort
Open: 10-4.30pm.

Central Museum
Open: Saturday to Thursday 9.30-4.30pm.

Kota
Fort
Open: Saturday to Thursday 9-5pm.

Festivals and Fairs

JAIPUR
Elephant Festival
1995, 20-21 March; 1996, 8-9 March; 1997, 27-28 March; 1998, 16-17 March; 1999, 5-6 March; 2000, 23-24 March.

Gangaur Fair
1995, 3-4 April; 1996, 22-23 March; 1997, 10-11 April; 1998, 30-31 March; 1999, 20-21 March; 2000, 7-8 April.

Teej Fair
1995, 30-31 July; 1996, 17-18
August; 1997, 6-7 August; 1998,
26-27 July; 1999, 14-15 August;2000,
2-3 August.

Pushkar Fair
1995, 15-18 November; 1996, 22-25
November; 1997, 11-14 November;
1998, 1-4 November; 1999, 20-23
November; 2000, 9-11 November.

KOTA
Dussehra Mela
1995, 1-3 October; 1996, 19-21
October; 1997, 9-11 October; 1998,
29 September-1 October; 1999,
17-19 October; 2000 5-7 October.

Accommodation

Ajmer
Mansingh Hotel
Circular Road ☎ 30855

Jaipur
Rambagh Palace
Bhawani Singh Road ☎ 75141

Hotel Jaipur Ashok
Jai Singh Circle
Bani Park ☎ 75121

Jai Mahal Palace
Jacob Road ☎ 73314

Samode Haveli Gangapol
☎ 42407

Kota
Hotel Brij Raj Bhavan
☎ 23071

Samode
Samode Palace Hotel
☎ (Jaipur) 42407

Sariska
Hotel Sariska Palace
☎ (Alwar) 722

Tourist Information Offices

Ajmer
Government of India Tourist Office
191 The Mall

Rajasthan State Information Office
Tourist Bungalow

Jaipur
Government of India Tourist Office
Hotel Khasa Kothi

Rajasthan State Information Office
Railway Station
☎ 69714

Kota
Chambal Tourist Bungalow
☎ 27695

Bikaner & Its Environs

The red sandstone city was founded in this geographically unpromising spot, due to its location on the trading
route from Jaisalmer, and because, in spite of appearances,
it is an oasis in the surrounding desert. Rao Bikaji, after whom
Bikaner is named, captured the region in 1472, but does not appear

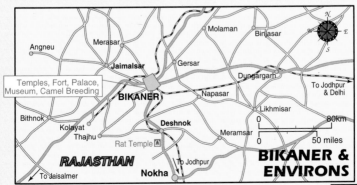

preceding page; Tourists enjoy stroking the young camels at Bikaner's Camel Breeding Station

to have built his fort until 16 years later; its ruins survive at the south end of the walled city. In the late sixteenth century, Rai Singh, an important general in Akbar's army and a descendant of Rao Bikaji, was rewarded sufficiently by the Emperor to commission a new fortress; his confidence was such that it was sited on flat land outside the protection of the city wall. This bravado was justified, the defences of Junagarh Fort proving impregnable. Although the many palaces within are amongst the most splendid in Rajasthan, Bikaner is equally renowned for its grand havelis, exquisitely carved in the local red sandstone, and its Jain and Hindu temples.

Bikaner is best reached from either Delhi, Jaipur or Jodhpur by comfortable night trains. There are also bus services but there is no airport. The railway continues only a short distance west of Bikaner.

✳ The Walled City of Bikaner

There are two good reasons for visiting the old city in the morning and Junagarh Fort in the afternoon: chronology and convenience (many temples close between 12.30 and 5pm). It is essential that a driver with local knowledge should be hired, either auto-rickshaw or taxi: bicycle rickshaws will not be found in Rajasthan outside Jaipur. A logical route (show the list to the driver) might begin at the city's Kota Gate, and include the thoroughfares of Mohto Ka Chowk, Acharyn Chowk and Ashanion Ka Chowk; the havelis of Rampuria, Bohar Niwas, Kothari and Daga; and the temples of Gordanath, Chintamani, Adinath, Bhanda Shah, Laksminath, Neminath, Ganesa and Naganachi. If it is early in the morning it is best to proceed directly to the temples. Leatherware should be left with the driver as it will not be permitted within many of them.

The **Chintaman Temple**, in Bare Bazar, only open 8am to 11am, is one of Bikaner's twenty-seven Jain temples, and was built of red sandstone in 1535. As usual, the carving is exquisite; particularly noteworthy are the splendid elephants which flank the entrance porch.

In Ashanion Ka Chowk, a marble haveli has been converted to the **Gardanath temple**.

The best of Bikaner's havelis were built in the first quarter of the twentieth century, all however, are difficult to locate, as they are not identified. To add to the confusion, the names given to the havelis are those of the families that originally built them; descendants subsequently commissioned their own, with the result that several havelis have acquired the same name. It was the existence of wealthy Mawari merchants in Bikaner, known as the 'Lombards of India', which led to so many splendid residences being built. Large plots of land were not available, so the havelis were built high, and the status of their owners was demonstrated by the quality of the carving.

Two of the best known, **Rampuria** and **Bohar Niwas** (built in the 1920s) are adjacent: the latter was converted to a small hotel in 1993. The **Kothari** haveli, built in 1919, is obviously influenced by European Renaissance work; note the carved arms of the United Kingdon and George V. **Daga haveli** is another picturesque example to be sought out.

On high ground, clustered around the old fort, is one of Rajasthan's most interesting temple complexes. Be prepared to shed different items of clothing as each is approached. The small **Adinath Temple** (Jain), a late sixteenth-century building, is reminiscent of the Chintaman Temple seen earlier, but its ceiling paintings are modern.

More important is the **Bhandasar Mandir Temple**, also Jain. Bhandasar is the name of the builder, whose brother, Neminath, was responsible for another Jain temple nearby. Begun in the late fifteenth century, it was completed in 1514. Strangely enough, leatherware does not appear to be proscribed here. Red sandstone is combined with gold sandstone, but most has been rendered and painted white, presumably to achieve a uniform effect. Much rebuilding, probably in extended form, took place in the seventeenth century, when the present *mandapa* hall and porches were constructed. Mural re-painting in the *mandapa* (rather garish) took place in 1985, but the sanctuary's decoration is early eighteenth-century work.

The **Laksminath Temple** is Vaishnavite, and its entry restrictions are severe — no leather, no shoes, no socks, no shorts, no cameras, wash hands before entry; one feels relieved that complete nudity is not demanded! The large courtyard is marble, but here again part of the red sandstone structure has been painted white, apparently a local preference.

Between the Laxminath and Bhandasar Mandir temples is Bikaner's most splendid Jain example, the **Neminath Temple**, named after its builder, the brother of Bhandasar, and completed in 1535. It is distinguished externally by a lofty tower (sikhara). The carving and decoration are exceptional, and the paintwork shimmers as if it were enamel. From within, the dome is surprisingly shallow considering its external height.

The **Ganesa Temple**, dedicated to the Hindu elephant-headed

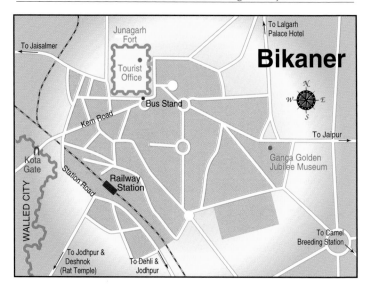

god Ganesh, is the best viewpoint from which to observe the ruined **fort of Rao Bikaji**, and the city wall. This fort appears to have been constructed in 1488, 16 years after Rao's conquest, and may therefore have been built on the site of an earlier structure. Rao Bikaji was a younger son of Rao Jodhaji, Maharaja of Jodhpur; not expecting to inherit his father's title, he founded his own city and state here at Bikaner, which was named after him.

Rao Bikaji's horse is represented in white marble in the wall of the small **Naganachi Temple** to Kali nearby, founded in 1515 and the city's oldest temple. A lone *chattri*, standing in the courtyard of the complex, is said to mark the point at which the city was founded.

It will be noticed that although Bikaner is classed as an oasis, monkeys find the region too dry; only rarely will they be seen in west Rajasthan. When monsoons have been regular, Bikaner's water level may be found at around 150ft (46m) below ground, but after a long dry spell this can increase to 300ft (91m). Some oasis!

Those with a taste for *lassi*, the cooling yoghurt-based drink, served either sweetened or salted, should ask to be taken to the tiny **Golden Restaurant** in Mohto Ka Chowk. Here, the *lassi* is kept refrigerated and, uniquely, each glass is given a topping of thickened yoghurt, which has developed the flavour of caramelized cream — absolutely delicious.

An amusing ritual takes place after lunchtime in the northern sector of Bikaner's old city. Men and boys will be seen throwing

(left) A delightful Bikaner temple
(above) Part of the temple complex at Bikaner (right) A unique creamy
topping goes on the lassi at Bikaner's Golden Restaurant

morsels of food as high in the air as possible. Great kites, in flocks, then swoop down to grab the titbits in their talons before they fall to the ground. After this, one wonders why so much fuss is made about feeding the pigeons in London's Trafalgar Square.

Junagarh Fort lies only a short distance to the north-east of the old city's Kota Gate. Allow around 2 hours for the obligatory guided tour and the museum.

ᕼ Junagarh Fort

The earliest part of the fort, including its entire wall and gateways, dates from Rao Singh's period, but many palaces were replaced, in the usual Rajput way, by his descendants in the eighteenth and nineteenth centuries. Like the Muslims, it seems that each successive ruler felt the need for a clean break from his immediate predecessor, frequently demolishing perfectly adequate accommodation and replacing it with a new pavilion. At Bikaner, there are also examples of additional storeys being added above exisiting structures.

Beside the entrance will be found a most helpful office of the Rajasthan Tourism Development Corporation. A series of gateways lead to the public entrance: **Karan Prole** (a local variant of the usual Pol, meaning gate) with elephant head-level spikes, **Daulat Prole**, beside which is a red hand-print in relief of a maharaja's wife who committed sati, **Fateh Prole**, **Ratan Prole** and **Suraj Prole**.

Suraj Prole faces east, hence its name, meaning Sun Gate. It displays more elephant spikes and sati prints. Painted on both sides of the gold sandstone gate are elephants with their mahouts. As in a Naubat Khana, musicians in the gallery above, now blocked, announced the arrival of important visitors.

On the left of the courtyard ahead, visitors to the palace must purchase tickets and wait for a guide. The entry charge for foreigners is rather steep by Indian standards but does include the guide; profits apparently go to a charitable trust set up to aid Bikaner's poor.

Visitors enter through the **Tripolia Gate**. Passed, left, is the **Har Mandir**, the private temple of the maharajahs; it is not open to visitors.

Karan Singh (reigned 1631-69) built the **Karan Mahal**, left, seen through a glass screen, which served as his Diwan-i-Am (Public Audience Hall). However, part of its decoration is the late seventeenth-century work of Anup Singh.

The pavilion in the courtyard is of imported Carrara marble from Italy; its basin is still filled with water in the hot season.

Approached from steps beside the **Karan Mahal**, and located on separate floors above it, are the **Gaj Mandir** and **Chattar Niwas**, but they are generally visited later, after the ground floor apartments to the west have been seen.

Next entered is the **Chandra Mahal** (Moon Palace). Sumptuously decorated, it was added by Gaj Singh (1746-87).

The **Anup Mahal**, built by Anup Singh in 1690, owes most of its present appearance to Surat Singh (1787-1828); it served as the Diwan-i-Khas (Private Audience Hall). Glass and vibrant paintwork combine to provide one of Junagarh's richest interiors.

A more recent addition, the **Badal Mahal** (Weather Palace), is the work of Dungar Singh (reigned 1872-87). The low level depiction of falling rain, a welcome event in Bikaner, gave the pavilion its name. Blue paintwork imitates ceramic tiles. Photos displayed of *Jogi* (holy men, the equivalent of Muslim fakirs) proving their faith by disregarding self-inflicted pain are not for the squeamish.

Further west, high buildings with a profusion of *jali* screens, indicate the female quarters.

A return is now generally made to the Karan Mahal, and the steps beside it ascend to the floor directly above; this comprises a five-room unit known as the Gaj Mandir, the most famous section of Junagarh. As may be expected from its name, Gaj Singh was responsible for this eighteenth-century addition. A central, slightly raised hall is surrounded by four interlinked rooms. Blue ceramic tiles, genuine this time, came from Persia. On display is a Krishna swing, but it is not contemporary with the building. **Shish Mahal**, one of the surrounding rooms, is decorated with mirror glass, stained glass and gold leaf.

More steps ascend to the Chattar Niwas, a pavilion built in the late nineteenth century by Dungar Singh. The single chamber is still furnished with a contemporary Rajput bed. Note that a mirror is positioned so that anyone can be seen approaching, an invaluable 'early warning system'. If apprehensive, a Rajput could immediately grasp his sword, which would be kept within easy reach beside the low bed.

Lying between the first two courtyards, the **Ganga Niwas**, now a museum, was built by the Indian prince who achieved greatest international fame: General H.H. Maharajah, Sir Ganga Singh Bahadur, GCSI, GCIE, GCVO, GBE, KCB, LL.D Ganga Singh was just 7 years old when he became maharaja in 1877, but did not effectively rule until his sixteenth birthday. In 1911, he was personally honoured by George V, who appointed him Knight Commander of the Star of India. He served in India's War Cabinet, and represented his country at the Imperial War Conferences, and the British Empire at the Peace Conference. Ganga Singh's long and eventful life ended in 1943.

Colonel Samuel Swinton Jacob, the architect of Jaipur's Albert Hall, was entrusted with this building in 1902, and as usual combined Indian and European styles resulted (this time Classical rather than Gothic). The two separate halls served as new and larger audience rooms, replacing the functions of Anup Singh's Diwan-i-Am and Diwan-i-Khas.

The imperial throne, of sandalwood, stands in the great **Durbar Hall**, for which it was made. Exhibits, almost as eclectic as the building in which they are housed, include the usual collection of weaponry, with devilish cunning shown in disguising a pistol to appear as a dagger, and simple devilry in the obscene knife, which opens out after it has entered the body of a combatant, severing his entrails. Only the strongest can even slightly raise the great double-edged sword of Rajkumar Padan Singh. Ganga Singh's ceremonial elephant howdah should not be missed, nor should the seductive miniature paintings of the Bikaner School. As might be expected, there are many exhibits from World War I, including a complete British bi-plane.

Immediately north-east of Junagarh Fort is the **Sur Sagar Tank**. Excavated for Sur Sing in the seventeenth century, its formal garden was laid out by Anup Singh in 1808.

❋ The Modern City

South-east of the fort, a short walk away, is the **Ganga Niwas Park**, in which stands an equestrian statue of Ganga Singh. For those who wish to boast, truthfully, that they have seen a live tiger in India, there are several specimens in the park's small zoo. Unfortunately, their conditions are terrible, and the sight of such magnificent creatures pacing neurotically in their tiny cages will arouse compassion in most.

If time permits, a visit should be made to the outstanding **Ganga Golden Jubilee Museum**, located in the Town Hall. Here is displayed Bikaner's most famous sculpture, an eleventh-century marble figure of Saraswati, consort of Brahma. The sinuous contours of the goddess and her enigmatic smile evoke an eastern Leonardo. Terracottas and, as would be expected, miniatures of the Bikaner School, are also on view.

Ganga Singh commissioned Swinton Jacob to design a new residence for him, which would be named **Lalgarh Palace** in honour of his father, Lal Singh. It lies to the north of Junagarh Fort, and is now operated by the Wellcome Group as Bikaner's highest grade hotel. Built entirely of red sandstone, the palace owes less to European styles than the same architect's other buildings in India. Ganga Singh was able to move to his new palace in 1902, but further stages took another quarter of a century to complete. As with most palace hotels, original furnishings add greatly to the appeal. Lord Mountbatten visited Lalgarh Palace in 1948, shortly before his return to England.

In 1976, part of the building was opened as the **Shri Sadul Museum**, commemorating the son of Ganga Singh, who died in 1950. Personal memorabilia of Bikaner's maharajas is displayed. The **Shiv Bilas** dining room, which seats 400, and the extensive grounds, in which peacocks are as numerous as sparrows on an English lawn, are worth visiting for a 'Last days of the Raj' atmosphere. However, take care at dusk, as the Lalgarh Palace Hotel's grounds seem to be where Rajasthan's mosquitoes go to in the winter time.

Cenotaphs of the maharajas of Bikaner, in the form of *chattris*, are grouped together in a walled enclosure above **Devi Kund Sagar**, a peaceful man-made lake, 5 miles (8km) east of the city on the main road to Jaipur: private transport is recommended. Some *chattris* are of red sandstone, but the most impressive are carved from marble, including the finest, which commemorates Surat Singh. The oldest cenotaph is that of Rao Kalyan, 1572. Sadal Singh's, the most recent, was constructed in 1950 and will be the last, as the enclosure is now full. A lotus flower denotes that the *chattri* commemorates a female, a sun denotes a male.

Located 6 miles (10km) south-east of Bikaner, near Shev Bur (private transport again advisable), the **Camel Breeding Station** accepts visitors every afternoon apart from Sundays. It is the head-quarters of India's National Camel Research Station, and each of the country's five distinct breeds are represented. Most important are the Bikaneri variety, renowned as a beast of burden, and the Jaisalmeri, faster and more suited to long-distance work. In truth, visitors are not particularly well catered for, and the lasting memory is likely to be of great numbers of camels disappointingly doing nothing in particular, which is mitigated by the tremendous appeal of the baby camels, often only a few hours old. Camel attendants all come from a caste known as Raika, and will tell visitors that the average life of a camel in Rajasthan is 26 years. Females first conceive at 5 years old, and the young are born after a 13-month pregnancy, perfectly formed. During World War I, the Ganga Risilla Camel Corps, comprising Bikaneri camels, served on behalf of the British Empire in Egypt.

From the Lalgarh Palace Hotel, accommodation may be booked at **Gajner Palace Hotel**, sited beside Gajner Lake, and formerly the summer palace of the Bikaner maharajas. It is located 20 miles (32km) west of Bikaner on the Jaisalmer road. There is a wildlife sanctuary (no big cats), which is never crowded, due to strict restrictions on numbers. **Gajner Lake's** birdlife is plentiful, but once, in a single day, it witnessed the slaughter of several thousand sand grouse; their descendants have apparently forgotten the event and once more migrate here from Siberia every winter.

Royal cenotaphs of Bikaner's maharajas at Devi Kund

Rat Temple

Those who are repulsed by rats will presumably give the rat temple of Karni Matra at **Deshnok** a miss, but others will be enthralled by the sheer numbers of rodents, bringing the legend of medieval Hamlin to life. Deshnok is 20 miles (33km) south of Bikaner, and regular buses from the bus station make the journey in around three quarters of an hour. Do not arrive before the temple opens at 5pm, and establish bus return times to Bikaner in advance as, once the temple has been visited, there is nothing else to see in the village. Also take a pair of thick socks that can be discarded afterwards.

Karni Matra, a member of the Charan minstrel caste, was believed to be, in her own lifetime, an incarnation of the goddess Durga, the fearsome aspect of Shiva's consort, Parvati. By tradition, Yana, the god responsible for dead souls, proved unable to restore to life a young male relative of Karni, and, in high dudgeon she decreed that henceforth all members of her caste would be reincarnated as rats, outside Yana's jurisdiction. Members of the Charan caste therefore built this temple as a refuge for the rodents.

It now seems probable that the first temple was built here in the second quarter of the sixteenth century, but the structure has since been replaced in enlarged form. A tradition that Karni Matra blessed Rao Singh immediately prior to his victory at Bikaner in 1472 led to the patronage of the temple by the maharajas; the silver doors to the entrance were the gift of Ganga Singh. All shoes and leather items must be deposited at the entrance; socks, however, appear to be permitted, a great boon, as the area is liberally covered with rat droppings, which squeamish tourists would not find entirely welcome between their bare toes — hence the reason why disposable socks should be worn.

Rats skuffle all around, but they are not in the least frightened of humans, and certainly do not bite. Their 'rat radar' also seems to be excellent as, in spite of their speed and jerky changes of direction, they unerringly manage to avoid human feet. Netting is draped above the courtyard to protect the rats from birds of prey. In the centre, they are served grain, while sweetmeats and milk are provided on either side for the dessert course. It can be seen that rat holes have been drilled in the temple's sandstone walls to encourage their occupancy. Non-worshippers are not permitted to pass the silver doors of the sanctuary, one panel of which depicts, in bas-relief, Karni Matra. The figure of the goddess within can be glimpsed; it is of gold sandstone from Jaisalmer, which has acquired an orange hue. As might be expected, the gathering together of such a quantity of rats does create a powerful odour, and few strangers will wish to linger for long.

Tourists of a hardy nature and with sufficient time at their disposal may now brace themselves for the rigours of proceeding south-westward to **Jaisalmer**, possibly the most beguiling of all Rajasthan's cities. Like Bikaner, Jaisalmer has an airport, but it is only for military use; the railway line runs eastward from Jaisalmer to Jodhpur, not Bikaner. One must, therefore, take either the day bus or the night bus from Bikaner to Jaisalmer, or else make an angular train journey, from Bikaner to Jodhpur as the first stage and Jodhpur to Jaisalmer as the second. However, this is not as bad as it sounds, as most will wish to see Jodhpur in any case, and a few days can split up the journey. Night trains are recommended for both stages. If the direct bus trip is made from Bikaner to Jaisalmer, the night 'Express' bus is somewhat faster, but forget any chance of sleep: internal lights flash off and on, the seats (if one is available) are hard, and the driver's youthful friends are convinced that passengers wish to hear Rajasthan folk music crackling full blast on a worn-out tape at 3am.

If travelling by bus between Bikaner and Jaisalmer, or by bus or train between Jodhpur and Jaisalmer, always take warm clothing for night journeys in the winter, as the temperatures regularly fall below zero, and neither heating nor blankets are automatically supplied. There are rumours that blankets can be provided, but only if they are booked at the same time as the sleeping compartment reservation is made. Good luck! The ancient trains currently plying between Jaisalmer and Jodhpur on metre-gauge track are, therefore, a refrigerated nightmare. Even when laying of the standard-gauge track has been completed no heating or bed-clothes are expected. As has been said earlier, the Bikaner/Jodhpur trains are comfortable and adequetly heated.

Additional Information

Places to Visit in and around Bikaner

Junagarh Fort
Open: Thurs to Tues 9.30am-5pm.

Shri Sadul Museum
Lalgarh Palace Hotel
Open: Thurs to Tues 10am-5pm.

Ganga Golden Jubilee Museum
Open: Sat to Thurs 10am-5pm.

Camel Breeding Station
Near Shev Bur
Open: Mon to Sat 2-5pm.

Accommodation

Lalgarh Palace Hotel
☎ 312
Dhola-Maru Tourist Bungalow
Pooran Singh Circle

Eating Out

Amber Restaurant
Station Road

Tourist Information Office

Junagarh Fort
☎ 5445

Jaisalmer & Its Environs

5

✳ JAISALMER

Jaisalmer (pronounced Jezel-meer), located in the middle of an inhospitable desert, is a long way from anywhere, and on route to nowhere apart from the Pakistan border, which is closed; it does not even possess architectural wonders of outstanding importance. Why then do all those who have been there insist 'you must get to Jaisalmer'? Primarily, it is a question of uniqueness: everything is built of gold sandstone, the walled hilltop fort encompasses the entire medieval town, not just royal buildings as elsewhere, and the exquisitely carved havelis are the most stunning in India. In addition, the atmosphere is extremely laid back and hassle-free in a way reminiscent of Pushkar. All tourists are made welcome, no matter how young or impecunious, and western standards of quality and service are approached in the delightful rooftop restaurants.

Jaisalmer is not large, and unaccompanied wanders through its streets, the best way of seeing the town, will take in the main sights

preceding page; Chattri *cenotaphs, and pedalos, at Gadi Sagar, Jaisalmer*

in a short time, without the need for laboriously studying plans or itineraries. Only from Jaisalmer is it possible in India to visit extensive Sahara-style sand dunes — camels and all (see the photograph on page 246).

Jaisalmer owes its fame as a tourist attraction to two factors: Prime Minister Indira Gandhi fell in love with the town and, following her visit in 1975, instigated its restoration and conservation; Jaisalmer was the final destination on the itinerary of the luxury railway carriages of The Palace on Wheels, which enabled wealthy tourists to make a 'whistle-stop' tour of Rajasthan in comfort. Tourists in Jaisalmer now tend to be those with plenty of time to spare, mostly youngsters and those on escorted tours of Rajasthan, the luxury coaches of the latter overcoming the rigours of public transport.

🏰 Jaisalmer Fort

Jaisalmer's fort, unlike Bikaner's, is picturesquely sited on steep-sided raised ground, daring any invader to come and have a go. In more pacific times the town's inhabitants left the protection of the fort's defences and built houses at the foot of the hill; a new wall eventually encircled the entire settlement. Most visitors, no matter where they are lodging in Jaisalmer, find the hilltop fort irresistible, and make their first ascent soon after arriving. An early morning start is recommended, as the Jain temples within the fort close at 12.30pm, and a unique library admits no visitors after 11am. It may, of course, be more convenient to make a separate visit specifically to see these.

Access to the fort is from **Manak Chowk**, the street which skirts the north side of its hill. Brilliantly attired ladies sell fruit and vegetables, and the thoroughfare has the appearance of a market. Formerly, it was a centre for the distribution of grain, some of which came from as far away as Egypt. For protection, merchants and their goods travelled here on camels, in groups known as caravans. Not only grain passed through Jaisalmer, which lay on the 'silk route', but also opium, ivory, coconuts, sandalwood, iron, dried fruits and, of course, silk. Immense wealth was acquired by the maharawals of Jaisalmer from transit duties levied on the goods that passed through the town. All this came to an end in the nineteenth century, with the opening up of the port of Bombay by the British; traders with India from the west now turned their backs on the dangerous, and slower, land routes.

Evoking a barnacled Noah's Ark stranded on Mount Ararat after the Flood, Jaisalmer's fort, founded by Maharawal Jaisal in 1156, occupies the triangular hilltop of Tricuta (three peaks), to the south-west of the town. Three walls buttress the escarpment, the lower wall, known as Patha, being constructed in the fifteenth century, and the second wall in 1578. Jaisal had ruled the nearby city of Lodurva, but decided to move here, with his subjects, as the steep-sided hill would be easier to defend. By tradition, a hermit advised Jaisal that Lord Krishna had prophesied the construction of a city and fortress on the site. The Moguls considered Jaisalmer to be of strategic importance and their emperors had to approve the appointment of its maharawals.

Much of the original twelfth-century wall of the fort has survived, but almost all its bastion towers, each with a cannon platform, are mid-seventeenth-century additions. The first of the fort's gates, **Akhai Prol**, was erected in the eighteenth century by Akhai Singh, and followed by three further gates, all built between 1577 and 1623: the **Suraj Prol**, **Bhuta Prol** (or Ganesh Prol) and **Hawa Prol**. Pictur-esquely rising above the Hawa Prol is part of the royal palace complex; *Jarokhas* and *jali* screens add delicate touches to the massive structure.

Immediately entered is the square facing the palace buildings, which will be returned to later. Cross to the south side of the square opposite, turn right and proceed ahead to the famous complex of **Jain Temples**, Jaisalmer's most important buildings, which straddle the thoroughfare. As at Bikaner and Mount Abu, Jains congregated here due to the isolated location, which gave them protection from the intolerance of orthodox Hindus. Additionally, in the case of Jaisalmer, however, resettlement was encouraged in the fifteenth century by the ruler, Maharawal Chachakdeo, who abducted Jain leaders and incarcerated them until they agreed to move their families to the town. Most temples close at 12.30pm, and no footwear or leather goods are permitted within.

First seen, on the left, is the **Chanda Prabhu Swami Temple**, built in 1509 and exhilarating profuse, intricate carving; more than 1,600 separate figures have been counted. It is permitted to ascend to the roof, from where the surrounding sikhara towers rising above the sanctuaries, may be admired.

On the opposite side of the alleyway is the **Rishabh Dev Temple**, built in 1636. Splendid carvings of *apsaras* (females who inhabit paradise) on the columns of the *mandapa* hall should be noted. Unusually for a Jain temple, there is no ceiling.

Temples to **Kuntha Nath** and, above it, **Santi Nath**, which follow, were built in 1536; the carving of the roof is particularly fine. Jaisalmer's most important group of temples, which should not be missed, is seen next, on the left side; incorporated is the Gyan Bhandar library, only open 10am to 11am. A magnificent *torana*

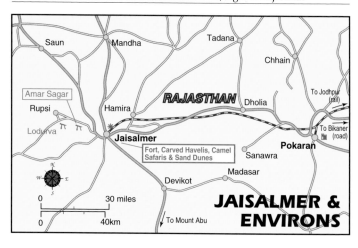

Saun
Mandha
Tadana
Chhain

RAJASTHAN
Dholia
To Jodhpur (rail)

Amar Sagar
Rupsi
Hamira

Lodurva
Jaisalmer
Fort, Carved Havelis, Camel Safaris & Sand Dunes
Sanawra
To Bikaner (road)
Pokaran

Madasar
Devikot

0   30 miles
0   40km
To Mount Abu

JAISALMER & ENVIRONS

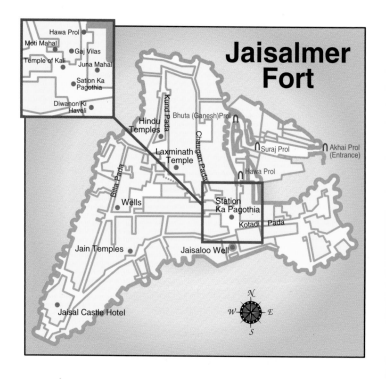

Hawa Prol
Moti Mahal
Gaj Vilas
Temple of Kali
Juna Mahal
Sation Ka Pagothia
Diwanon Ki Haveli

Hawa Prol
Kund Pada
Bhuta (Ganesh)Prol
Hindu Temples
Chaugan Pada
Suraj Prol
Akhai Prol (Entrance)
Laxminath Temple
Hawa Prol
Bilta Pada
Wells
Station Ka Pagothia
Kotadi Pada
Jain Temples
Jaisaloo Well

Jaisal Castle Hotel

Jaisalmer Fort

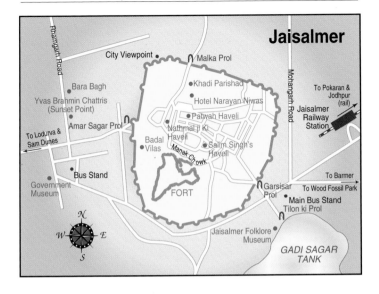

Jaisalmer Fort looms over the eighteenth-century extension to the town like a barnacled Noah's Ark

archway forms the entrance. In the centre of the complex is the Chintamani Parshvanath Temple and, to its left, the Sambhava Nath Temple, both built in the 1470s. Added later, to the right, in 1497, is the Shital Nath Temple. At the time of writing, photographs of the temples were not permitted but, for a fee, photography of the library's exhibits was allowed. Such rulings appear flexible and may change.

The **Chintamani Parshvanath Temple** is undoubtedly the finest of all; its carvings include a multitude of figures, the most impressive being the bas-relief dancing girls in varied poses, some of them naked. It is said that the main figure of Chintamani Parshvanath, of clay inset with pearls, was made in 55BC, and brought from Lodurva. Only slightly less exuberant is the **Sambhava Nath Temple**, with more female dancers, this time accompanied by just one, fortunate, male instrumentalist.

Beneath the **Shital Nath Temple** is located the **Gyan Bhandar Library**, one of three established by Jin Bhadra Suri in 1500; the others, at Jalore and Nagaur, were destroyed by Muslims. The library does not deal exclusively with religious matters, art, history and astrology also being covered. Some of the manuscripts, dating from the eleventh century, are written on dried palm leaves and blocks of wood; paintings are also exhibited. It is not possible to enter the library itself, which is kept locked, unless an appointment for research purposes has been made; the exhibits are displayed in cases outside. Kept within the library for security is a large emerald, carved to represent Sambhava, the third tirthankara; it originally occupied the most prominent postion in the sanctuary of the Shital Vath Temple above.

The lane continues, following the wall, to the **Jaisal Castle Hotel**, in the south-west corner of the fort. This has twelve letting rooms, each with private facilities, and retains a great deal of character; the views are naturally splendid. The hotel's only drawback is that it is somewhat distant from Jaisalmer's tourist restaurants. The thoroughfare now swings northward and soon leads to two of the fort's three wells, the **Jaislu** and **Ranisar**; the former is reputed never to have dried up, even after the long drought of the 1980s.

Further ahead lies a group of minor **Hindu temples**, but more interesting is the **Laxminath Temple**, a short distance to the south. This was built in 1494 and incorporates ninth-century columns retrieved from a disused temple in Lodurva.

The square fronting the royal palace buildings, seen earlier on entering the old town, is now reached; it is called **Sation Ka Pagothia**. In this square, johar took place two and a half times. Johar was the custom by which, rather than face rape or slavery, Rajput women and their children, were immolated by fire, in the manner of sati. The women were dressed in their bridal gowns, and are said, as they stood on the pyres, to have shown neither fear nor pain: no doubt they were heavily drugged with opium. Their menfolk, also wearing wedding robes, and certainly drugged, rushed out of the gate fighting valiantly until struck down. Full johar took place here in 1315, prior to defeat by the Muslim forces of Ala-ud-din-Khalji and again, 10 years later, by those of Ghiyas-ud-din-Tughlaq. In the sixteenth century, Maharawal Loon Karan was tricked into allowing soldiers of Amir Ali, a supposed friend, into the fort dressed as women; interestingly, they were called 'doli' men. When fighting began, Loon Karan panicked and, unnecessarily as it transpired, put the women and children to death by the sword, there being no time to prepare fires: as the rules of johar had not been strictly observed, the event is referred to as half johar (*sako*).

Stability arrived when the ruling Bhati family became vassals of the Moguls and, partly due to Jaisalmer's isolated position, no more battles were fought in the town, the British taking over as its 'protector' in 1818. Although Jaisalmer's fort is Rajasthan's second oldest (Chittaurgarh predates it by at least 400 years), the royal palaces within have been rebuilt from time to time, and were not evacuated by the maharawals until the late nineteenth century.

The **Jaisaloo Well**, now covered, which supplied the palace with drinking water, stands to the south of the square. Looking to the north from this point, from right to left, are the **Juna Mahal** (built around 1500), right of the gateway, now abandoned and in disrepair; **Gaj Vilas**, immediately left of the gateway, and **Moti Mahal** (Pearl Palace), of 1813, further to the west and now accommodating a school. The free-standing building in the foreground is the royal **Temple of Kali**.

Gaj Vilas was built around 1844, and is open to visitors; there is, however, very little of interest within.

Most havelis of importance lie in the town below the fort, but the **Diwanon Ki haveli**, immediately in front of the wall, is worth noting. It is typical of Jaisalmer that the ground floor, generally used for storage, is undecorated, intricate carving being reserved for the residential storeys. The area within the fort wall is not large, and many will also wish to stoll around its intimate lanes in the northern and eastern extremities.

A tour of the 'new' town generally follows, once the fort above it has been explored. This was laid out in the eighteenth century, during the reign of Akhai Singh (1722-62), and its streets basically follow a grid pattern. A 3 miles (5km) long wall was constructed around Jaisalmer by Muiraj II (1762-1820); the most important of its original six gates are located to the north, east and west: **Malka Prol**, **Garsisar Prol** and **Amar Sagar Prol** respectively. Thanks to tourism, the main streets are now in a reasonable state of maintenance, their havelis occupied and commercial premises thriving. Once these are left, however, much remains dilapidated, the delicately carved buildings apparently uninhabited apart from cows, goats and pigs, all of which are so numerous in Jaisalmer that the impression is given of a vast farmyard, surrounded by palaces rather than barns. Some of Jaisalmer's animals apparently have a mean streak. 'Please paying attention, sir, he very naughty cow', warned one solicitous owner, pointing out the bovine rogue as his herd ambled past, through an alarmingly narrow lane.

The town's wealth reached its zenith in the nineteenth century, and it was then that the splendid havelis of the merchants were built; stylistically, little had changed since Jaisalmer's foundation 800 years earlier, and the craftsmanship remained superb. Jaisalmer's merchants migrated to the new sea ports from the mid-nineteenth century and, at the same time, the Brahmins, who were persecuted by the state's chief minister, Salim Singh, left for other states: the city's population fell from 35,000 to 4,000 and most of the havelis were deserted. In spite of the coming of the railway to Jaisalmer in 1948, the town continued to decline, and its fate appeared to be sealed when trade routes via Pakistan were severed in 1950, following Jaisalmer State's acquisition by India; the consequent movement of the city's Muslims to Pakistan added to the desolation.

An unexpected lifeline was thrown to Jaisalmer by the Indo/Pakistan wars of 1965 and 1971, as it immediately became a strategically important military base. Shortly afterwards, following discovery of oil reserves in Rajasthan, an administrative centre for the Oil and Natural Gas Commission was established in the city. The development of tourism, which began in the 1980s, proceeded apace and is now the city's most important industry. Jaisalmer's population is once more estimated to be in excess of 30,000, and the laying of the broad-gauge railway track to Jodhpur in place of the metre gauge will undoubtedly increase the potential of this remote city. Geographical difficulties, which would be expensive to overcome, appear to prohibit a direct rail link with Bikaner for many years, and there is, as yet, no sign of Jaisalmer's small airport being reopened for civil flights.

Salim Singh's haveli, in the southern part of Jaisalmer, is situated near the approach road to the fort. It was probably built for Swaroop Singh, a member of the wealthy Mehta family, in 1815, but alternative suggestions of earlier and later dates have also been made. Swaroop, the chief minister of Maharawal Mool Raj II, excercised almost complete power over the state as the maharawals were heavily in debt to him. A member of the royal family assassinated the overbearing Swaroop in 1824, but when his young son Salim Singh came of age, Mool Raj appointed him to succeed his father as chief minister. A tyrannical rule followed, the citizens being taxed by Salim at a burdensome rate. In 1880, Salim Singh, like his father, was assassinated.

The six-storey building still towers above this part of the town, but originally it is said to have possessed a further two storeys, built of timber and known, respectively, as the Rang Mahal and Kach Mahal. Allegedly, these were demolished by order of Maharawal Gaj Singh (ruled 1820-46) but, in view of his indebtedness to Salim Singh, this hardly seems likely. As is frequently the case in Jaisalmer, only the upper part of the haveli is profusely carved. This overhanging storey is sometimes referred to as the Jahaz Numa (Hanging Apartment), or the Moti Mahal (Pearl Palace). No doubt, Salim Singh would sit within the arcades at sundown during the stifling summers, to take advantage of any evening breezes. Those who have visited the Gothic Quarter of Barcelona may recall a similar rooftop feature. It is sometimes possible, with a little persuasion, to ascend to the top floor of the restaurant opposite for a closer view.

The **Nathmal ji Ki haveli** lies to the west, in the direction of the Amar Sagar Gate. This was completed in 1885 for Salim Singh's successor as chief minister, Nathmal, another member of the Mehta family, and an inscription on a stone tablet records that the haveli was presented to him by Maharawal Beri Sal Singh. It is alleged that Salim Singh had seriously considered connecting his haveli directly with the fort by means of a bridge, and perhaps the Maharawal felt that this unwelcome proposal would be finally quashed by providing his new chief minister with another haveli.

The building was completed in 1885 by two famous stone carver brothers, Laloo and Hathi. Laloo was responsible for the left hand side (facing the house) and Hathi for the other, which is why they do not match up. Unusually in Jaisalmer, every storey is exuberantly carved, the balconied *jarokhas* being particularly outstanding. Most of Jaisalmer's best carving, including that of this haveli, is the work of Muslims who, it is apparent, adopted Hindu rather than Muslim styles. When the Muslims vacated the city for Pakistan at partition, they included most of the finest carvers (*silavatas*), and the few Hindu craftsmen left had to take on responsibility for the vast amount of restoration work that had become necessary in Jaisalmer.

Uniquely in Rajasthan, photographs of the building's two carvers, Laloo and Hathi, are displayed in the haveli; they are now somewhat faded but can be seen in the left spandrel of a window. The haveli's courtyard can be entered, as may the first storey room, once the dance hall but now a souvenir shop. Displayed in the shop is a hand-coloured photograph of Maharawal Beri Sal Singh, who commissioned the house. An assistant may well be prevailed upon to show other parts of the building. Before leaving, note that as in the murals of Shekhavati's havelis, which are contemporary with this house, European introductions such as steam trains and bicycles are depicted in the carving.

Not far away, slightly to the north-east, is the **Patwah haveli**, a great mansion divided vertically for the five sons of Guman Chand, a wealthy brocade (*patwah*) merchant, in the first half of the nineteenth century. All the sons prospered, mostly in other Rajput areas, and only one, Pratap Chand, stayed in Jaisalmer. One wonders if, eventually, he had the run of the entire building. Numbers three and five are now owned by the Rajasthan State, and may be entered. Sixty-six projecting *jarokhas*, profusely carved and surrounded by *jali* screens, are the glory of this haveli. Views through the archway further up the street are extremely picturesque and much photographed. A further vantage point is directly opposite the haveli, where properties of no architectural interest were demolished by order of Mrs Gandhi, so that the façade of the Patwah haveli might be examined more easily: the owners received compensation. As usual, ground floors were used exclusively for storage, residential areas being located high above as a protection from the street's dust and sand, still a problem in Jaisalmer when a hot blast of wind hits the city in summer. Both houses may be ascended to roof level, passing through the souvenir shops. Some mural fragments have survived, and many of the rooms form a museum of local art.

North of this haveli is **Hotel Narayan Niwas**, central Jaisalmer's most prestigious hotel — Princess Anne stayed here on one occasion. Bedrooms are designed to exclude the burning sun, and some find them rather claustrophobic.

A return south-westward, passing the cinema, leads to the Amar Sagar Prol. South of this rises the lofty tower of **Badal Vilas**. The palace was built by Shi'ite Muslims, and presented, in thanks for his protection, to Maharawal Bairisal, who vacated the fort and adopted it as his official residence around 1880. Its delicate tower represents the bamboo tazlas constructed by Shi'ites as a sign of reverence for Hasan and Huseyn bin Ali, whom they believe should have inherited the caliphate, rather than the Ummayads. As the descendants of Bairisal still live here the building is not open to the public.

The royal cenotaphs are grouped above a dammed lake at **Bara Bagh** (Great Garden), approximately 4 miles (6km) north-west of Jaisalmer, and transport will be needed. Jait Singh began the complex of *chattris* around 1585, to commemorate the cremation here of the maharawals of Jaisalmer and their families; the oldest date from the sixteenth century, the most recent being that of Jawahar Singh, who died after India's partition. While the latter was under construction, Girdhar Singh, Jawahar's son, died; this was regarded as a bad omen, and the *chattris* were never completed. Within the *chattris*, the maharawals are depicted on horseback, while their maharanis stand, usually separately. If both are shown together it indicates that the maharani committed sati on her husband's funeral pyre. Some favoured concubines are also represented. The importance of the person commemorated is indicated by the size of the *chattri*; those of the maharawals are therefore the largest. The lake is effectively an oasis and much of the city's vegetable produce is grown here. There are even mango trees, a rare sight in the Thar Desert.

On returning to Jaisalmer, a stop should be made at the **Yvas Brahmin Chattris**, primarily for the view from them of the city at sunset. This is one of two 'sunset points', the other being from raised ground just outside the north-west corner of the wall, which gives a closer view but includes no desert. As the sun sets, the walls of Jaisalmer shimmer like a crown of gold at melting point. Although Jodhpur's fort is significantly higher, it is not so isolated, and therefore does not have the same 'desert mirage' appeal. The walled city of Carcassone in south-west France is the nearest European equivalent.

Amar Sagar

A brief stop on the way to Lodurva should be made at Amar Sagar, a water tank and garden built for Amar Singh in 1740; the water usually dries up in the early summer. Three Jain temples have been erected, the most recent, and finest, being to Adeshwar Nath, in 1928. The usual high standard of craftsmanship indicates that twentieth-century carvers have lost little of their ancestors' great skill. Few tourists visit Amar Sagar, and lone visitors will usually have the entire complex to themselves. Nearby, work is continuing, laboriously, on a new Jain temple of Parshvanath. Construction will not be completed for many years, and visitors can observe the age-old craftsmanship still being exhibited. Few carvers, however, appear to be local, most coming from the Udaipur region.

Lodurva

The remains of Lodurva are 5 miles (8km) further north. Like Pompeii, most of this ancient city lies below ground, but it is covered by drifting sand and stones rather than lava; very little has been excavated. Lodurva, a walled city with twelve gates, fell to Deoraj, a Bhatti Rajput, who, in 853, had founded Deorawal, the first capital of

Desert Excursions from Jaisalmer

India's Sahara, camels and all, at Sam Dunes in the Thar Desert, near Jaisalmer

Safaris into the Thar Desert are popular excursions from Jaisalmer, and may be booked through hotels or direct from one of the many tourist agencies. It is best to shop around, paying particular attention to precisely what is included. The Hotel Narayan Niwas has had long experience in arranging these trips and still represents the top end of the market. Most tours are based on groups, although individual arrangements, at a price, can be made. It is essential that blankets, food and drink are supplied by the operator, and warm clothing must be taken, as the desert nights are very cold in winter. Lengths of safaris vary from half a day to eleven days (all the way to Bikaner), but the most popular long trip is the four-day circular tour around Jaisalmer by camel. It must be said, however, that those who are not used to camels may become acutely saddle sore, and some protection for the thighs is advisable — ask for a spare pillow or cushion at the hotel. For those who prefer not to emulate Lawrence of Arabia, four-wheel drive vehicles are provided for the shorter trips. Overnight camping in the sand dunes, under the most brilliant of starry skies, can be very romantic. A tip for first-time camel riders is that, on rising, the camel will throw its passenger backward; on kneeling down, forward. Hold tight and adjust your balance accordingly.

Obviously, those on escorted tours will not be able to take advantage of the longer safaris, and the elderly would find them too uncomfortable; most participants, therefore, tend to be young and have plenty of time available. However, if a half-day 'sunset' trip by jeep to Sam Dunes is taken, the most exciting part of the safari will be seen in any case. The Thar Desert, unlike the Sahara, has only limited areas of silky smooth sand dunes, the nearest to Jaisalmer being just south of Sam village, 27 miles (44km) distant. Another good stretch exists north of Ramgarh, but this area is out of bounds to all but the military, due to its proximity to the Pakistan border. On arriving at Sam, tourists are met by camelmen and given (usually included in the tour price) a short ride across extensive dunes; a small additional payment will encourage the driver to get away from the rather crowded standard route. Sunset is the most popular time for a visit, as then the sinuous shapes of the dunes throw deeper shadows, and take on a richer hue. Surprisingly, there is an abundance of wildlife in the Thar Desert, but almost all the animals are nocturnal. Most spectacular is the Great Indian Bustard, a bird that was, until recently, on the verge of extinction but now numbers 1,000.

On the way to the dunes, a stop is generally made at a small settlement, to view life in a typical Jaisalmer village. Some villagers have purchased a solar energy panel (there being no electricity), which they usually connect to the solitary street lamp. Another stop may be made on route at **Mool Sagar**, 6 miles (9km) from Jaisalmer, where a small royal palace is set in a garden with a water tank; it was laid out for Maharawal Mool Raj II in 1815.

A villager's home in the Thar (Great Indian) Desert

the Indian desert region. Lodurva stood on the River Kak, which has now dried up due to the encroachment of the desert sands. Majez Khan destroyed the city in 1103 but he was subsequently killed by Jaisal in a desert battle. It is not clear how much time Jaisal spent in the ruined city of Lodurva, but presumably he rebuilt part of it, as his move to Jaisalmer did not take place until 1156.

Still in perfect condition, the Jain temple of Parshvanath is a seventeenth-century replacement of a much earlier building, probably destroyed by Majez Khan. The fortified wall that protects the temple area was needed due to the hostility shown towards Jains by both Muslims and orthodx Hindus. Subsidiary temples in the four corners were built in 1618 and form the oldest part of the complex. The serpentine *torana* arch at the entrance is one of the finest examples in India. Formerly, a sacred tree of 'enlightenment' is said to have grown within the compound, which was symbolically replaced by the present metal version. Allegedly, a black cobra has lived within the wall of the temple since it was rebuilt, and a sighting of the snake on one of its rare appearances is considered to be an omen of good fortune.

A palace known as **Moomal Ki Meri** stood on the banks of the River Kak, but only its ruins survive. By tradition, Moomal was a beautiful princess, whose lover, Mahendra, discovered her with her sister, disguised as a minstrel (for the usual complicated reasons). Believing that Moomal had been unfaithful to him, Mahendra abandoned her with great sorrow. Eventually, on reuniting, the passionate excitement appears to have been too much for the lovers, and they expired in each others arms.

Excavations will continue in Lodurva, and some further discoveries of importance are expected.

❋ Gadi Sagar

Jaisalmer's water supply once depended on the Gadi Sagar (or Gadsisar, or Garsisar) Reservoir, excavated by Maharawal Garsisar in 1367. It lies a short distance south-east of the Gadsisar Gate, and is picturesquely surrounded by Hindu temples and *chattri* cenotaphs. The complex is entered through an imposing arched gateway, known as **Teelon Ki Pol**. Teelon, a devoutly religious Hindu lady, was born in Jaisalmer, but moved to Hyderabad (now in south Pakistan), where she made a fortune as a courtesan. Every year, in the wet season, she returned to her birthplace, and decided to construct, at her own expense, a splendid entrance to the tank. It is said that the Maharawal refused to permit this, as he objected to passing through a gateway paid for by a prostitute. However, it was erected during one of his many absences from Jaisalmer. On the return of the Maharawal the gateway's destruction was ordered but, on the advice of Hindu priests, Teelon speedily added a Krishna temple to the superstructure, which ensured that it could not be demolished. It is possible to hire pedalos from the tank's steps. Forming part of the complex is the **Jaisalmer Folklore Museum**.

Further south-eastward, at Akal village, 9 miles (14km) from Jaisalmer, just off the road to Barmer, is Jaisalmer's own 'Jurassic Park', where fossilized trunks of great trees from the Jurassic period, estimated at 175 million years old, have been proclaimed a conservation area. If driving directly from Jaisalmer to Mount Abu, the Fossil Park may be seen on route.

Although Jaisalmer lacks five-star accommodation, there is a fairly wide choice of hotels below this grade, the modern **Jawahar Niwas Palace**, outside the town, offering the best rooms. This is followed, as already mentioned, by the **Narayan Niwas** and **Jaisal Castle**; another recommended upper-grade hotel is the centrally located **Hotel Sona**. Most of Jaisalmer's establishments are budget grade, like the friendly **Hotel Jaisal Palace** (not as grand as its name), and appear to be run entirely by amusingly cheeky teenage boys. Those who have endured the excessive politeness of obsequious hotel staff in the grander establishments will find the change refreshing.

Restaurants abound, and the standard is surprisingly high. Extremely popular are the **Trio**, **Sky Room** (exceptional tandooris) and **Natraj**. Those who have become addicted to the vegetarian *marsala dosas* will find them at the cinema's restaurant, the only South Indian food outlet in the town.

Since 1979, a three-day **Desert Festival** has been held annually at Jaisalmer, generally in February but occasionally in late January, depending on the full moon. Hotels are always full at this time, and a complex of tented accommodation is set up by the Rajasthan Tourism Development Corporation. The festival has no historic basis, and primarily exists to entertain tourists; in consequence, some may find the regional dancing, camel polo matches, camel racing and turban tying competitions a little too commercial for their taste. The Son et Lumière display at Sam Dunes, beneath a full moon, is the festival's highlight.

Most holidaymakers continue their tour of Rajasthan from Jaisalmer by taking the bus or train to Jodhpur. Mention has already been made of the 'ice box' quality of the night train. There is also a day train, but the journey is rather tedious. The bus journey should take no longer than 5 hours, generally somewhat quicker than the trains.

Pokaran   ❋

Some may wish to make a halt, after 2 hours on route by bus or train to Jodhpur, at Pokaran. Like Jaisalmer, **Pokaran Fort** is constructed of gold sandstone; it is set on raised ground, and the streets and houses of the town's inhabitants are protected by its walls. Founded towards the end of the sixteenth century, the fort contains a temple, but its most attractive feature is the upper storey **Phul Niwas** (Flower Pavilion), *jali* screens denoting that the ladies of the palace resided within. Overnight accommodation is available at the **Dak Bungalow**, but most will wish to continue to Jodhpur (or Bikaner).

Additional Information

Places to Visit in Jaisalmer

Gaj Vilas (palace)
Open: 10am-5pm.

Gyan Bhandar Library
Open: 10-11am.

Jain Temples
Close: at 12.30pm.

Jaisalmer Folklore Museum
Open: 9am-12noon and 3-6pm.

Patwah Haveli
Open: 10am-5pm.

Desert Festival Dates:
1995, 13-15 February; 1996, 2-4 February; 1997, 20-22 February; 1998, 9-11 February; 1999, 29-31 January; 2000, 17-19 February.

Accommodation

Jaisal Castle Hotel
☎ 2362

Narayan Niwas Hotel
Malka Pole
☎ 2408

Jawahar Niwas Palace Hotel
Amar Sagar Road
☎ 2206

Hotel Sona
Gajroop Sagar Road
☎ 2732

Eating Out

Moti Mahal Restaurant
Faces Salim Singh Haveli

Sky Room Restaurant
Nachna Haveli

The Trio Restaurant
Gandhi Chowk

Natraj
near Salim Singh's Haveli

Tourist Office

Moomal Tourist Bungalow
☎ 2406

JODHPUR & ENVIRONS

To Bikaner (rail)
Bara Bara
Osiyan
Danwara
Baonri
Umednagar
Meherangarh Fort/
Palaces, Blue City &
Umaid Bhavan Palace
Ancient Temple
Complex
To Jaipur
(rail)
Mandore
JODHPUR
Jhanwar
To Jaipur
(rail)
Ancient Capital,
Ruins of Palaces
& Temples
To Udaipur (rail)
Kankani
Bhetanda

0   20 miles
0   40km

Jodhpur & Its Environs

6

✳ JODHPUR

Jodhpur is visited primarily for its great fort, one of Rajasthan's finest, perched on a cliff face 393ft (120m) above the surrounding plain, a height only exceeded in the state by Chittaurgarh Fort's 500ft (152m). The walled city itself, however, is one of India's most attractive, its blue-painted, cubist-style houses clustered below the fort being reminiscent of Greece. Once the fort and its palaces have been seen, however, there are few other 'sights' of major importance, and most will find that two full days in Jodhpur will suffice. It has already been noted that Jaipur is a more convenient base from which to visit Ajmer and Pushkar, which lie almost equidistant between the two cities.

As at Amber, the maharajas of Jodhpur, bearing the family name of Rathore, claim legendary descent from Rama, the seventh avatar (incarnation) of Lord Vishnu. They ruled from Kanauj, in the state of Uttar Pradesh, from 470 until defeated by Muhammad Ghuri's

preceding page; A triumph of bougainvillea in the grounds of the Umaid Bhavan Palace Hotel. In the background rises the omnipresent bulk of Jodhpur's Meherangarh Fort

Muslim Afghans in 1194. Two itinerant centuries followed before the Rathores captured Mandore in 1453 but within 6 years, Rao Jodha, then still a teenager, decided to build a new fort on the more easily defended 'Bird's Nest' outcrop 5 miles (8km) to the south. Allegedly, a hermit put the idea into Rao Jodha's head, but this is such a recurring tale in Rajasthan that its authenticity must be doubted. Jodha founded the city of Jodhpur, which bears his name, probably at the same time as the fort, but its wall was not completed until 1573; his descendants were to rule seven of India's former states, including Bikaner and Kishangarh.

Although a footpath provides an easy descent from the fort, it is recommended that an auto-rickshaw is hired for the steep ascent. Just before the fort is reached, a halt should be made at the **Jaswant Thada Cenotaph**, erected in 1899 to commemorate the cremation of Jaswant Singh II on its site; it is not the usual simple *chattri*, but resembles a temple. The cenotaph is approached by steps of red sandstone, however, it is the monument itself is of Makrana marble. Although the building appears to be closed, it may always be entered from the east side.

Within, an orange glow prevails, the walls being so thin that the bright sunlight pentrates. It must be hoped that, eventually, the RSJs supporting the roof, which strike a discordant note, will be decorated. All maharajas were greatly respected by their subjects, but here this respect appears to have approached idolatry. Prayers to Maharaja Jaswant Singh II are still made by devout Hindu citizens of Jodhpur, who believe that by so doing they will be cured of ailments. To encourage the healing process, money is placed in a dish, and offerings, such as handkerchiefs and ribbons, deposited. Three *chattris* to later maharajas have been erected to form part of the complex; prior to 1899, all had been cremated at Mandore.

A spice and tea seller is usually to be found at his stall outside the entrance to the fort; he blends all the varieties himself and is a mine of information on their respective merits. A post-home service is offered. The fort is approached via a zig-zag path, which is interrupted by an unusually large number of gates, beginning at Jey Pol.

Meherangarh Fort

When Rao Jodha built his fort in 1453, it was called Chintamani, but is now known as Meherangarh (Majestic), a very apt name. As at Jaipur, the rulers of Jodhpur formed a close liason with the Moguls, Rao Udai Singh being appointed maharaja by Akbar, and his son, Sur Singh, leading the Emperor's victorious armies in Gujarat and the Deccan. Jaswant Singh I supported Shah Jahan and his eldest son Dara Shukoh, against Aurangzeb in 1658. Aurangzeb, of course, was the victor and, following the death of Jaswant Singh, took control of Jodhpur, vexed by the unreliability of Rathore support. Immediately following Aurangzeb's death, in 1707, Ajit Singh regained Jodhpur for the Rathores and, with the divided Moguls now mortally weakened, began to remodel and enlarge the palace complex within the fort. On consolidating his position, Ajit Singh, who died in 1731, also expelled the Moguls from Ajmer to the east. As was usual in the princely states, a treaty with the British was signed in 1818 and stability ensued — at the price of British suzerainty.

Jey Pol (or Jai Pol) and the stretch of wall as far as Dodh Kangra Pol were built to commemorate Man Singh's defeat of Maharaja Jagat Singh of Jaipur in 1808. This was just one of the internecine Rajput battles that occurred during the chaotic period between Mogul and British rule. Jai means victory in Hindi, but the satirically punning reference to Jaipur is obvious. The structure of the gate was designed to incorporate the bronze doors that had been taken from Ahmedabad by Abhas Singh (1724-49), when he threw out the Moguls. Above the gate is a pump for obtaining water from Gulab Sagar in emergencies such as siege or drought.

Seen immediately left, after passing through the gate, the memorial *chattri* commemorates Kirat Singh, who died fighting courageously against Jaipur's invading army.

Fateh Pol (Fateh also means victory, but in Urdu) was built similarly to commemorate a military triumph: in this case the expulsion of the Moguls from Jodhpur by Ajit Singh in 1707 and the subsequent restoration of the Rathore dynasty.

Two more gates follow, and the site of another, which has been demolished. **Dodh Kangra** (or Lakna) **Pol** was erected in the mid-sixteenth century by Rao Maldeo. Indentations in both the gate and the fort's wall at this point were made by Jaipuri cannon. Plaques below refer to events at the 'Historic Iron Gate' in 1708 and the 'Heroes of 1808' (who fought off Jaipur's invaders); the heroes are also commemorated by an adjacent *chattri*.

The path rises to **Amrit Pol**, another of Rao Maldeo's mid-six-teenth-century gates. A red sandstone plaque 'Rao Jodhaji's Falsa

1459' identifies the cream painted stone with two holes in which lengths of timber were inserted to provide a makeshift barrier.

Loha Pol (Iron Gate) was first built in the fifteenth century, but remodelled by Rao Maldeo. On the left hand side, within the gate's archway, are impressed the hand prints of royal widows and concubines who commited sati. Although the British made sati illegal in 1829, the custom was ingrained and difficult to eradicate. This seems to have been particularly so at Jodhpur, where India's last example of sati took place as recently as 1953.

Tickets for entering the palaces, which together accommodate a museum, are purchased at this point; an additional levy is made on cameras. Immediately right is the usual **Naubat Khana**, from where musicians announced important arrivals. Opposite the museum's entrance, a member of the Mirashi caste of musicians 'plays in' today's visitors with his pipe and drum.

Although the entrance fee to **Meherangarh Fort** is high by Indian standards, it does include the services of a guide for every party — even a party of one — each of whom is extremely well-trained and knowledgeable; unaccompanied visits are not permitted, nor would they be possible bearing in mind the maze of courtyards and buildings that make up the palace. Entrance to the museum is gained at **Suraj Pol** (Sun Gate).

The first courtyard visited was formerly part of the female quarters (*zenana*) and will remind those who have seen it already of Bikaner Fort's Anup Mahal courtyard, with which it is contemporary. All is of red sandstone but, as at Bikaner, the ground floor has been painted. The order in which the rooms are seen and the names by which they are known may vary but will include the following:

Khabka Mahal. The name indicates that this was the sleeping quarters. Ajit Singh built the palace in the 1720s, and the European

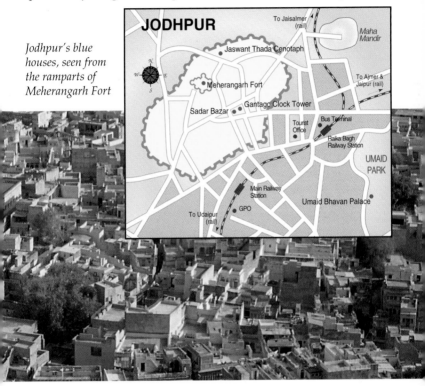

Jodhpur's blue houses, seen from the ramparts of Meherangarh Fort

influence of classical capitals may be noted. The ceiling is of sweet-smelling sandalwood.

Dipak (Light) Mahal. This chamber was used by Jodhpur state's chief minister for meetings and receptions.

Jhawki (Glimpse) Mahal. Royal ladies in purdah could observe pageants from behind the *jali* screens of this long gallery. A display of royal cradles includes one (the first seen) of 1948 vintage, which is gently rocked by electric power rather than the action of a nurse.

Moti (Pearl) **Mahal**. Niches in the walls of this room, the Diwan-i-Am (Private Audience Hall), once supported lamps which, when lit, gave the room the appearance of a pearl: hence its name. It is said that the five screened openings represent the five wives of Sur Singh (ruled 1595-1619), who is accredited with building the Moti Mahal. Shah Jahan's throne may be returned here after restoration.

Sardar Vilas. Articles of exotic woodwork displayed include some exceptional lacquering.

Umaid Vilas. Gilded examples of the Jodhpur School are naturally pre-eminent in the collection of miniature paintings.

Sheesh (Mirror) **Mahal**. Bas-reliefs of Hindu gods in this room indicate that it was formerly a prayer hall. Although fine, the mirror-glass does not approach the magical quality of Jaipur's or Bikaner's. Coloured glass balls in the ceiling will remind some Westerners of Christmas tree decorations.

Amkash Mahal. Musical instruments of Rajasthan are seen before returning to Sardar Vilas for superb views of Jodhpur city from its upper storey.

Takhat Vilas. This, the most important bedroom in the palace (the bed and cradle are original), was built above Umaid Vilas by Takhat Singh in the second half of the nineteenth century. Frescoes illustrate legends and scenes from the life of Krishna. A servant stationed outside the door operated the fan manually throughout the night.

Ajit Vilas. Costumes are displayed, pride of place being given to highly decorated jodhpurs. These were a World War I invention of Regent Sir Pratap Singh, who led the Mounted Lancers Regiment. He disliked the horsemen's usual cloth wrapping of the legs (patti) worn beneath knickers, and devised jodhpuri, a combination of trousers, pyjamas and salwar. A London tailor was given the specifications and an order for a dozen, which he mistakenly described as jodhpurs — the name stuck, and jodhpurs soon became standard wear for polo players. Today, jodhpurs are still worn for equestrian events, although they are now generally tighter than those styled by Pratap Singh.

Phul (Flower) Mahal. Built by Abhai Singh (around 1730), the hall originally served as the Diwan-i-Khas (Public Audience Hall). Jaswant Singh II commissioned its redecoration in the late-nineteenth century. The one painter, who worked for 10 years on the project, died with the scheme still uncompleted, and it was decided, in deference to him, that the hall would be kept as he had left it. Hindu gods and Jodhpur maharajas are depicted on the gilded ceiling, while the frieze illustrates various styles of dancing. Exhibited here, unless returned to the Moti Mahal, is the throne of Shah Jahan, presented to the Maharaja of Jodhpur by Aurangzeb (loyalty to the Mogul Emperor having been at least temporarily re-established).

Daulat Khana. Lying directly beneath the Phul Mahal, this room exhibits the most exotic collection in the palace. Pride of place is given to the maharajas' sedan chair, originally curtained, which needed twelve men to carry it. Other exhibits include decorated wooden boxes (look for the opium box), metalwork, wine bottles and hookahi, which are smoking pipes similar to hubble bubbles.

The **Armoury** displays great locks and keys, Rao Jodha's sword (seven pounds in weight), Akbar's sword, and shields studded with semi-precious stones. The mural, by A.H. Müller, 1893, depicts Durga Das, who guarded the infant Ajit Singh until he was able to regain the throne of Jodhpur from the Moguls in 1707.

Displayed at the end of a long corridor is the Sangar Choki, a red sandstone chair made in the fifteenth century, on which all rulers of Jodhpur since Rao Jodha have been enthroned;its white marble overlay was added in the mid-eighteenth century. Silver elephant haudahs are all two-seater; the maharaja sat in front, his mahout/ guardian behind; one of them was presented by Shah Jahan to Jaswant Singh I in 1657.

Palki Khana. Royal palanquins (sedan chairs) are exhibited. The museum is now left and a path followed to the ramparts, where ancient cannon are stationed.

Three small temples ahead may be visited. **Nagnechiji Temple** (closes at 11am) remains the private temple of the Rathore family; its idol was transferred here from Marwar. **Salimkot Temple**, for a period, accommodated aristocratic Rajput prisoners. **Chamunda Devi Temple** was rebuilt in the mid-nineteenth century following an accidental gunpowder explosion; its Durga idol, brought from Mandore by Rao Jodha in 1459, survived the accident.

Jodhpur City   ✳

Steps descend to the **Sadar Bazar market**. Ahead rises the **Gantago clock tower**, built in 1912 and reminiscent of many an English market square's clock of the period. A pleasing feature of Jodhpur's streets is that although they are colourful and vivacious, they are not uncomfortably overcrowded. Just behind the market's archway is the unpretentious **Mishrilet Hotel**, a mecca for lovers of *lassi*, where here it is made with butter (*makhan*). Yellow in colour, rich and creamy *lassi makhani* is only to be found in Jodhpur.

From Sadar Bazar it is convenient to stroll westward along Jodhpur's ancient streets, keeping reasonably close to the base of the fort's escarpment, the further one proceeds westward, the bluer the houses become. Originally, only members of the Brahmin priest caste were permitted to paint their houses blue, all others had to be white, but as they moved out and non-Brahmins took over their former properties, the rules were relaxed. Now, anyone who wishes may paint their property blue, although most roofs are kept white in order to reflect the burning sun.

Jodhpur's top hotel, the **Umaid Bhavan Palace**, administered by the Wellcome Group, is worthy of a visit, even by non-residents. The great pile was begun in 1929, but not completed until 1944, Maharaja Umaid Singh moving in the previous year. A wing of the hotel still serves as the residence of the head of the Rathore family. The architect of the palace, H.V. Lanchester, had worked closely with Lutyens, and the influence of the latter's work at Viceroy's House, New Delhi, is unmistakeable. Even for a maharaja, the project was grandiose. The building's location, on Chittar Hill, is superb, but no water supply existed, a 12 mile (20km) rail link with the stone quarry had to be laid, half a million donkey loads of earth were needed for the foundations, and more than 4,000 workmen laboured on the project. Although undoubtedly impressive, the architecture exhibits a certain aridity and coldness that even Rajasthan's blue skies and

Still partly occupied by the former Maharaja, Jodhpur's Umaid Bhavan Palace has been remodelled as a hotel

bright sunlight cannot quite dispel. The gardens, however, are a different matter. Rows of bougainvillea, cut as box hedges, lead the eye from the hotel's terrace to the distant Meherangarh Fort on its 'Bird's Nest' hill. Quite a background for breakfast or afternoon tea where, in spite of the hotel's grandeur, the atmosphere is most relaxed and friendly.

A basement-level swimming pool is also available to non-residents for a small fee. In the museum, the usual stuffed animals include a lion, which surprises those who believe that this animal is unique to Africa. It virtually is nowadays, but a few Asian lions remain, under protection, in Gujarat State: none have survived in Rajasthan. Of greater interest are the collections of clocks/watches, glass/ceramics and, in the former Diwan-i-Am, weapons. A buffet dinner in the vaulted **Marwar Hall**, built for durbars, is a memorable experience — although more for its setting and musical accompaniment than its gastronomic quality, which is average. In fact, buffet meals in India's tourist hotels, no matter what grade they may be, appear to differ little in standard. They are always perfectly adequate, but rarely sensational. Nearby, on Umaid Bhavan Palace Road, is **Lalji's Emporium**, an exotic department store.

For those with time to spare, Jodhpur's **Umaid Park** has a zoo with a good aviary, and the **Sardar Museum**, which displays handicrafts, weapons, sculpture and paintings. In contrast, a section of a meteorite which fell nearby in 1937 is also exhibited: it is claimed that the meteorite's impact could be heard 37 miles (60km) distant. As with most of Rajasthan's provincial museums (apart from those within the larger palaces) the presentation is poor and rundown. This is particularly unfortunate at the Sardar Museum, as its collection of sculptures is outstanding and would attract visitors from far and wide if displayed in a Western city. Figures of Vishnu from the ninth, tenth and twelfth centuries, and of three Jain tirthankaras from the fifteenth century (in the main gallery) are magnificent, but some of the smaller figures, such as a delicately carved dancing girl from the tenth century, are equally delightful.

A royal concubine's residence, the **Talaiti Mahal**, which dates from the early seventeenth century, is the oldest palace in Jodhpur. Now a women's hospital called the Hewson Dispensary, it is to be found near Juni Dhan Mandi.

Apart from those located within Jodhpur's handful of tourist hotels, the city is short on restaurants. Most that do exist lie between the Sojati Gate and the railway station, just south of the walled city. Near the station, try the Adarsh Niwas Hotel's **Kalinga Restaurant** or, facing it, the **Renuka**. Beside Sojati Gate, **Agra Sweet Home** also serves buttery *lassi makhani*, and **The Coffee House** is renowned for its *masala dhosas*; **Dimples Snack Bar**, nearby, provides satisfying meals which are rather more than snacks. Apart from *lassi makhani*, Jodhpur's only other claim to gastronomic fame appears to be *mawa kachori*, a dessert, extremely sweet of course, which differs little from the Greek baclava.

As an alternative to the Umaid Bhavan Palace hotel, the **Ajit Bhavan Palace**, and **Hotel Ratanada International** also offer high quality accommodation. From the cheaper range, the **Adarsh Niwas Hotel**, the restaurant of which has already been referred to, and the **Ghoomar Tourist Bungalow**, beside the Umaid Gardens, are clean and comfortable. The latter is particularly convenient, as the local tourist information centre and Indian Airlines office are located within.

Jodhpur has direct daily flights to Jaipur, Udaipur, Delhi, Bombay and Ahmedabad. The Udaipur flights are extremely popular, and reservations should be made in advance. Buses and trains to Udaipur take around 10 hours and are not to be recommended.

⊓ MANDORE

Mandore, only 5 miles (8km) north of Jodhpur, is reached by a frequent bus service, and may be viewed in 2 or 3 hours; it is therefore ideal as a tourist's late-afternoon 'filler'. Locals visit the ruined city primarily for its gardens because, unlike Jodhpur, the area is well-watered. In times of drought, women were required to trudge from Jodhpur to Mandore and back to collect water for the fort. How they managed it, particularly in view of the long and tiring ascent to Meherangarh Fort, is almost inconceivable. Even now, visitors to India are astonished to observe the heavy manual labour expected of women: gangs of them, clad in their colourful sarees, work on construction projects, hacking away at rock with heavy implements, like flocks of industrious butterflies.

From the sixth century until Rao Jodha's foundation of Jodhpur, Mandore was the capital of Marwar State, ruled by the Parihar Rajputs. Marwar means 'Land of Death', and it was hardly surprising that this depressing nomenclature was eventually changed to that of its new capital city — Jodhpur. A member of the Rathore family, Rao Chanda, married a Parihar princess when he settled at Mandore. The city was originally called Mandavyapur, but the British found this too difficult to pronounce, and the present abbreviation evolved.

When Mandore, on its rocky plateau, was abandoned for Jodhpur, the city was left to decay, and is now little more than scattered rubble;

in the centre, however, ruins of a temple may still be distinguished. Also remaining from earlier times, sited on higher ground, are an eighth-century **Gupta temple** and a **memorial** to Mandore's last Parihar ruler Rao Nahur.

It is probable that the site of the **gardens**, where outstanding memorials to Jodhpur's rulers from the sixteenth to the eighteenth century survive, has long had religious significance, each cenotaph marking the spot where a maharaja was cremated. The relative lushness of Mandore attracts abundant wildlife; peacocks, para-keets, squirrels, even monkeys (rare in this region), giving animation to the grounds.

The **cenotaphs of Rao Maldeo** and **Uda Singh**, the earliest exam-ples, are separated by that of **Sur Singh**, a seventeenth-century maharaja. Also from the seventeenth century are the memorials to **Gaj Singh** and **Jaswant Singh I**. The finest of all, and the loftiest, is in temple form and commemorates **Ajit Singh**, who died in 1731. On his funeral pyre, six wives and fifty-eight concubines committed sati, one of the most horrifying examples of peacetime immolation in India.

Carved in the rock, also within the garden, is **The Hall of Thirty Three Crore Gods**, created early in the eighteenth century. A crore is the Indian equivalent of 10 million, but visitors will be relieved to learn that rather less than 330 million sundry gods, spirits and holy men are depicted within.

Adjacent, the **Hall of Heroes** is much smaller. To western eyes, the primitive style of its fifteen gigantic figures carved from rock is endearing rather than awe-inspiring, and the unremitting bright-ness of the gaudy colours becomes tiring.

Nearby is a **palace**, built of stone by Ajit Singh's successor, Abhai Singh. Also within the gardens is a temple with a rare dedication — to **Bheru**, an early Indian god, symbolized by a dog, and a small **temple** to **Shiva** guarded, as usual, by a Nandi bull and displaying a Shiva lingam.

OSIYAN

Now an entirely modern village, but once an important city on the Jaisalmer trading route, Osiyan lies 36 miles (58km) north of Jodhpur, sand dunes indicating the Thar Desert situation. Osiyan is visited for its Jain temples, some of the earliest and finest in India, and those who are unable to visit Ranakpur or Mount Abu from Udaipur are particularly recommended to make the journey. Buses and trains link Jodhpur with Mandore and Osiyan and it is easy, therefore, to visit both in one day.

As has been seen, many important merchants were Jains, and Osiyan's remoteness, providing some security from opression by members of other religions, was an attraction for them. Temples are concentrated in two separate complexes; they date from the eighth to the twelfth centuries and include some Hindu examples.

The first group, on the outskirts of the village, is the most important. Three small temples are dedicated to **Hariham**, a typically complicated deity, combining Vishnu with Shiva. As at Ranakpur, there is also a temple to the Vedic sun god **Surya**, but this tenth-century example is 300 years older. The gracefulness of the structure, with its conical sikhara, is greatly admired. Within is a figure of Durga.

A temple dedicated to the last Jain tirthankara, **Mahavira**, is the most impressive of Osiyan's set. Built in the late eighth century, extensions and alterations made in the tenth and eleventh centuries include the towering sikhara, *nal mandapa* (staircase hall), and *torana* arch, with its sinuously carved maidens. The vase/foliage decorative theme was to become a popular architectural embellishment in India.

Supported by thirty pillars, the tenth century *mandapa* hall of the **Pipla Devi Temple** is original.

Osiyan's second and much smaller complex of temples is located on a hill to the east of the modern village. Most important here is the **Sachi Mata** temple, founded in the eighth century but greatly enlarged and remodelled 400 years later; its rather fussy sikhara is entirely twelfth-century work.

Additional Information

Places to Visit in Jodhpur

Meherangarh Fort
Open: daily 9am-5pm.

Umaid Bhavan Palace Museum
Open: daily 9am-5pm.

Festivals

Marwar Festival 1995, 7-8 October; 1996, 25-26 October; 1997, 15-16 October; 1998, 4-5 October; 1999, 23-24 October; 2000, 12-13 October.

Accommodation

Umaid Bhavan Palace Hotel
☎ 22316

Ajit Bhavan Palace Hotel
Airport Road
☎ 20409

Hotel Ratanada International
☎ 25911

Tourist Information Office

Ghoomar Tourist Bungalow
High Court Road
☎ 25183

Udaipur & South-West Rajasthan

7

✳ UDAIPUR

Udaipur, with its picturesque lakes, is undoubtedly the most serenely located city in Rajasthan. Surrounded by high, undulating hills, which do not quite aspire to mountains, the views put one in mind of Scottish lochs at the end of an unusually dry summer. Udaipur is predominantly a white town, reflections of its gleaming lakeside buildings shimmering in the waters. There are some thirty Jain temples but, apart from the scenery, it is the former royal palaces which primarily draw visitors to the city. Most of Udaipur's attractions may be seen in two full days, although an additional day is needed for each of the three important excursions in the vicinity.

🏛 City Palace

Dominating much of the east side of Lake Pichola is the City Palace, by far the most important architectural feature of Udaipur. It is the largest palace ever built in Rajasthan, and consists of four major and

preceding page; The City Palace at Udaipur

numerous minor buildings; although these were constructed at various times since the mid-sixteenth century, a surprisingly homogenous appearance has been achieved. As the palace straddles a low ridge instead of a steep-sided promontory like most Rajasthan forts, unusually high walls were needed for its defence.

Of Rajasthan's 'Salute' states, Udaipur, named from its founder Udai Singh II, had precedence, its ruler uniquely boasting the title maharana (great warrior). Udaipur's maharanas bear the family name Sisodia, and claim descendance from Lord Rama; they are the leaders of the Rajput 'solar' clan and display a stylized sun as their emblem. The Sisodias moved to Udaipur after finally losing their stronghold at Chittaurgarh to Akbar in 1567. Maharana Pratap of Udaipur and the Maharao Raja of Bundi were the only Rajput princes who refused to acknowledge Akbar's suzerainty. A brief incursion by the Marattas took place at Udaipur in the eighteenth century and the British imposed their protection, by treaty, in 1818.

The foundation stone of the City Palace was laid in 1579, an earlier Udaipur palace, built in 1567, being abandoned, apparently because its site prohibited extensions. It was built to face east, emphasizing the 'solar' inheritance of the Sisodias. The finest aspects of the great complex are therefore gained from that side, at which a unifying terrace runs the length of the palace, supported by arches where the ridge falls. It should be noted that the palace may only be entered from the north side; no access is permitted at its southern extremity from the former guesthouse of the palace, now the Shivniwas Palace Hotel.

Unlike most of Rajasthan's fortresses, the City Palace of Udaipur has few defensive gateways, and there is no steep zig-zag path between them. The **Bari Pol** (Great Gate) of 1600 is followed by a marble **Tripolia Gate**, erected in 1725; its arches support a nine-teenth-century **Hawa Mahal** (Wind Palace), with *jali* screens through which the royal ladies could view processions, in the manner of Jaipur.

Bada (or Bara) **Chowk** was planned to provide a great courtyard, separating the stables and guardrooms on the north side (now converted to shops) from the residential areas of the palace. It also served as a parade ground, where 100 elephants could be assembled. Ahead, on the south side of the courtyard, the **Toran Pol** forms the entrance to the **City Palace Museum**. On the wall to its right, at upper level, is the sun emblem of the Mewar rulers and, below this, the elephant dismounting platform, known as the **Padgadi Hathni**.

The small **Ganesh Deorhi** gate leads to **Rajya Augan** (Royal Courtyard), created in 1559 as one of the earliest features of the palace. Within stands Udaipur's earliest surviving building, the **Dhuni Mata shrine**, in which are depicted the four pre-eminent gods venerated by the Mewars.

Displayed in rooms on the north side of the courtyard are the armaments of Pratap Singh (ruled 1572-92), the warrior who valiantly continued his father Udai Singh II's struggle against Akbar.

Steps ascend to the raised garden of **Bada Mahal**, from which are gained superb views over Lake Pichola. A passage from the garden leads to the arcaded courtyard of **Shiv Praina Amar Vilas**, built in 1694.

Displayed in the **Chandra Mahal** (Moon Palace), a single, open room, is the throne used for coronations of Mewar rulers until 1710. It is said that the room's central marble basin was filled with gold pieces to celebrate maharanas' birthdays; these were then distributed amongst the poor.

Karan Singh built the four-roomed **Dilkushal Mahal** in the seventeenth century; its mirrored walls display outstanding miniature paintings. A combination of red and clear glass in the Kanch-ki-Burj chamber has an appearance which is not dissimilar from the metallic wallpapers recently in vogue in Europe. Another of the rooms, **Chitram-ki-Burj**, decorated with murals in 1780, portrays contemporary scenes. Hunters are depicted rather unsportingly shooting bears and panthers from the top of a tree. In the vestibule of the Dilkushal Mahal note the illustrations of crocodiles on Lake Pichola; apparently they were introduced to discourage unwelcome visitors bent on mischief from swimming to the palace.

Udaipur's **Moti Mahal** (Pearl Palace) seems rather strangely named, as its coloured glass and mirrors hardly evoke the soft hues of a pearl.

By tradition, all maharanas ritually greeted the sun each morning at dawn from **Bhim Vilas**. Its sun window, Suraj Gokhala, was installed in a corridor by Bim Singh in the late eighteenth century.

Priyatama Vilas was built in the late nineteenth century by Sajjan Singh. Its courtyard, **Mor Chowk** (Peacock Court), was named from the mosaic peacocks with which it is decorated. On the north side of the courtyard, built as a throne room, the **Manek Mahal** (Ruby Palace) displays a collection of glass and porcelain. A second throne room, the **Surya Chopar**, occupies the south wing.

It is now usual for visitors to be guided back to Rajya Angan, although much of the City Palace has not been seen. This includes the Rang Bhawan, with its state treasures, and the adjacent Laxmi Chowk, in the centre of which stands the Peacock Pavilion, and the Durbar Hall. Applications to make a more extensive tour may be made, in advance, to the palace.

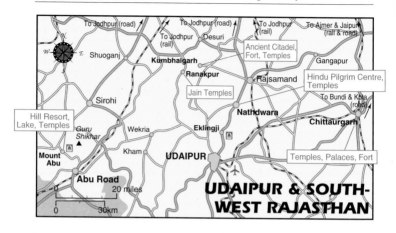

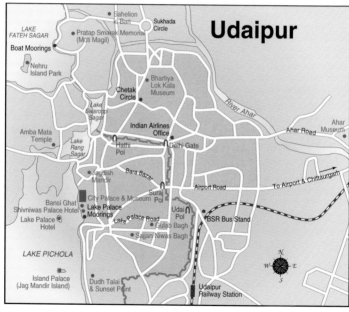

Wood carvings within the City Palace, Udaipur, demonstrates
the importance of animals in Rajasthan

✳ Udaipur City

Udaipur's most interesting temple, the **Jagdish** (or Jagat Nath) **Mandir**, is conveniently located 150 yards north of the City Palace entrance, at the west end of Bara Bazar. Approached by steps, which are flanked by elephants, the temple is dedicated to Vishnu, and was built around 1640. A black stone figure depicts Vishnu as Lord of the Universe of Jagat Nath. Profusely carved dancing girls, horses and elephants decorate both the main building and the *chattri* facing it, which shelters a bronze Garuda, Vishnu's mount.

On the opposite (south) side of Bara Bazar, the sixteenth-century **Adinath Mandir** is the most important of Udaipur's Jain temples.

Bara (Great) **Bazar** leads eastward, serving as Udaipur's 'High Street'. Although lively, it is not as congested as similar ancient shopping streets in most Indian cities. **Delhi Gate**, at the far end of Bara Bazaar, is the north-east gate in Udaipur's ancient wall, much of which survives. Others include: **Hathi Pol**, to the north-west, **Suraj Pol** and **Udai Pol** to the east, **Kishan Pol** to the south and **Jal Burj** to the south-west.

Few will now be able to resist making for Udaipur's best-known attraction, **Lake Pichola**, with its Lake Palace Hotel. It is reached by following Bhatina Chotta southward from Bara Bazar's clock tower (there is a sign on the corner). The downhill walk is most pleasant, skirting, as it does, the east façade of the City Palace. A right turn leads directly to the lake, passing, left, the **Roof Garden** restaurant, with its superb views of the City Palace and excellent food.

Lake Pichola, Udaipur's oldest is, like the others, man-made. A merchant created it in the fifteenth century by damming a tributary of the Ahar River and laying a causeway across it. Shortly after founding Udaipur in 1567, Udai Singh extended the lake and rebuilt the dam with stone. The lake's name commemorates a small village which once stood on the west bank. In times of drought, the water level can be very low: as recently as 1972-3 and again in 1988-9 Lake Pichola completely dried up, and visitors to the Lake Palace Hotel had to be transported to it by wading camels. Lake Pichola covers an area of approximately 2½ miles (4km) by 1½ miles (2km).

The **Lake Palace Hotel**, administered by the Taj Group, occupies all Pichola Lake's **Jag Niwas Island**, and incorporates sections of several palaces, the most important of which, the Jag Niwas Palace, was completed by Jagat Singh II in 1746. As recently as 1955, the Maharana of Udaipur resided on the island during the summer to take advantage of the lake breezes. Conversion to a hotel began 4 years later, 75 rooms being added. The hotel, built entirely of white marble, opened 1 February 1963, precisely 217 years after the inauguration of the Jag Niwas Palace, and is acknowledged as one of the world's loveliest. Unfortunately, it is always fully-booked many months in advance, however, on occasions, a telephone call just after 9.30am can be successful in discovering a cancellation for that night. If not, book a table for lunch or dinner, and the complex may then be explored. Do not miss the exquisite lily pond, the swimming pool and the terraces, with their stupendous views of the lake. Access is from the east bank of Lake Pichola by the hotel's private ferry service (free), which departs from below the drive to the Shivniwas Palace Hotel. All prospective visitors will be checked-out on the intercom, and no booking may well mean no admission. If they are unoccupied, it is sometimes possible to view some of the royal suites, in particular the **Sajjan Niwas Suite**, an eighteenth-century room with original murals, the **Khush Mahal Suite** with delicate stained glass, and the **Udai Mahal Suite**.

From the hotel, but also from the lakeside, afternoon boat trips call for half an hour at **Jag Mandir Island** to the south. The domed Gul Mahal pavilion was built on the island by Karan Singh in 1622 and extended by his successor Jagat Singh. Prince Khurram, later to become Shah Jahan, was given shelter on the island during his dispute with his father, Jahangir, from 1623 to 1624. In 1857, Jag Mandir also served as a sanctuary for European women and children while the Indian Mutiny was being quashed; Maharana Sarup Singh, their protector, is reputed to have threatened that he would personally kill anyone who attacked his guests.

Gul Mahal, unusually in Rajput architecture, incorporates rooms with curved walls; on the top floor, one of the earliest, if not the earliest examples of petra dura inlay work in India may be seen. The three **pavilions** to the west were built by Sangram Singh II early in the eighteenth century; some of their rooms are also partly curved. Facing the lake are eight statues of elephants.

On the east bank of the lake, note the picturesque castellated building: this disguises Lake Pichola's purification plant, which supplies Udaipur's drinking water (still, unfortunately, not safe enough for foreign visitors). A little further south of the plant is **Sunset Point**, from where the finest views of Lake Pichola, with the romantic pavilion of Jag Mandir Island in the foreground, are obtained. This may be reached either on foot or by the road which skirts the east shore south of the City Palace.

If it is not possible to stay at the Lake Palace Hotel, an enchanting alternative is the **Shivniwas Palace Hotel**, originally built in 1909 by Fateh Singh as a single storey pavilion for his own accommodation within the City Palace. Bhupal Singh used the building to entertain foreign visitors, and it later served as a nine-room guest house. The first floor was added recently when the palace was converted to a

opposite; The internal areas of Udaipur's Lake Palace Hotel are as enticing as its lakeside views

Peacock Courtyard of the City Palace, Udaipur

hotel; each of the upper rooms has a private terrace garden for sunbathing, and even for sleeping in the hot season, when beds will, on request, be moved outside. Ground floor public areas, particularly the gardens, are a delight, and visitors are welcome; the hotel's suites are amongst the most splendid in India — try to see the immense Imperial Suite.

Immediately south of the hotel, Lake Palace Road runs eastward; on its south side, the 100 acre (40 hectare) garden, **Sajjan Niwas Bagh**, was laid out in the late nineteenth century by Sajjan Singh. Incorporated are the Gulab Bagh (Rose Garden), the name by which the entire garden is now better known, a small zoo, and a children's ride. Before proceeding northward to Udaipur's next most important lake, Fateh Sagar, a visit should be made to **Bansi Ghat** fronting the northern section of the City Palace, where scenes are reminiscent of Pushkar and Varanasi (Benares).

A vehicle will be needed to reach **Sahelion ki Bari** (Maids of Honour Garden), laid out by Sangram Singh II in 1734 as a summer palace for the royal ladies, but now a public water garden fed by Lake Fateh Sagar. The lotus pool, marble elephants and fountains (imported from England) are a delight.

A short distance southward, on Moti Magri (Pearl Hillock), is the **Pratap Smarak Memorial**, a bronze equestrian statue of Maharana Pratap Singh riding his horse, Chetak. The statue overlooks Lake Fateh Sagar, with its Nehru Island Park, which is accessible by boats from the point below the municipal Rock Garden.

Lake Fateh Sagar was created by Jai Singh in the seventeenth century, but in times of flood it drowned the Sahelion ki Bari, and the east bank was built up by Fateh Singh in the nineteenth century to protect the garden. **Nehru Island Park**, originally conceived in 1937 as another island palace, was never completed. It is a favourite picnic spot, and there is a cafeteria. Views from here of the lake, which is more rural in aspect than Lake Pichola, are superb, and the whole atmosphere is enjoyably tranquil.

Above Lake Fateh Sagar, the **Laxmi Vilas Palace Hotel** is another converted royal palace; it has a pretty terrace and swimming pool with sensational views. Adjacent, the **Hotel Anand Bhavan** is equally well sited.

Udaipur provides a wide range of hotels to suit all budgets and, apart from the Lake Palace Hotel, on-spec visitors can normally be catered for with ease. Restaurants in the city tend to be grouped around Chetak Circle (**Berry's Restaurant** is the best here), Suraj Pol (mainly vegetarian restaurants) and, as mentioned, immediately south of the City Palace.

Panch Vati runs northward from Chetak Circle passing, on the right, a folk museum, **Bhartiya Lol Kala Museum**. Puppets and puppet shows are the chief attraction, performances being held throughout the day. Local costumes and musical instruments are also exhibited.

Day Excursion to Kumbhalgarh, Ranakpur, Nathdwara and Eklingji

This enjoyable day excursion is one of Rajasthan's most varied. Not only is the scenery magnificent, including as it does lakes, rivers and mountains, but the locations visited are also outstanding: an ancient, walled fort, exquisite Jain temples and important Hindu temples. Local bus services exist, but they are slow and inconvenient and their use would preclude completing this itinerary in one day. This is one occasion, therefore, when a private car is really essential; the cost, if vigorously bargained in advance, will not be horrendous. Insist on an 8am start from Udaipur, arriving at Kumbhalgarh by 11am.

Kumbhalgarh Fort

It is the hilltop location and length of its walls that are the most memorable feature of Kumbhalgarh Fort. First seen as the complex is approached are the black, snaking fortifications, their castellations resembling a succession of spoutless teapots. Situated 3,800ft (1,159m) above sea level, the fort is the highest in India, and the height of its 22 mile (36km) stretch of wall is only exceeded by that of the Great Wall of China. There are seven gates in the wall, which in parts has become ruinous.

The origins of Kumbhalgarh are a second-century fortress founded by Jains, which was completely rebuilt in the fifteenth century by Rana Kumbha, after whom the present fort is named. Kumbha was a warrior who never lost a battle, and Kumbhalgarh is the oldest of the Mewar fortifications. It eventually fell to Akbar in the sixteenth century.

Less than one hundred tourists, on average, visit the fort each day in the dry season, the majority of them on escorted tours, and by mid-day most will have departed, leaving the individual visitor in tranquillity to soak up the atmosphere of great battles fought long ago; the only sound heard will be birdsong.

A group of temples within the fort may be inspected, the most important of which, the **Kumbhaswami Temple**, is almost Grecian in its colonnaded purity. Shiva is worshipped here, faced, as is common, by his Nandi bull vehicle. Other temples are the **Nilkanth Mahade** and **Mahadeo**.

Rana Kumbha is commemorated by a *chattri*; although undefeated in battle, he was murdered by his son. Another *chattri* serves as a memorial to Prithviraj, brother of Rana Sanga.

Most of the fifteenth-century fort is in ruins, but visitors are now permitted to inspect the **Badal Mahal** (Cloud Palace) on the summit. Begun in the eighteenth century, much of the building was remodelled in the late nineteenth century by Maharana Fateh Singh. As may be imagined, views from the ramparts of the palace are sensational. A guardian will show visitors the bedroom of the Maharani, last occupied as recently as 1984; its walls create an unusual echo, which will be demonstrated. Apparently, the palace has been abandoned, and rapid decay will no doubt take place.

Kumbhalgarh Fort's wall evokes the Great Wall of China, and is, reputedly, India's longest

Ranakpur

Those travelling to Udaipur by bus from Jodhpur may like to bear in mind that the slow ones stop at Ranakpur on route. The bus journey to Udaipur, however, takes a further tedious 5 hours, while from Kumbhalgarh, only a 30 minute drive is involved. Located in a secluded wooded valley is a remarkable cluster of four Jain temples, dating from the thirteenth, fourteenth and fifteenth centuries. Before entering the complex, deposit all items of leather with the driver, as they will not be permitted within the temples.

Dominating the group is the **Adinath Temple**, dedicated to the first tirthankara, and completed in the mid-fifteenth century. The building was donated by Maharana Dharna Shah, and designed, in 1433, by the great Jain architect Dipak, who appears to have based his work on the existing (single storey) temple to Adinath, at Mount Abu, built four centuries earlier. The temple opens at midday; photography of the structure (but not the idols) is permitted for a fee.

A surprisingly symmetrical ground floor plan incorporates many prayer halls. In the centre, the figure of Adinath is depicted with four faces (a *chanmukha*), each directed at a cardinal compass point. Beneath the floor, idols were hidden from Muslims during periods of their religious intolerance. Everywhere, the gleaming white marble is profusely carved, some of the figures rivalling in eroticism the Hindu sculptures of Khajuraho (some of which are Jain), although it is unlikely that any of the craftsmen would have seen them. Particularly impressive are the 1,444 pillars, none of which is identical in design. Stairs lead up to the roof terrace, with its elephant carvings. From here, the sikhara can be observed more closely.

Smaller temples in the group are dedicated to **Parvanath** (fourteenth century) and **Neminath** (fifteenth century).

To the south, the **Surya Temple**, built in the thirteenth century and the oldest at Ranakpur, may not be entered by non-Hindus. Surya,

The fantasy Jain temple of Adinath at Ranakpur, north of Udaipur

god of the sun, is one of the three most revered gods in the early Vedic scriptures. One of the many external friezes depicts Surya in a horse-drawn chariot. The temple's sikhara was restored in the fifteenth century.

For those who would like to experience almost complete isolation, it is possible to stay overnight within the complex in its dharamsala (guesthouse), where a simple meal is provided; there is no set charge, but donations are expected. Other accommodation in Ranakpur is available at the state-run **Shilpi Tourist Bungalow**.

Nathdwara

The next destination, the **Shri Nathji Temple**, at Nathdwara, lies 20 miles (32km) north-east of Udaipur (there is an hourly bus service); arrival should not be made before 3.30pm, when the temple enclosure re-opens. Non-Hindus, however, are at no time permitted to enter the temple itself. Its figure of Nath (Krishna) was brought here from Mathura in 1669, to escape the iconoclasm of Aurangzeb. A full length black stone figure represents the god, which is said to have been worshipped at Mathura since Krishna's deification (between 1100 and 1200BC).

Eklingji

Approximately half way between Nathdwara and Udaipur, a distance of 14 miles (22km), lies the lakeside village of Kailashpuri, better known as Eklingji (single phallus lord), a reference to its famous temple, in which Shiva has been venerated for centuries. A regular bus service links Udaipur with the village.

Before entering the **temple complex**, which is surrounded by a high wall, socks as well as shoes must be removed; no photography is permitted. Proceed to the centre of this 'village of temples', where the important **Shiva temple** will be found, dominated by its pyramidal sikhara tower. The first temple on the site was built in 734 by Rana Bappa, to commemorate his acquisition of Chittaurgarh for the Mewar dynasty, which he had founded. At the time, Bappa ruled from Nagda, a short distance to the west of Eklingji, and had worshipped his guru's Shiva lingam. Henceforth, Shiva, in his lingam form, was to be adopted by the Sisodias as their 'patron' deity.

Elephants flank the entrance to the temple, with its many-columned hall. Having discovered the derivation of the name Eklingji and the importance of the single phallus symbol of Shiva to the Mewars, it is a surprise to discover that within the temple, surrounded by a screen of silver, Shiva is depicted not as a lingam, but as a four-faced black marble figure — such are the complexities of Hindu worship.

Facing the temple, one behind the other, are two figures of Shiva's bull Nandi: in bronze and black marble respectively.

A **Vishnu temple**, ascribed to the fifteenth century, is also worthy of note; it is faced by a black marble Garuda.

For those with time to spare and a car at their disposal, the ruins of **Nagda** (or Nagada), destroyed by Muslim forces in the thirteenth century, survive ½ mile (1km) west of Eklingji, and are reached by a side road. Of greatest interest are the eleventh-century **Sus Bahu** (Mother and Daughter-in-Law) **temples**, dedicated to Vishnu, in which some vaguely erotic carvings may be seen. A Jain temple bears the unusual name **Adbadji** (the strange), referring to its extraordinary idol. Additional ruined temples and shrines from earlier periods are also of interest.

MOUNT ABU

Mount Abu is famed for its group of Dilwara temples, which display what is regarded as the finest marble carving in India. However, it is the hill station's cool position, 3,936ft (1,200m) above sea level, which attracts the majority of visitors, most of whom are Indian. Buses from Udaipur take around 7 hours, whereas those with a hired car are able to complete the journey in half that time. The last stretch of road winds upward, and the views are dramatic, however, most of the route passes through a flat plain, and is nowhere near as appealing as the drive to Ranakpur. Although the description of the Mount Abu excursion follows that to Ranakpur in this book, this is for ease of comparison: to make both excursions on consecutive days would be too fatiguing for all but the most enthusiastic admirer of Jain temples. A point to bear in mind is that from mid-November to the end of February, Mount Abu, due to its height, is decidedly chilly. The visitor to Udaipur with limited time at his disposal (ie less than 4 days) must decide whether the Dilwara temples accolade of 'the finest' warrants the long, whole day trip, particularly if Ranakpur has already been seen. Some holidaymakers on escorted tours will automatically be taken to Mount Abu and then, of course, this difficult decision will not have to be made.

Mount Abu spreads over a plateau at the south-west extremity of the Aravalli range of hills, which runs diagonally north-eastward through Rajasthan before petering out on the outskirts of Delhi's North Ridge. The Dilwara temples may be visited from mid day and, as they are the chief reason for making the journey, most day-trippers make for them immediately on arrival at Mount Abu.

The complex of Jain temples lies 3 miles (5km) north-west of Mount Abu, and is located within a walled enclosure, at the gates of which shoes and all leather items must be deposited. Check on arrival if photography is permitted — the situation varies.

The temples are predominantly of Makrana marble, although structural elements are mostly of stone. Each one is known under a variety of names, which can be confusing; in this book, those given on the identification boards are shown first. Unlike the Adinatha Temple at Ranakpur, Dilwara's two major examples are single-storey buildings.

First seen after entry, on the left, is the **Khartar Vasahi Temple**, a three-storey structure dedicated in 1458 to Parasnath. Carved pendants are suspended from the domes on each side and there is some erotic carving. Behind doors are four-faced *chanmakhu* idols.

Facing the **Vimal** (or Adinath) **Temple** is the **Donor's Pavilion**, in which stand ten stone elephants bearing donors who contributed towards the cost of the temple. The elephants are believed to be a reminder that the marble for the temple was transported here all the way from Makrana, near Jaipur, by elephants.

Vimal Shah, sponsor of the temple, was a minister of Bhim Deva, King of Gujarat, and the work was completed in 1031, making this one of the oldest known Jain temples in existence. Set within an arcade forming a cloister, the temple consists of a double portico and a *mandapa* hall. It is reached via an unprepossessing entrance.

The first section of the portico is circular and domed, the second rectangular, with a small cupola. Forty-eight columns support the two- section portico, linked by scrolled *torana* arches, which are so delicate that they look more like paper chains than carved marble. The marble in this temple has acquired a creamy appearance, which is definitely not white as so often described. It has been suggested that chiselling could never have achieved such intricate lightness of detail, and that material must have been gently and laboriously scraped away with delicate tools from solid blocks of marble. In the centre of the *mandapa* is the figure of Adinath. To the rear of this, the building material used is stone, not marble, suggesting, perhaps the need for economy towards the end of the project.

It is worth exploring the surrounding cloister, the columns of which create two side aisles and one end aisle, entirely built of marble. Fifty-two cells are formed, each one accommodating an idol representing a tirthankara; all are virtually identical in appearance. As is common in Buddhism, the figures are depicted cross-legged.

Immediately left of the exit is the **Luna Vasahi** (or Neminath, or Tejpal) **Temple**, where the carving is even more miraculously delicate. The building is dedicated to Neminath, the twenty-second Jain tirthankara, and its patron was Tejpal (according to an inscription), another but much later minister of a Gujarat king. The layout is similar to that of the Vimal Vasahi Temple, but the marble is much whiter, and the donor's elephant hall forms the rear of the cloister, behind a patterned marble screen. The exquisite lotus pendant suspended from the ceiling of the *mandapa* is an unrivalled example of the delicacy of Jain carving.

Other temples of interest are the tiny **Mahaveer Swarmi Temple** of 1582 with, to its left, the **Pittalhar Temple** of 1468, its 'gold' idol in fact being made from an alloy of five metals. Right of this stands the **Shimashah Temple**, built by Bhimashu of Gujarat.

Four miles (6km) north of Dilwara, a right turn leads to **Achalgarh**, another of the more than thirty forts ascribed to Rana Kumbha. Built in 1452, little has survived; it is Achalgarh's group of temples, particularly the Shiva temple of **Achaleshwar Mahandeva**, that hold the greatest interest. To the south, on the bank of the Lake Manda Kini Kund, which was excavated more than 1,000 years ago, is the **figure of King Adil Pal** holding a bow from which he has shot arrows into the three stone buffaloes nearby. This set of figures commemorates a legend that the lake was once filled with ghee (clarified butter) and demons in the form of buffaloes came nightly to consume it; the King put a dramatic stop to their activities.

Guru Shikhar, only 2 miles (4km) further on, is not only, at 5,648ft (1,722m), the highest of Mount Abu's peaks, but also the highest point in Rajasthan. A shrine to Shiva, the Atri Rishi Temple, has been built on the summit. As would be expected, the views in clear weather are dramatic. It will be noted that Mount Abu is separated from the rest of the Aravalli range by a flat plain; due to this, the spur, of which it forms a part, has been named separately as the Abu Hills.

Most will now wish to make the 9 mile (15km) return journey to the centre of Mount Abu and its pretty, man-made lake. This is named **Lake Nakki**, a reference to the legend that it was created by a god, who used only his fingernails (*nakk*) for its excavation. The lake, with its many islets, may be explored by pedalos. Interestingly-shaped rocks overlook it, Toad Rock, resembling a toad of course, being the most dramatic. On the lake's south bank, the fourteenth-century **Raghanath Temple** (Hindu) may be visited. Two miles (3km) north-east of the lake is the **Adhar Devi** rock temple.

An important site in Vedic mythology, 5 miles (8km) south-east of Mount Abu, may be visited by those staying overnight (a long walk is involved). It is the tank of the **Gaumukh Temple**, Agni Kund, where four of the most important Rajput dynasties were traditionally created by the gods in a fire purification ceremony: the Chauhans, Paramars, Pratiharas and Solankis. The name of the **Gaumukh** (Cow Mouth) **Temple** is a reference to its marble cow, from the mouth of which spouts spring water. Within the temple, idols of Rama and Krishna flank Vasishta, their tutor.

The RTDC operate twice-daily tours of Mount Abu's most important sights, the afternoon tour being the most popular, although often booked up well in advance. Due to its cool climate, which particularly appeals to Indians, and its inaccessibility, Mount Abu is well-endowed with hotel accommodation; a good, centrally-located establishment is **Hotel Hill Tone**, its **Madhuban Restaurant** being one of Mount Abu's best. For those in desperate need of a break from curries, excellent Chinese food is served at the **Nina Shuba Restaurant**.

♜ Chittaurgarh (or Chittor) Fort

Situated almost 500ft (152m) above sea level, Chittaurgarh, although partly ruinous, is Rajasthan's highest-located fort, as well as its most historic. The fort's unique Tower of Victory is one of India's most famous structures. 'Private' buses from Udaipur make the 71 miles (115km) journey in 2 hours — pretty fast for Rajasthan. There is also a rail connection, but services are much less frequent and slower. Although the journey offers little of scenic interest, great fields of white poppies are passed, prompting reflection as to what use the crop might be put.

Until 1568, **Chittor** town was sited within the walls of the fort, but it now lies at the foot of the high plateau, and is known as Talaiti (Lower Town). There is nothing of particular interest to be seen here, and most will wish to proceed immediately to the fort. Transport is essential, and an auto-rickshaw should be hired, not only for the journey to the fort, but to provide transport between its buildings, which spread over 3½ miles (6km) — allow for 2 to 3 hours. It should be borne in mind that no food or drink is available at the fort. If convenient, some may prefer to take the RTDC escorted tour by minibus, which leaves from the Tourist Bungalow in the town centre. As the plateau is approached, it will become apparent that it consists of a long, squat, steep-sided rock, rising out of a flat plain in the manner of Australia's Ayer's Rock.

Legends aside, the Sisodia dynasty of Udaipur's maharawals may be traced back to the sixth century, when it was founded by Guhil (meaning cave born). His descendants are known to have lived near Ahar village, outside Udaipur, before transferring to Nagda, the now ruined settlement beside Eklingji. Bappa Rawal, the Guhilot leader, gained Chittaurgarh around 728 as part of his wife's dowry. A fort almost certainly existed at the time; allegedly, it had been founded by Bhim, one of the heroes of the Mahabharata. Although

beautiful wife of the young Maharana's uncle and adviser, Bhim Singh. Initially, the attack was repulsed, but Ala-ud-din returned and took the fort. Before it fell, the royal ladies, clad in their wedding dresses, marched to an underground chamber, where they were immolated by fire in a ritual johar; the men, wearing their bridal saffron robes, then rushed through the gates and were slaughtered by the Muslim troops: it is said that more than 7,000 Rajputs died. In spite of this carnage the Sisodias regained Chittaurgarh within 10 years.

Bahadur Shah, Sultan of Gujarat, in 1535, was the next to conquer the fort. Once more a johar took place and, on this occasion, 13,000 women are recorded to have been immolated and 32,000 Rajputs killed: no prisoners were taken. Bahadur Shah's victory, however, was short-lived, as the Mogul Emperor Humayun dispersed the invaders, returning the fort to the Sisodias; Prince Udai Singh II who, as an infant, had been smuggled out of the fort, ruled as Rana from 1541.

In 1567, Akbar besieged Chittaurgarh because Udai Singh would not accept Mogul suzerainty, and the fort was taken for the third and last time; however, the vastly superior Mogul force was kept at bay for four months. At the south end of the plateau, Akbar built a mound from where his troops could fire cannon balls over the wall into the fort. This was called Mohar (a gold coin of the Moguls) Magri (Mound) as, to encourage his men in their dangerous task, Akbar is said to have paid them one *mohar* for every container of earth added to raise the height of the mound. As defeat became inevitable, johar again was ordered; this time, nine ranis and five princesses being amongst those who perished in the flames. Around 8,000 Rajput warriors were slaughtered, 1,700 of them members of the Sisodia family, and Akbar, with untypical venom, ordered the murder of 4,000 peasants sheltering in the fort. Rana Udai Singh II, the Sisodia's leader, escaped as, perhaps disingenuously, he had left the fort earlier, apparently in order to carry out guerilla raids on Akbar's soldiers. Having survived the battle, he then took his relatively small band westward to found Udaipur, which bears his name. Almost 50 years later, in 1616, Emperor Jahangir, Akbar's son, gave Chittaurgarh back to the Sisodias, but by then the family's base had become established at Udaipur, and they preferred to remain there rather than return to Chittaurgarh, with its grim, though heroic, memories. An added disincentive to move was Jahangir's insistence that Chittaurgarh's defences should not be restored.

The road to the fort crosses the River Gambheri, the mile long ascent of the jungle-clad slopes of the plateau, with its two zig-zag bends, passing six defensive gates before reaching the Ram Pol Gate,

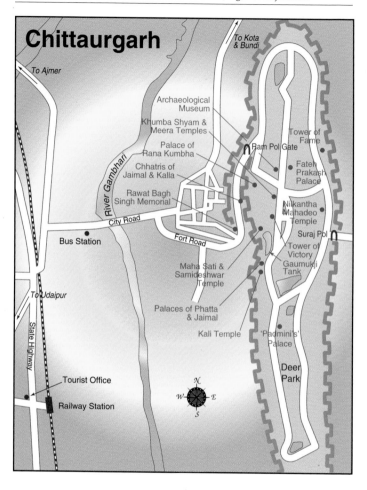

Chittaurgarh

To Kota & Bundi

To Ajmer

Archaeological Museum

Khumba Shyam & Meera Temples

Palace of Rana Kumbha

Chhatris of Jaimal & Kalla

Rawat Bagh Singh Memorial

River Gambhiri

City Road

Fort Road

Bus Station

To Udaipur

State Highway

Maha Sati & Samideshwar Temple

Palaces of Phatta & Jaimal

Kali Temple

Tourist Office

Railway Station

Ram Pol Gate

Tower of Fame

Fateh Prakash Palace

Nilkantha Mahadeo Temple

Suraj Pol

Tower of Victory

Gaumukji Tank

'Padmini's' Palace

Deer Park

which gives access to the fort. Ask the driver to pass them slowly: all the structures are large, and incorporate watchtowers with guard-rooms and spikes fixed to the doors at elephant-head level.

To the left of the first gate, **Padal** (Buffalo) **Pol**, a stone marks the spot where Bagh Singh, chief of Deolia, was killed during Bahadur Shah's assault of 1535. **Bhairon Pol** commemorates another Rajput warrior who was slain nearby; an alternative name for it had been Tuta (Broken) Pol, but the damaged structure was rebuilt. Within this gate, on the right, *chattris* commemorate where teenage Rajput heroes, Jaimal and Kalla, were struck down in 1567, the former being shot by Akbar himself. Another *chattri* ahead similarly marks where Phatta, Jaimal's 15-year-old cousin, died in the same battle. **Hanuman** and **Ganesh Pols** refer to the Hindu monkey and el-ephant-headed gods, the latter being worshipped at an adjacent altar. **Jorla** (Joined) **Pol's** name simply reflects that it is attached to the Lakshman Pol. The **Ram Pol**, which gives access, at last, to the fort, is built beside a temple to Rama, hence its name. The peristyle **hall** surmounted by *chattris*, facing the Rama Pol, is believed to have served as the main guardroom of the fort.

Most of interest at Chitta-urgarh lies roughly within the central third of the long, narrow enclosure. A road skirts the walls, its west and east stretches being linked by short roads; it is recommended that an anti-clockwise route is followed. Apart from the two famous tow-ers, few buildings are easy to identify, and a knowledgeable guide will prove useful for those not on a conducted tour.

It will be noted that a modern settlement has been established just within the entrance. Imme-diately ahead is the **Tulja Tem-ple**, followed by the circular **Nau Lakha Bhandar** (Nine Hundred Thousand), the former Treasury. The fourteenth-cen-tury **Shantinath Temple**, exqui-site Jain work, was built in the

Chittaurgarh Fort's unique Tower of Victory, easily reached from Udaipur

wall which connected the Treasury with the Nan Katha Magazine.

Two gateways, **Bari Pol** and **Tripolia**, lead to the fifteenth-century **Kumbha Palace** which, although ruinous, still impresses. Its builder, Rana Kumbha, was murdered in 1468 by his son Udai Singh I. Hated by his people for this patricide, Udai Singh became known simply as Hatyara (Murderer); by tradition, he was killed by lightning in 1473 but, in view of his deep unpopularity, it seems likely that a human hand was involved. By tradition, the third johar took place in the cellars of this palace. *Jali* screens indicate that the building was linked with the female quarters. To the south-west, the palace of Kumbha's murderous son, known as the **Kanwar Pade-Ka Mahal** (palace of the Heir Apparent), survives in part.

Continuing eastward to the next junction, a right turn passes the huge **Khumba Shyam** (or Vriji) **Temple**, rebuilt in 1448; its great sikhara tower is particularly impressive. Vishnu's winged Garuda faces the building, which incorporates a small **Meera Temple**. Past this, the **Jata Shankar Temple** of Shiva was reputedly built by Princess Mira Bai, who died heroically, battling against Bahadur Shah's troops.

Ahead, rising to 122ft (37m), Chittaurgarh's most famous building, The **Tower of Victory** (Jaya Stambh), was erected by Rana Kumbha, possibly to mark his victory over Muhammad Shah in 1440. Construction took 10 years, from 1458 to 1468, and the work is regarded as a high point in the fifteenth-century revival of Jain architecture. All surfaces are profusely carved, and each of the nine storeys clearly delineated. A staircase within (157 steps) connects each level, and visitors may ascend to the top floor. The original dome, damaged by lightning, was replaced by the present structure in 1861.

To the south-west, the wooded terrace, **Maha Sati Chowk**, was the cremation square, where royal widows and concubines committed sati on their husband's funeral pyres; some sati stones may be seen. Excavations have revealed a thick layer of ash, indicating that the 1535 johar probably took place here. To the south, the **Samideshwar Temple**, a structure of 1428, was built by Rana Mokal on the site of an earlier shrine. A Nandi bull guards the temple, within which is a three-headed image of Shiva. There are good views from this temple of the blue houses of Brahmins below the fort, reminiscent of Jodhpur.

Steps descend to a pool of green water, known as the **Gaumukh** (Cow Mouth) **Tank**, due to the stone heads of cows, from the mouths of which flows spring water; the adjacent Hathi Tank is usually dry outside the monsoon season. A cave nearby is reputedly where Padmini took part in the johar of 1303.

Further south, side by side, are the two mid-sixteenth-century **palaces of Phatta and Jaimal**, the teenage heroes killed in the struggle with Akbar. The adjacent **Kali** (or Kalika) **Temple** was built by Rana Hamir in the fourteenth century, on the site of an eighth-century **Surya** (Sun) **Temple**, which had been destroyed by Ala-ud-din Khalji's Muslim raiders in 1303. Kali, the fearsome aspect of Shiva's consort, is particularly venerated at Chittaurgarh.

'**Padmini's Palace**', south of the road junction, is an 1880s rebuilding of its thirteenth-century predecessor, the history of which is uncertain. The same can be said of Padmini herself, who some believe to have been the wife of Bhim Singh, uncle and adviser of the young Rana Lakshman; others ascertain that she was the Rani and favourite wife of Rana Rattan Singh I. By tradition, it was Ala-ud-din Khalji's passion for Padmini which led to his sack of Chittaurgarh in 1303. Apparently, he saw a reflection of the Princess in a mirror within the palace, which aroused his unquenchable desire to possess her. There is, however, no verification of this, or any of the other fanciful events which are supposed to have led to Ala-ud-din's assault on the fort — in spite of a mirror placed in the rebuilt palace to 'prove' the truth of the legend. It is certain, however, that this palace stood within the *mardana* (men's area); and if it had any connection with Padmini at all this would only be because her husband lived there.

The palace overlooks an artificial lake, in the centre of which stands an island pavilion, another nineteenth-century replacement of a thirteenth-century building. It is ascertained that Padmini used this as her summer palace, and a variation on the legend mentioned above is that Ala-ud-din saw her reflection in the lake rather than a mirror in the palace. It is known that Akbar took the bronze gates of the original pavilion to his new fort at Agra, where they may still be seen.

A return northward, followed by a right turn south of the lake, leads to the **Suraj Pol** gate on the east side of the plateau. Ahead, on the left, the **Nilkantha Mahadeo Temple** is believed to date from the thirteenth century. A black stone Shiva lingam is worshipped in its sanctuary.

North of this temple, passing the left turning, rises the 75ft (23m) high **Tower of Fame** (Kirti Stambh). Formerly, this was known as the Tower of Allata (ruled 953-972), and thought to have been erected in 895; however, its style indicates a twelfth-century date, which is now generally accepted. By tradition, the tower was built by a Jain merchant, and dedicated to the first tirthankara, Adinath. A multiplicity of carved nude figures of tirthankaras indicate that the structure was erected by the ascetic Digambara sect of Jains, who practise total nudity, at least within their homes and temples. As with the Tower of Victory, narrow steps may be climbed to the top.

Further north is the remodelled sixteenth-century **Rana Ratan Singh II Palace**, distinguished by its six great towers.

To the west of the Tower of Fame lie two museums. The **Fateh Prakash Palace**, built for his own occupancy by Maharana Fateh Singh in 1925, displays sculptures discovered in the fort. Facing it, on the west side, is the **Archaeological Museum**.

Near the Fateh Prakash Palace, the **Mira Temple** was built by Rana Kumbha in the fifteenth century, and named in honour of Mira Bai, the poet-princess.

Planes leave Udaipur daily (airport 15½ miles / 25km from the city) for other cities in Rajasthan in addition to Delhi, Ahmedabad and Bombay.

If proceeding to Ajmer or Bundi, it is unnecessary to return from Chittaurgarh to Udaipur.

Additional Information

Places to Visit

Udaipur
City Palace Museum
Open: Saturday to Thursday
9.30am-4.30pm.

Bhartiya Lola Kal Museum
Open: 9am-6pm daily.

Lake Pichola
Boat Trips 3-7pm daily.
Sakelion Ki Bari Gardens
Open: 9am-6pm daily.

Eklingji
Temple Complex
Open: 10.30am-1.30pm and
5.30-7.30pm daily.

Mount Abu
Dilwara Temples Complex
Open: 12noon-6pm.

Nathdwara
Shri Nathji Temple
Open: 3.30-6pm daily.

Ranakpur
Adinath Temple
Open: 12noon-5pm daily.

Festivals

Mewar/Gangaur Fair
1995, 3-4 April; 1996, 22-23 March;
1997, 10-11 April; 1998, 30-31 March;
1999, 20-21 March; 2000, 7-8 April

Accommodation

Lake Palace Hotel
☎ 23241

Shivniwas Palace Hotel
☎ 28239

Laxmi Vilas Palace Hotel
☎ 24411

Rang Niwas Palace Hotel
☎ 23891

Tourist Information Offices

Kajri Tourist Bungalow
Shastri Circle (☎ 23605)

Dabok Airport (☎ 23011)

Udaipur Railway Station

Fact File

8

Accommodation

India possesses some of the world's finest hotels, with all services well up to international standards. Pre-eminent are those run by the Taj Group and the WelcomGroup (Sheraton). Most luxury hotels are situated some distance from city centres, which can be inconvenient, particularly in Delhi. During the hot season (April to October), air-conditioning is a definite boon, and in the cold season (November to February), heating is certainly welcome from sundown to sunrise in west Rajasthan.

For those on limited budgets, medium-grade accommodation of varying standard, but always with private shower/toilet, is available.

An increasing number of Rajasthan palaces owned by former maharajas are being converted to hotels, and provide a unique experience; most, although not all, are operated by the larger hotel groups. Accommodation is naturally more limited than in the purpose-built hotels, and should be reserved in advance if at all possible.

In theory, all foreign visitors should pay their bills in foreign currency, but many smaller establishments do not insist on this. Ensure that a currency receipt is issued and keep it for exchanging rupees at the airport when returning home.

Climate (See graph on page 290)

The climates of Delhi and Agra are virtually identical, but Rajasthan is significantly dryer, with greater extremes of day and night temperatures. In the cool season, November to March, a jacket or cardigan will often be needed from early evening to mid-morning.

The hot season begins in April and ends in October; it is interrupted by the south-west monsoon, which should arrive in mid-June. Apart from the years in which it fails, torrential rain can be expected for 3 months. In Rajasthan, rainfall is always much less than in Delhi, and often peters out completely as the monsoon proceeds westward.

Credit Cards

Leading credit cards are accepted in most of the higher-rated hotels, restaurants and tourist agencies, but check in advance if unsure. It is always safer to carry sufficient cash for small purchases, but practically all shops accept cards for major items.

Currency Regulations

A maximum of 250 rupees may be brought into or taken out of the country. In theory, amounts of foreign currency or travellers cheques in excess of US$1,000 should be declared on arrival in India, but in practice this appears to be unnecessary. Visitors staying more than 90 days have to apply for an income tax exemption certificate; to obtain this, currency exchange forms must be produced (see Money, page 294).

Customs Regulations

One bottle of spirits and 200 cigarettes may be brought into India. Valuable items, such as cameras, transistors, etc may have to be entered in a Tourist Baggage Re-Export form to ensure that they will not be re-sold in India, where they are extremely expensive. The form and the items concerned must be shown on departure.

Electricity

Throughout India, voltage is 230-240 AC. Varying types of sockets are used, and an adaptor may be necessary. Men should always take razors (and blades) in case of difficulties. A current stabilizer is recommended. Large hotels have their own generators, but in other establishments power cuts can occur at any time.

Festivals and Holidays

Indian festivals are many, and most of them are held on dates which vary each year, according to religious calendars. Ascertain precise dates on arrival. The most picturesque festivals are in Rajasthan, and their dates until the year 2000 are given in the Additional Information section that follows each centre.

Name of Festival	Date	Venue
Republic Day	26 January	Throughout India, but particularly in Delhi
Shivaratni	February/March	Throughout India
Holi	February/March	Throughout India
Mahavir Jayanti	March/April	In Jain areas of India
Ramanavami	March/April	Throughout India
Independence Day	15 August	Throughout India, but particularly in Delhi
Janmastami	August/September	Throughout India, but particularly in Agra and Mathura

Dussehra (Ram Lila in Delhi)	September/October	Throughout India, but particularly in Delhi
Gandhi Jayanti	2 October	Delhi
Diwali	October/November	Throughout India
Govardhana Puja	November	Throughout India

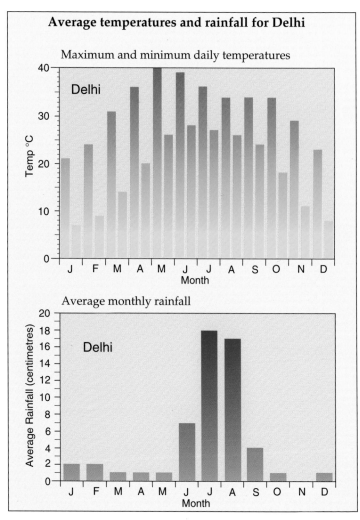

Average temperatures and rainfall for Delhi

Maximum and minimum daily temperatures

Delhi

Average monthly rainfall

Delhi

Food Vocabulary

A general review of food and drink in India forms part of the introduction (page 41). Please note that spelling of the following will vary widely.

Aloo	Potato
Aloo chole	Diced potatoes and chick-peas in a spicy sauce
Anda	Egg
Bingan bharta	Charred egg plant mixed with onions, tomatoes and chillis
Bhaji	Dry, cooked vegetables
Bhatura	Leavened bread made from wheat flour and yoghourt; deep-fried, crisp and spectacularly puffed-up
Bhindi	Okra (ladies fingers)
Biriani	A combination of steamed, aromatic rice, meats, vegetables and spices (also without meats)
Boondi	Tiny dumplings with yoghourt
Brinjal	Egg plant
Chai	Tea
Channa	Chick-peas
Chapatti	Unleavened bread of flour and water
Chat	A snack of any type
Chawal	Rice
Chini	Sugar
Dahi	Yoghourt
Dahi budi	Wheat flour dumplings with yoghourt
Dahi idli	Rice flour dumplings with yoghourt
Dhal	Curried lentils
Dhansak	Pureed lentils cooked with meat and vegetables. Traditional Sunday fare for Parsees. (NB not hot and sweet as served in the UK)
Dopiaza	With onion
Dosa	Pancake made from a mixture of lentil and rice batter; it is deep-fried, crisp and puffed-up. Served either plain or filled with lightly curried potato
Dudh	Milk
Firnee	Rice pudding with nuts and dried fruit
Ghee	Clarified butter
Gobi	Cauliflower
Gosht (or Josht)	Meat (usually lamb or goat)
Gulab jamun	Reduced milk and flour dumpling fried in ghee and simmered in sugar syrup
Gushtaba	Spongy meat balls with yoghourt and onion sauce

Idli .... Steamed rice dumpling
Idli dosa .... As masala dosa, but the bread is replaced by dumplings
Jalebi .... Crisp, fried twirls of flour and milk batter seeped in sugar syrup — sold in the streets
Kachori .... Short pastry, fried and usually stuffed with dry lentils
Keema .... Minced meat
Korma .... A Moghlai meat stew with almonds, cashew and whole spices
Kulfi .... Hard ice-cream, generally pistachio, mango or malai (cream and cardoman) flavoured
Makhan .... Butter
Makhanwalla ..... A sauce of tomatoes, cream and butter
Masala .... A blend of spices (the base for all curries)
Masala dosa .... The dosa is filled with curried potato and served with coconut chutney
Mattar .... Peas
Mattar panir ...... Peas and cottage cheese in a spicy sauce
Murgi .... Chicken
Nan .... Leavened bread baked in a clay tandoori oven
Nimbu .... Lime
Pakora .... Chick-pea flour fritters, deep fried with
(or Bhujia) .... onions, potatoes, egg plant and chillis in various combinations
Pani .... Water
Pani .... Small and crisp puffed-up pieces of deep-fried
(or Papri) puri ... bread filled with a sauce. Sold on the streets: beware of the water (*pani*) that is added
Palak .... Spinach
Paratha .... Unleavened, layered bread cooked in ghee
Papads .... Crisp, thin bread made from rice and lentil flour
Pulao .... Fried rice with flavourings, often peas or mixed vegetables
Raita .... Savoury yoghourt with a chopped vegetable or date or tomato
Rogan .... Red sauce used for cooking, and previously obtained by skimming the juices of cooked meats
Rumali roti .... Large chapattis folded to resemble handker-chiefs. Sold on the streets, particularly around Delhi's Jama Masjid
Sabzi .... Vegetables
Sag .... Spinach or a green-leafed vegetable
Samhar .... Lentil and vegetable spicy broth with tamarind
Sheek kabab .... Skewered, minced lamb

Tandoori	A charcoal-fired clay oven in which is cooked meats previously marinated in herbs and yoghourt
Thali	A large metal platter with compartments for various dishes and accompanying sauces, generally, but not always, vegetarian food
Tika	Boneless pieces of meat

Health

Currently, it is recommended that visitors to India are injected against typhoid, paratyphoid, tetanus, polio and hepatitis A. During the dry season, few mosquitoes are seen in north-west India, and malaria is rare, nevertheless, many may wish to take precautions. Seek advice on the current situation some weeks before leaving from a pharmacy or a general practitioner. Drugs such as chloroquine and proquanil offer 70 per cent protection, but take insect repellent — and use it. Also enquire about qinhaosu, an ancient Chinese remedy now being researched. If visiting the remoter areas, insect repellant coils may prove useful. If particularly worried about health dangers, specialist hospitals will give detailed advice; in the UK contact the Hospital for Tropical Diseases Travel Clinic ☎ 0171 637 9899.

Rabies is common throughout India, and visitors are recommended not to pat dogs or hand-feed monkeys. If bitten, seek medical advice immediately.

Most stomach upsets in India are caused by an excess of chillies, and quickly disposed of by proprietary medicines, such as Immodium. It is best that these are brought by the visitor so that action can be taken as soon as discomfort is experienced. Tap water should be rigorously avoided outside the luxury hotels, as should any fresh fruit and salad vegetables that may have been rinsed in it. Check with the establishment to ensure that the water that they provide has been purified. Ice made from unpurified tap water can also be dangerous, as the freezing process does not kill the microbes which cause the problems. Indians have developed immunity to them and can drink most water without fear. Bottled mineral water is readily available in tourist areas, but should be bought in advance if travelling elsewhere. It is recommended that teeth are brushed in purified or mineral water whenever possible. Purification tablets should be brought for use in an emergency.

If worrying symptoms develop on returning home, contact a specialist hospital immediately, eg in the UK the Hospital for Tropical Diseases, 4 St Pancras Way, London NW1 0PE ☎ 0171 387 4411. Help is also available regionally in Birmingham, Liverpool and Glasgow.

Insurance

It is imperative that adequate insurance is taken out, particularly health cover. Those travelling on package tours will be offered a recommended policy by their operator.

Maps

An excellent map of the region is Nelles India 2: Western India, scale 1:1500,000.

Measurements

The metric system is used throughout India. Spirits are poured in 'fingers', which almost equal an English triple measure. The following conversions apply:

1 kilogram (kg) = 2.2lb
1 litre = 1¾ pints
4.5 litres = 1 gallon
8 kilometres (km) = 5 miles

Money

The basic Indian currency is the rupee, which is divided into 100 paise (pronounced pies). Formerly, the rupee was also divided into sixteen annas, but the anna is no longer in use. Although the rupee was made convertible in 1993, the amount of foreign currency that Indians may purchase in India remains strictly limited, and a black market, therefore, continues to flourish: the most popular unit is the British £50 note, for which quite a high premium is offered. It should be remembered by all visitors that to exchange money with non-authorized dealers is a punishable offence. American dollars and sterling are the simplest currencies to exchange in India, whether they be in note or traveller cheque form.

Many hotels in India are able to change money for their guests, and the rate given is now very little less than that obtainable from banks. Indian banks should be avoided whenever possible, as the infamous red tape and form-filling involved means that a simple transaction may take several hours. Banking hours are: Monday to Friday 10am-2pm, Saturday 10am-12noon. Always insist on plenty of low-value notes, as no-one ever has any change. Never accept torn or damaged notes, because Indians are loth to take them. Ensure that currency exchange forms are given for each transaction, and keep them, for exchanging any remaining rupees when leaving India, or for obtaining a tax clearance certificate if staying more than 90 days. It is best to pay a travel agent to obtain this certificate, in order to avoid the tiresome official procedure:

involving a solicitor, a local Income Tax office, a main Income Tax office, and a return to visit the latter 3 days later. Most banks in small towns will not be able to change travellers cheques. The most welcome travellers cheques in India are those issued by American Express and Thomas Cook, both in dollars.

Packing

As little warm clothing will be needed in India, and hotels provide a fast, reliable laundry service, it is unnecessary to pack a large amount of clothing. The standard allowance permitted by most tour operators is 20kg plus hand baggage. Toiletries, a simple medical kit and camera film (particularly for colour slides) should be brought, but all clothing is cheap throughout India, and much of it of excellent quality, particularly in the large towns. Jackets and trousers, for example, can be made to measure in a couple of days, so leave plenty of room, or bring items that can be discarded. A particularly useful buy, soon after arrival, are leather sandals which can easily be removed before entering religious buildings or tombs.

Passports

All visitors to India must have a full passport (*not* a one year British Visitor passport), valid for 6 months after their return date. Holders of Indian passports are not permitted to travel to India on chartered flights, which virtually rules out most package tours to India for them. A visa for India is required by all visitors (see Visas, page 298).

Police

If police assistance in Delhi is urgently required, telephone 100, however, it is initially preferable to seek advice from a hotel.

Postage

Stamps may be purchased at larger hotels or post offices, but the latter always involve long, slow-moving queues. The postal service is remarkably quick, efficient and honest. Mail sent home should arrive in one week. Never even think about sending a parcel out of India, the procedure demanded is a nightmare. Look with suspicion on offers by stores to post goods overseas; they may or may not arrive. This does not, of course, apply to state-run emporiums or shops sited within large hotels. Post offices are open Monday to Friday 10am-5pm and Saturday 10am-12noon.

Religious Buildings

In general mosques can be visited daily from dawn to dusk; only on special occasions will non-Muslims be refused entry. In general, tombs and mausoleums (always Muslim) can be visited at any time during the day; when this is not so opening times are shown.

Hindu and Jain temples are more restricted in their opening times, many of them closing throughout the afternoon. Wherever possible, such restrictions are referred to.

When visiting mosques, tombs or temples shoes must always be removed at the entrance. Sometimes socks and leather articles must also be left outside (particularly in Jain temples). Slip-off footwear is advisable, in order to avoid repeatedly tying and untying shoelaces.

Telephones

Overseas calls should be booked well in advance outside Delhi. Always telephone from a hotel room whenever possible, despite the premiums charged, as waits in a telephone office can be very long. Local calls may often be made from the larger shops.

Time

India is 5½ hours ahead of GMT and 9½ hours ahead of USEST.

Tipping

Tipping (*backsheesh*) is widely practised in India, as in most Third-World countries. Only very small amounts are usually expected, so carry plenty of low-denomination notes and coins to give for minor services. It is usual for the service charge to be included in restaurant bills, if not, tip the waiter 10 per cent. Taxi drivers and auto-rickshaw operators will always quote an inclusive price, but for good service, a small additional tip is appreciated.

Tourist Information

Much information can be obtained from hotel reception staff and representatives of tour operators, many of whom make daily visits to the larger hotels. Information Centres will be found in all Indian cities and major towns frequented by tourists. There is a 24 hour counter at Indira Gandhi International Airport.

India Government Tourist Offices:

UK
7 Cork Street
London W1X 1PB
☎ 0171 812 0929

USA
Suite 204
3550 Wilshire Boulevard
Los Angeles CA 90010
☎ (213) 380 8855

Room 15
North Mezzanine
30 Rockefeller Plaza
New York, NY 10020
☎ (212) 586 4901/2/3

Canada
West Suite No 1003
60 Bloor Street
Toronto
Ontario M4W 3B8
☎ (416) 962 3787/88

Australia
Level 5
65 Elizabeth Street
Sydney NSW 2000
☎ (2) 232 1600/1796

Travel

Air

Most visitors to the area will arrive at Delhi's Indira Gandhi International Airport. Those travelling with tour operators will automatically be met by buses to take them to their accommodation. Luxury hotels will also meet individual guests. International return flights from India on scheduled (not chartered) aircraft must be confirmed, usually one week in advance of departure. Check the situation immediately on arrival in India, as it can be almost impossible to contact international airlines, apart from Air India, by telephone from outlying areas. It is imperative to remember that a departure from India tax of 300 rupees is levied at all Indian airports. Airports for internal flights are located at Agra, Jaipur, Jodhpur and Udaipur.

The internal flights terminal at Delhi's Indira Gandhi International Airport is located 6 miles (9km) distant from the international terminal.

Bus

Only the most intrepid of foreigners will use public buses in the major cities; routes are confusing and vehicles jam-packed, services can also be infrequent outside the rush hour. In Rajasthan, however, buses are often the best bet, and on occasions, such as between Bikaner and Jaisalmer, Ajmer and Pushkar, and throughout much of the Shekhavati region, the only means of public transport available.

Express buses link Delhi, Agra and Jaipur, many of them being quicker than all but the fastest trains. Never expect a 'luxury' bus to approach the standard of ordinary buses in the west; the description is merely comparative. This does not, of course, apply to most vehicles provided for escorted tours.

Tickets for longer distances are usually purchased at bus station kiosks, not on the vehicle. Ask for a window seat, preferably in the centre, so that some reduction of the crackling noise of ethnic music is gained; it is often played at full blast — even through the night. Partly for this reason, night travel by train is always preferable. An idiosyncracy to look out for is that some Indian ticket sellers will ask 'How much?'. They are not reversing roles and pretending that you are selling the tickets. What they want to know is how many tickets are required.

Train
First-class, air conditioned compartments offer the best accommodation on Indian railways. Standard second-class should be avoided wherever possible. Reservations are essential for all sleeping accommodation, preferably through an agent — ask at your hotel for the nearest operator. Always book a super-fast or express train — others will be infuriatingly slow.

In the United Kingdom, India Rail Passes (and reservations) may be obtained from S D Enterprises, 103 Wembley Park Drive, Wembley HA9 8HG (☎ 0181 903 3411)

Taxis
Vehicles hired in the manner of taxis are in three categories; these are, in descending order of cost: taxis, auto-rickshaws (partially enclosed three-wheel motorbikes) and cycle-rickshaws (in Old Delhi, Agra and Jaipur only). All except cycle-rickshaws have meters but, on spotting a tourist, their drivers are almost always loath to use them — 'meter no working'. Ask for usual fares at your hotel reception to avoid being fleeced too badly. For long distances it is always essential to bargain.

Car Hire
Some may wish to hire a car for travelling in the remoter parts of Rajasthan, and there are a multitude of hiring organisations. Those non-resident in India are not permitted to hire self-drive cars, however, the supplement for including a driver is surprisingly low.

Visas

All foreign passport holders need a visa to enter India. In the case of the United Kingdom, this measure was introduced as a tit-for-tat by Indira Gandhi, when the British government decided to require Indians visiting the UK to obtain a visa, thereby ensuring that they were not immigrating illegally. It is advisable to make postal application for visas at least 2 months in advance, although personal applicants are usually able to collect their visas on the same day — after a lengthy queue, a wait, and then a return. Tourists can specify 1 or 6 month visas; a 6 month visa is always recommended, and it is essential to specify multi-entry validity if trips to Sri Lanka or Nepal are envisaged. Business visas are available for a 12 month period, but can rarely be obtained on the same day. The validity of the visa commences on the date that it is stamped, not the date of arrival in India. Would-be visitors to India without a valid passport and visa will not be permitted to board the plane, nor can any refunds be expected. Travel agents are able to advise on the current procedure. In the United Kingdom, visas must be obtained from the High Commisioner for India, India House, Aldwych, London WC2 B4NA (☎ 0171 240 2084) or the Indian Consulate in Birmingham, 86 New Street (☎ 0121 643 7444). Three passport-size photographs are required. If a visa is needed urgently, and personal application is difficult, passport and visa courier services exist which will simplify and speed up the process for a fee; a visa can generally be obtained in 7 days by this means. One such organisation is Thames Consular, 363 Chiswick High Road, London W44 HS (☎ 0181 995 2492).

A Note to the Reader

Thank you for buying this book, we hope it has helped you to plan and enjoy your visit. We have worked hard to produce a guidebook which is as accurate as possible. With this in mind, any comments, suggestions or useful information you may have would be appreciated.

Please send your letters to:

The Editor
Moorland Publishing Co Ltd
Moor Farm Road West
Ashbourne, Derbyshire, DE6 1HD

The Travel Specialists

INDEX

Going to Goa ?

While intensive sightseeing in north India is a magical experience, it can be exhausting, and many holidaymakers feel in need of some relaxation before returning home. A week or so on the idyllic golden beaches of India's western state of Goa

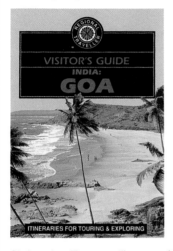

will provide this, simply and economically. Direct flights from Delhi to Goa are met automatically by private transport operated by many of the resort hotels.

Goa's winter temperatures are much higher than those in north India, and the dry season, from October to April, provides perfect beach weather, with balmy seas and a great winter suntan guaranteed.

A companion volume to this book *Visitor's Guide India: Goa*, also written by Christopher Turner, will prove of invaluable assistance. Goa's beaches and their facilities are intensively researched, and fascinating inland excursions described. These include the magnificent churches of Old Goa (the 'Rome of the Orient'), the unique Hindu temples of Ponda, Panaji, the charmingly intimate capital, and India's highest waterfall, at Dudhsagar.

Visitor's Guides

Itinerary based guides for independent travellers

MPC

MPC Visitor's Guides are available through all good bookshops. Free catalogue available upon request from Moorland Publishing Co Ltd, Moor Farm Rd, Ashbourne, Derbyshire DE6 1HD, England ☎ 01335 344486.

Mail Order In case of local difficulty, you may order direct (quoting your Visa/Access number) from Grantham Book Services on ☎ 01476 67421. Ask for the cash sales department. There is a small charge for postage and packing.